a dictionary of
contemporary
SPAIN

WITHDRAWN
WITHDRAWN

SANDRA TRUSCOTT & MARÍA J. GARCÍA

Hodder & Stoughton
A MEMBER OF THE HODDER HEADLINE GROUP

ACKNOWLEDGEMENTS

The authors would like to thank the following for their assistance: Michael T. Newton and Peter J. Donaghy, authors of *Institutions of Modern Spain: a political and economical guide* (1997), and CUP, publishers of the same; Christopher J. Ross, author of *Contemporary Spain: a Handbook* (Arnold, 1997); Ian Gibson, author of *Fire in the Blood* (Faber & Faber/BBC, 1992).

Cover photo from Life File.

Order queries: please contact Bookpoint Ltd, 39 Milton Park, Abingdon, Oxon OX14 4TD. Telephone: (44) 01235 400414, Fax: (44) 01235 400454. Lines are open from 9.00–6.00, Monday to Saturday, with a 24 hour message answering service. Email address: orders@bookpoint.co.uk

A catalogue record for this title is available from The British Library

ISBN 0 340 65517 8

First published 1998
Impression number 10   9   8   7   6   5   4   3   2   1
Year   2002   2001   2000   1999   1998

Typeset by Wearset, Boldon, Tyne and Wear.
Printed in Great Britain for Hodder & Stoughton Educational, a division of Hodder Headline Plc, 338 Euston Road, London NW1 3BH by Cox & Wyman, Reading, Berks.

ABASCAL, NATI
Top model, former *duquesa de Feria*, she is a member of the Spanish jet set and frequently appears in gossip magazines such as HOLA.

ABC
The leading conservative independent newspaper with a circulation of 300,000 on weekdays and 700,000 on Sundays. *Blanco y Negro* is the title of its Sunday magazine. The newspaper is readily available throughout the country (which is not always the case with other newspapers). An edition is printed in SEVILLA with a circulation of 57,000. It is the newspaper most widely read by the Spanish right and by army officers. For many years it was edited by Luis María Anson; he resigned in 1997. ABC is published by *Editorial Española*.

ABERRI EGUNA
Basque National Day. It was first celebrated on 26th March 1932 in BILBAO, to commemorate the anniversity of the PNV (PARTIDO NACIONAL VASCO) party. Nowadays it is celebrated on Easter Sunday.

ABERTZALE
From the Basque *aberia* (*patria*/country) and *zale* (*amante*/lover), this word is used to describe Basque nationalists.

ABERTZALISMO
Basque nationalism.

ABORTION
Abortion is permitted in Spain in the case of rape, mental or physical danger to the mother, and of an abnormal foetus. The law liberalising abortion was passed in March 1983. Although in

principle abortion is legal in these circumstances, it can be difficult to obtain in those clinics where medical staff are opposed to the practice on moral and ethical grounds.

ABRIL MARTORELL, FERNANDO (1936–)

Spanish politician. *Ministro de Agricultura* in the government of ADOLFO SUÁREZ (1976–1977), *ministro de Economía* from 1978 to 1979 and *vicepresidente*, responsible for the economy from 1979 to 1980.

ABRIL, VICTORIA (1959–)

Film and television actress. She has worked extensively with VICENTE ARANDA, notably in *La muchacha de las bragas de oro* (1980), *Tiempo de silencio* (1986) and *Amantes* (1991). She has also appeared in a number of films directed by PEDRO ALMODÓVAR, including *¡Átame!* (1989) and *Tacones lejanos* (1991). In 1995 she appeared in the very successful *Nadie hablará de nosotros cuando hayamos muerto*, directed by AGUSTÍN DÍAZ YANES. Her latest film is *Libertarias*, directed by VICENTE ARANDA, in 1995.

ACADEMIA GENERAL MILITAR

Officer training college at ZARAGOZA, the Spanish equivalent of Sandhurst.

ACERÍA COMPACTA DE BIZKAIA

Basque steelworks. One of the very few steelmills which is investing in new plant, it will open a new mill in 1996 in Sestao (Vizcaya) with a workforce of 320 people.

ACERINOX, S.A.

This company manufactures and sells flat stainless steel products. Its factory is located in Cádiz. It also has trading subsidiaries abroad and in other regions of Spain.

ACOGIMIENTO FAMILIAR

At the same time as the rules on adoption were modified (1987), the possibility of ACOGIMIENTO FAMILIAR or long-term fostering was introduced into Spain. Families who wish to invite a child on a long-term basis into their home undertake to feed, house, clothe and educate him or her. The child is visited at six monthly periods by the relevant authorites to ensure that s/he is cared for competently.

ACOSO SEXUAL
ACOSO SEXUAL, or sexual harrassment at work, is now an offence according to legislation passed by FELIPE GONZÁLEZ' government at the end of their third term of office.

ACTUALIDAD ECONÓMICA
Weekly business magazine, founded in 1958. It specialises in financial news, economic reports and details of new companies.

ACUERDO ECONÓMICO Y SOCIAL
A type of social contract, to which the government, UGT and the employees' associations were all party and which covers wages, job creation, public spending, social security and industrial relations.

ACUERDO MARCO INTERCONFEDERAL
A type of 'social contract', signed in 1980 by the employers' organisations and the UGT. It dealt with wages, job conditions, job creation and industrial relations.

ACUERDO NACIONAL DE EMPLEO
A type of 'social contract', to which the government, trade unions and employers' associations were all party. It dealt with wages, social security and industrial relations.

ACUERDO SOBRE SOLUCIÓN EXTRAJUDICIAL DE CONFLICTOS LABORALES
This agreement or out-of-court settlement of industrial disputes, was signed in 1996. Disputes must go to arbitration: this process is entrusted to impartial individuals appointed by SIMA.

ADENA See: *ASOCIACIÓN PARA LA DEFENSA DE LA NATURALEZA*

ADOPTION
In the case of a Spanish child, at least one of the parents must be more than 25 years old and at least 14 years older than the child. Adoption takes place through the 'servicios de protección de menores' in the AUTONOMÍAS. It is legal to adopt children from

abroad, but the law of the country from which the child comes must be followed, as well as Spanish law. The parent must be approved by the child adoption service and the documentation authorized, translated and sent to the country of the child in question.

AEB See: *ASOCIACIÓN ESPAÑOLA DE LA BANCA PRIVADA*

AECI See: *AGENCIA ESPAÑOLA DE COOPERACIÓN*

AEDENAT
Organisation which works towards the protection of the environment.

AENA See: *AEROPUERTOS ESPAÑOLES Y NAVEGACIÓN AÉREA*

AEPI See: *ASOCIACIÓN DE ESCRITORES Y PERIODISTAS INDEPENDIENTES*

AEPSA See: *ACUERDO PARA EL EMPLEO Y LA PROTECCIÓN SOCIAL AGRARIOS*

AEROPUERTOS ESPAÑOLES Y NAVEGACIÓN AÉREA
Organisation responsible for the management, maintenance and development of the 40 airports in Spain. It was established in 1990 and is directly answerable to the MINISTERIO DE FOMENTO.

AES See: *ACUERDO ECÓNOMICO Y SOCIAL*

AFEITADO
An illegal practice by which the horns of bulls are shaved prior to entering the bullring. This affects the bulls' balance and allows them to be fought more easily.

AFORAMIENTO
Immunity from prosecution. Members of the government (DIPUTADOS and SENADORES) enjoy the *fuero* or privilege of not being liable to prosecution from the courts. This can only be overturned by a joint decision of the CONGRESO DE LOS DIPUTADOS. Recently, JOSÉ BARRIONUEVO, member of parliament and former

ministro del Interior, invoked this privilege in order to avoid prosecution for his alleged collaboration with GAL.

AGENCIA DE CONTRATACIÓN
Private employment agencies. These were introduced in the employment legislation of 1994. Previously, the only employment agency was the state-run INEM.

AGENCIA DEL MEDIO AMBIENTE
Environmental agency set up by the autonomous region of ANDALUCÍA. It was the first of the regions to demonstrate practical concern for the environment within its own borders.

AGENCIA ESPAÑOLA DE COOPERACIÓN INTERNACIONAL
This agency is responsible for relations between Spain and Latin America. Its work in bringing about peace in Central America has, to date, been its most successful enterprise.

AGENCIA INDUSTRIAL DEL ESTADO
This agency was created in 1996 to control those loss-making public enterprises which formed part of the INI (INSTITUTO NACIONAL DE INDUSTRIA) holdings. These companies will either be restructured or closed. See also: INI.

AGENCIA TRIBUTARIA
Government agency responsible for tax-collection, inspection and eliminating tax-evasion. Its current director is Jesús Bermejo Ramos.

AGROMAN EMPRESA CONSTRUCTORA, S.A.
Group of companies whose construction activities include civil engineering projects (roads, railways, hydraulic works), house building and the construction of factories and industrial plants. The group also purchases and develops land.

AGRUPACIÓN
Political party founded by JOSÉ MARÍA RUIZ MATEOS.

AGRUPACIÓN DE INTERÉS ECONÓMICO
These associations exist to enable those companies who so wish,

to share facilities such as research and development or information technology. They are registered with the *Registro Mercantil*.

EL ÁGUILA
This company's principal activity is the production and sale of beer. It has factories in MADRID, VALENCIA and ZARAGOZA. The company also manufactures other beverages as well as carbon dioxide.

AGUIRRE GIL DE BIEDMA, ESPERANZA (1952–   )
Lawyer, ex-*senadora* for Madrid and currently (1996) *ministra de Educación y Cultura*. She was *concejala* for the PP (PARTIDO POPULAR) in MADRID until 1996. Her priority during the 1996 legislature is to implement the LOGSE (LEY ORGÁNICA DE ORGANIZACIÓN GENERAL DEL SISTEMA EDUCATIVO).

AHV See: *ALTOS HORNOS DE VIZCAYA*

AI See: *ACUERDO INTERCONFEDERAL*

AIE See: *AGENCIA INDUSTRIAL DEL ESTADO*

AIE See: *AGRUPACIÓN DE INTERÉS ECONÓMICO*

AIGUES TORTES Y LAGO SAN MAURICIO
This area was declared a national park in 1955. It is situated in the Pyrenees in Lérida and is representative of the countryside of the area, which is mountainous with numerous lakes and waterfalls.

AIR EUROPA
Originally a charter airline, it is now the third largest travel company in Spain. Its retail outlet is *Viajes Halcón* and it has a fleet of 24 aeroplanes.

AJURIA ENEA
Residence of the chief minister of the Basque autonomous government. It has given its name to the PACTO DE AJURIA ENEA, an agreement signed by the Basque political parties to combat terrorism.

AL KASSAR, MUNZER
International arms dealer. He has worked for the MINISTERIO DEL INTERIOR on several occasions as an agent and intermediary.

ALASKA (1964–)
Born in Mexico, ALASKA's real name is Olvido Gara. Originally a punk singer who first rose to fame in the MOVIDA in MADRID, she became popular with the Spanish public at large through her role as Truca in the TV series *La bola de cristal*. She is now a night-club owner.

ALBERDI, CRISTINA (1946–)
Spanish politican, born in Los Rosales, Sevilla. In 1993 she became *ministro de Asuntos Sociales* in the Socialist government of FELIPE GONZÁLEZ. She was the first woman to become a member of the CGPJ (CONSEJO GENERAL DEL PODER JUDICIAL). In her own law firm, she specialised in women's rights in the field of discrimination in the work place, divorce and abortion.

ALBERTI, RAFAEL (1902–)
Andalucían poet who belongs to the *Generación del 27*. He first became famous through his collections of verse, *Marinero en tierra* and *Sobre los ángeles*. He is known for his political and surrealist verse. Among his most famous collections of poetry are *Cal y canto* and *Oda marítima*. He has been a life-long member of the Communist party. He went into exile during the FRANCO régime but returned to Spain in 1977. He won the PREMIO CERVANTES in 1983.

ALBORCH, CARMEN (1948–)
Politician and member of the PSOE (PARTIDO SOCIALISTA OBRERO ESPAÑOL). She was a university lecturer in commercial law for many years and dean of the Faculty of Law in VALENCIA. For 5 years she headed the IVAM, the *Instituto Valenciano de Arte Moderno*. She is a well-known feminist who belongs to the *Asociación de Mujeres Universitarias* and the *Asamblea de Mujeres de Valencia*. She was *ministra de Cultura* in GONZÁLEZ's last government. She is currently a member of parliament for VALENCIA.

ALCALÁ DE HENARES
This university was refounded in 1977 in the city of Alcalá. Originally founded in 1499, it was a very prestigious institution until the 19th century, when it was decided to remove it to MADRID. When the need for more university places became pressing, Alcalá was chosen to house this institution once again. Its name comes from the Arabic *Al-Kala Nahar*.

ALCALDE
The Mayor of a MUNICIPIO, he is normally elected by his CONCEJALES or town councillors at the first council session after elections. He or she will have headed the party list in the elections. The position of mayor is an important one both politically and as a representative of the MUNICIPIO. Among his or her functions are: to lead the town council, to convene and chair meetings, to direct, inspect and promote municipal works, to issue edicts (BANDOS) and to head the police force.

ALCAMPO
Third largest chain of supermarkets in Spain. In 1995, it had 22 stores, 9,300 employees and a turnover of 263,400 million pesetas.

ALCÁNTARA, THEO (1941–   )
Conductor, born in Cuenca in 1941. He worked first in Frankfurt and since then in the United States, latterly with the Pittsburgh Opera and the Phoenix Symphony Orchestra.

ALCÀSSER
Small town, 20 kilometres from the city of VALENCIA, where the bodies of three murdered girls were found buried in shallow graves in 1993. Various television reality shows seized on this event and made programmes designed to attract mass audiences. See: CASO ALCÀSSER

EL ALCÁZAR
Evening newspaper, originally published in MADRID. It was extremely right-wing with a large input on and by the military. It ceased publication in 1988.

ALDAYA ETXEBURUA, JOSÉ MARÍA (1942–   )
Basque entrepreneur, owner of a small haulage company, ALDAYA was kidnapped on the 8th of May, 1995, by the Basque terrorist organisation ETA and held captive for almost a year. He was freed on the 14th of April, 1996.

ALDERDI EGUNA
Basque for the 'day of the party'. It refers to the 'fiesta' or feast day of the PNV.

ALDITRANS
The company owned by JOSÉ MARÍA ALDAYA, who was kidnapped by ETA in May 1995.

ALIANZA ATLÁNTICA
Alternative name for NATO, known is Spain as OTAN (*Organización del Tratado del Atlántico Norte*).

ALIANZA NACIONAL
Extreme right-wing political party, headed by Ricardo Sáez de Ynestrillas.

ALIANZA POPULAR
This party was formed in 1976 to represent the Spanish centre right. FRAGA IRIBARNE was its leader, aided by other well-known politicians of the FRANCO years, including Fernández de la Mora, Silva Muñoz and Antonio Carro Martínez. Originally, the party was composed of seven right-wing groups in a loose coalition, most of which were led by ex-FRANCO ministers like FRAGA.

ALMARAZ
Site of a nuclear power-station which produces 10% of electricity in Spain. Inhabitants of Cáceres, the region in which it is sited, fear that there is a higher than normal incidence of cancer in the area.

ALMEIDA, CRISTINA (1944–   )
Feminist lawyer, ALMEIDA has been a member of parliament for IU (IZQUIERDA UNIDA) since 1989. She first joined the PCE (PARTIDO COMUNISTA DE ESPAÑA) at the age of 19 and remained a member until 1981. She is a founder and active member of the PARTIDO

DEMOCRÁTICO DE LA NUEVA IZQUIERDA. Currently she is working as a defence lawyer in the CASO ARNY.

ALMODÓVAR, PEDRO (1949–   )

Enfant terrible of the modern Spanish cinema. The author/director of films such as *Tacones lejanos* (High Heels) (1991), *Kika* (1993), *¿Qué he hecho yo para merecer esto?* (What Have I Done to Deserve This?) (1984) and *Mujeres al borde de un ataque de nervios* (Women on the Edge of a Nervous Breakdown) (1988). The first of the Spanish directors apart from LUIS BUÑUEL to gain a truly international reputation, ALMODÓVAR depicts a Spain of transvestites, gays and drug addicts, but always with humour, compassion, melodrama and at breakneck speed. *La flor de mi secreto* (The Flower of my Secret) was screened in 1995, and *Carne Trémula* appeared in 1997. It is based on a novel by Ruth Rendell.

ALMUNIA, JOAQUÍN (1948–   )

Basque politician, he became *secretario general* of the PSOE when FELIPE GONZÁLEZ resigned in June 1997. He is a DIPUTADO for MADRID and *presidente* of the *Grupo Parlamentario Socialista*.

ALONSO MANGLANO, EMILIO (1926–   )

Director-general of CESID (CENTRO SUPERIOR DE INFORMACIÓN DE LA DEFENSA) from 1981 to 1995, when he was forced to resign due to a telephone-tapping scandal. In 1995, he was accused of telephone tapping, perversion of justice and embezzlement of public funds. He was allowed bail of one million pesetas.

ALONSO, ODÓN (1925–   )

Musician and conductor. He was leader of the *Sinfónica de Radio y Televisión Española* from 1978 to 1984.

ALSA

Well-known coach company which operates between all the major cities in Spain and with many in Europe. It also has a service in China.

ALTOS CARGOS

Name commonly given to senior civil servants. They are often *cargos políticos* or political appointees.

ALTOS HORNOS DE VIZCAYA

Important steelworks, sited on the left bank of the River Nervión in BILBAO. Founded in 1902, the company is to be found at the heart of the district of Barakaldo. In its heyday, it employed more than 16,000 workers. In common with steelworks throughout the world, its future is gravely threatened and it has recently joined a conglomerate of steelmills called the *Corporación Siderúrgica*.

ÁLVAREZ CASCOS, FRANCISCO (1947–)

A former engineer, ÁLVAREZ CASCOS became *senador* for ASTURIAS in 1982. He was later a member of parliament (1986) and has been *secretario-general* of the PP since 1986. In 1996, he became *vicepresidente* of the Spanish government and *ministro de la Presidencia*.

ÁLVAREZ DEL MANZANO, JOSÉ MARÍA (1937–)

ALCALDE of MADRID since 1991 in which he stood for the PP and gained an absolute majority. His administration broke with that of earlier mayors such as TIERNO GALVÁN and JOAQUÍN LEGUINA, both of whom were socialists. Earlier ÁLVAREZ DEL MANZANO had been a member of the UCD (UNIÓN CENTRO DEMOCRÁTICO) and then of the PDP (PARTIDO DEMÓCRATA POPULAR).

AMA See: *AGENCIA DEL MEDIO AMBIENTE*

AMADOR, ÁNGELES (1950–)

Politician, currently *ministro de Sanidad*.

AMARILLISMO

Name given to the phenomenon of the sensationalist press in Spain. Spain does not really have a history of this sort of press, but with the advent of democracy, some newspapers and magazines have attempted to appeal to a mass audience by using this journalistic style.

AMEDO, JOSÉ (1946–)

Ex-*subcomisario de policía*, AMEDO was sentenced to 108 years imprisonment, together with his colleague, MICHEL DOMÍNGUEZ, for his role in the CASO AMEDO, (later to be known as the *Caso* GAL). They were accused of incitement to murder, illicit association, falsification of public documents, use of assumed names and battery. In 1994, AMEDO's sentence was changed to that of *tercer grado penitenciario* in which prisoners are allowed freedom during the day but must return to prison at night.

AMENÁBAR, ALEJANDO (1973–   )

Winner of one of the PREMIOS GOYA for the best film of 1996, *Tesis*. *Tesis* is AMENÁBAR's first feature film. *Abre los ojos*, his second film, was released in 1997.

AMI See: *ACUERDO MARCO INTERCONFEDERAL*

ANDALUCÍA

ANDALUCÍA occupies most of the southern part of Spain and is an autonomous region or AUTONOMÍA. Geographically, it is very varied, with a climate ranging from sub-tropical near the coast, to the mountain ranges of Granada. Its main industries are tourism and agriculture. It produces olive oil, vegetables and tropical fruits as well as cereals and tobacco. Cádiz is an important shipbuilding and fishing port and Huelva is the petrochemical centre for most of Southern Spain. Algeciras is a centre for international shipping and has a large container port, oil refinery and a major stainless steel plant. SEVILLA is the capital of the region and an important tourist centre. It is a river port set in a very fertile region, and has important lead and copper mines. See also; AUTONOMÍAS (ESTADO DE)

ANDREU, BLANCA

Poet. She has published collections such as *De una niña de provincias que se vino a vivir en un Chagall*, *Báculo de Babel* and *Elphistone*.

ANE See: *ACUERDO NACIONAL DE EMPLEO*

ANETO

Highest peak in the Pyrenees rising to 3,404 metres in the province of Huesca.

ANGLÉS ANTONIO (1965–   )

Principal suspect in the ALCÀSSER case, in which three young girls were murdered. He was able to resist police arrest and fled to Lisbon and then to Dublin. Latest sightings have been in Uruguay.

ANGUITA, JULIO (1941–   )
The leader of the coalition of left-wing parties, IU or IZQUIERDA UNIDA. He has been a member of parliament since 1989 and was ALCALDE of CÓRDOBA from 1979 to 1986, the only Communist mayor in Spain since the Civil War. He is the leader (*secretario-general*) of the PCE and was elected to that post in 1988.

ANOETA STADIUM
Large sports' stadium in SAN SEBASTIÁN, scene of the HB (HERRI BATASUNA) 1996 elections rally in which 30,000 people watched the Spanish and French flags being burned and witnessed a multitude of banners which demanded the return of political prisoners to the PAÍS VASCO, and the release of HB leaders from prison. Hooded individuals harangued the crowd and the stadium was invaded by teams of horses whose riders brandished the Basque flag.

ANSON, LUIS MARÍA (1934–   )
Journalist and editor of ABC for many years, he is currently the *presidente* of *Televisa España*. He was elected to the REAL ACADEMIA ESPAÑOLA in 1998 where he occupies the chair for ñ.

ANTENA 3
One of three private television companies broadcasting nationally. The Spanish government invested in the company in 1995 through the TENEO group. It is one of the most popular channels with a large audience share.

ANTEPROYECTOS DE LEY
These are draft bills, usually preceded by a LIBRO BLANCO or White Paper.

ANTOÑETE (1932–   )
Antonio Chenel, ANTOÑETE, was an important Spanish bullfighter. He retired in 1988.

AOIZ, FLOREN (1967–   )
Spokesman (with JON IDÍGORAS) for HERRI BATASUNA, he is a member of its *Mesa Nacional* (or cabinet) and of the autonomous government in NAVARRA. He represents both the hawks and the younger generation within ETA which rejects negotiation and preaches permanent mobilisation against the Spanish state.

APARCERÍA
System of farming based on share-cropping. This system is steadily declining in importance and today counts for less than 3,5% of cultivated land.

APD See: *ASOCIACIÓN PARA EL PROGRESO DE LA DIRECCIÓN*

APE See: *ASOCIACIÓN PARA EL PROGRESO EMPRESARIAL*

APOYO A LAS MIGRACIONES INTERIORES
Under this scheme, workers who find jobs at some distance from their homes are given help with removal costs.

APRENDIZAJE
A certain number of apprenticeships are available in Spanish firms. To qualify, the apprentice must be aged between 16 and 25. At least 15% of the working day must be devoted to training. In the first year, the apprentice earns at least 70% of the minimum wage, in the second 80% and in the third, 90%.

APS See: *ATENCIÓN PRIMARIA DE SALUD*

ARAGÓN
ARAGÓN is one of the AUTONOMÍAS and is in the north-east of Spain between NAVARRA and CATALUÑA. It has a population of 1.2 million and covers an area of 47,650 square kilometres. It is an important agricultural centre with most production centred on Huesca. This area produces quality fruit such as peaches and apricots. The main industries in ARAGÓN are car production (there is an Opel assembly plant in ZARAGOZA, the manufacture of electrical goods, animal feed and automobile accessories. ZARAGOZA is the regional capital.

ARANDA, VICENTE (1926–)
An important film-maker who has worked extensively with VICTORIA ABRIL. Among his later films are several adapted from contemporary Spanish novels, such as *La muchacha de las bragas de oro* (1980), *Si te dicen que caí* (1989), *El amante bilingüe* (1993) and *Tiempo de silencio* (1986). He has also worked in television, notably on a series entitled *Los jinetes del alba* (1990) and on *El*

crimen del capitán Sánchez (1985). In 1996 he directed *Libertarias* with VICTORIA ABRIL, ANA BELÉN and Ariadna Gil, the story of three women anarchists fighting in the Spanish Civil War. His latest film, completed in 1997, is entitled *La mirada del otro* and is based on a novel by Fernando Delgado.

ARARTEKO
Name of the Basque DEFENSOR DEL PUEBLO.

ARCHIPIÉLAGO DE CABRERA
National park in the BALEARES. Famous for its coastline and sea birds.

ARCHIVO HISTÓRICO NACIONAL DE SALAMANCA
Certain historical documents belonging to the GENERALITAT were seized during the Civil War and re-housed in Salamanca. In 1995 central government authorized their return, but this was refused by the authorities in Salamanca. This controversy has yet not been settled and has given rise to a general debate on where documents of national historical importance should be held.

ARCO See: *FERIA INTERNACIONAL DE ARTE CONTEMPORÁNEO*

ARDANZA, JOSÉ ANTONIO (1941–   )
Spanish politician and mayor of Mondragón in 1979. He has been the member of parliament for Guipúzcoa since 1983. President (or LEHENDAKARI) of the Basque autonomous government since 1985 when he succeeded CARLOS GARAIKOETXEA. He won the 1989, 1990 and 1994 elections on the PNV ticket and currently governs in a coalition with the socialists.

ÁREA DE SALUD
District health authority. Typically it serves a population of between 200,000 and 250,000 people and has one *Centro de Salud* (that is, a general hospital and other medical facilities).

ÁREA METROPOLITANA
A government department which covers a metropolitan area and may represent several MUNICIPIOS within the conurbation. There are examples in the BARCELONA, VALENCIA and ZARAGOZA regions.

ÁREAS
These are departments within a DIPUTACIÓN and as such are responsible for sectors such as education, culture, traffic and social welfare.

ARECES, RAMÓN (1905–1989)
Spanish business-man who founded EL CORTE INGLÉS. He started his career in Cuba as a shop-assistant in a department store. On his return to Spain, he set up a small clothes shop which he called EL CORTE INGLÉS. It has since become the largest retail chain in Spain and has diversified into supermarkets and real estate. At his death, a foundation (the *Fundación* RAMÓN ARECES) was created to administer his business empire. The foundation also sponsors many cultural events.

ARGENTARIA
Large financial holding company, originally created in 1991 by amalgamating the state's banking interests such as the BANCO EXTERIOR DE ESPAÑA, the *Caja Postal de Ahorros* and banks belonging to the former *Instituto de Crédito Oficial*. The first stage of privatization began in 1996 when the government's stake in the company was reduced to 25%.

ARGUIÑANO, KARLOS
Famous television cook from Zarautz in the Basque country, he has a daily cookery programme on RTVE. He has compiled several books of recipes and has a popular restaurant in his home town.

ARIAS IMANOL (1956–   )
Actor brought up in the PAÍS VASCO. His first important role was in *Cecilia* (1981), directed by Humberto Solás in Cuba. He has worked with VICENTE ARANDA in *Tiempo de silencio* (1986) and in a series of films about *El Lute*, a modern-day rogue who has almost become a Spanish folk hero. ARIAS achieved great popularity through the television series made with Pedro Masó, *Anillos de oro* (1983) and *Brigada central* (1989) and also *Mi querido maestro* in 1997.

ARIAS NAVARRO, CARLOS (1908–89)
First civilian prime minister since the Civil War, ARIAS NAVARRO was appointed to the post by FRANCO after the death of CARRERO BLANCO in 1974. He resigned in 1976. He stood for *senador* for the PP in 1977, but was not elected: he was considered incapable of adapting to the new democratic régime by the electorate.

ARMADA, ALFONSO (1920–   )
ARMADA was condemned to 30 years imprisonment for his role in the attempted coup d'état of the 23 DE FEBRERO, 1981. He was released in 1988. At the time he was arrested, he held an important post as *segundo jefe del Estado Mayor del ejército*. He was a former military instructor and had been personal secretary to the King.

ARMERO, JOSÉ (1927–95)
The intermediary between the government of ADOLFO SUÁREZ and SANTIAGO CARRILLO, leader of the Communist Party in Spain. He was instrumental in the legalisation of the party and it was in his house in Pozuelo that the first interview took place between ADOLFO SUÁREZ and the Communist leader.

ARRABAL TERÁN, FERNANDO (1932–   )
Playwright and novelist, born in MELILLA (North Africa). Has written almost exclusively in French. Among ARRABAL's most important plays are *El cementerio de automóviles* and *Ceremonia por un negro asesinado*. He received the PREMIO NADAL in 1983 for his novel *La Torre herida por el rayo*. In 1987 he received the gold medal of the *Academia de Bellas Artes*. He calls his type of theatre '*teatro pánico*'.

ARRENDAMIENTO
System of land rental by which the farmer pays the land-owner a rent in either cash or kind. This type of tenure accounts for 14% of cultivated land in Spain.

ARRESTO MENOR
Minor offences subject to a maximum prison term of three years.

ARRESTOS DE FIN DE SEMANA
In accordance with the 1995 CÓDIGO PENAL, full-time imprisonment may be substituted by weekend imprisonment (for terms of

up to two years, at the rate of two weekends per week of imprisonment).

ARROYO, EDUARDO (1937–   )
Painter in the pop tradition. He spent several years in exile as a result of satirical works on subjects such as FRANCO, Salazar and Mussolini, which he showed in the Third Paris Biennial in 1963.

ARZAK, JUAN MARIA (1938–   )
Internationally famous restaurateur and chef. His restaurant in SAN SEBASTIÁN is considered to be one of the best in Spain. He was elected *Caballero de la orden de las artes y las letras*. He writes for EL PAÍS in the Sunday supplement and also presents a radio programme entitled *A vivir, que son dos días*, for CADENA SER.

ARZALLUS, XABIER (1932–   )
Basque politician, currently presidente of the PNV. Formerly a Jesuit priest, he first joined the PNV while living in Germany in the sixties. He was a member of parliament for Guipúzcoa in 1977 and 1979.

AS
One of the leading sports newspapers, with a circulation figure of 163,000 during the week and 214,000 for its weekly edition.

ASAMBLEA FEDERAL
Supreme body of the IZQUIERDA UNIDA and equivalent to the CONGRESO FEDERAL of the PSOE. Among its functions are: analysis and debate, approval of the programme for government at national and European level, decisions on party strategy and election of members to the *Consejo Político Federal* which is the main governing body of the party between assemblies.

ASAMBLEA REGIONAL
Each AUTONOMÍA has an assembly, elected by the inhabitants of the region according to a system of proportional representation. The ASAMBLEA works according to the central government model, apart from the fact that there is no upper chamber. Some ASAMBLEAS are much bigger than others, depending on the number of inhabitants per AUTONOMÍA.

ASEC See: *ACUERDO SOBRE SOLUCIÓN EXTRAJUDICIAL DE CONFLICTOS LABORALES*

ASENSIO, ANTONIO (1947–   )
President of the *Grupo* ZETA, a conglomerate of newspapers and magazines, and head of the private television channel ANTENA 3 since 1992. He founded the magazine INTERVIÚ.

ASISTENCIA SANITARIA
Those Spaniards and their dependents who have contributed to the SEGURIDAD SOCIAL have the right to free health care. Up till 1996, prescriptions were free. One may choose any doctor within one's own health district, providing that doctor's list is not full.

ASOCIACIÓN DE ESCRITORES Y PERIODIASTAS INDEPENDIENTES
This professional association for writers and journalists was founded in 1994.

ASOCIACIÓN DE VÍCTIMAS DEL TERRORISMO
Association founded to give help and advice to all those who have suffered from terrorist attacks in Spain. In 1997 they denounced companies and organisations who placed advertisements in the daily newspaper EGIN, alleging that such advertising revenue helps swell the coffers of the Basque terrorist organisation ETA.

ASOCIACIÓN ESPAÑOLA DE LA BANCA PRIVADA
This association represents the banking sector and publishes monthly and annual statistics. It is a powerful lobby within Spain although its interests are now economic rather than political.

ASOCIACIÓN PARA EL PROGRESO DE LA DIRECCIÓN
This body has 3,000 members and organises conferences, training events and seminars on management issues.

ASOCIACIÓN PARA EL PROGRESO EMPRESARIAL
An organisation allied to the CÍRCULO DE EMPRESARIOS, which provides management education and training.

ASOCIACIÓN PARA LA DEFENSA DE LA NATURALEZA

First environmental group to be set up in Spain and headed, in the early days, by the TV journalist Félix Rodríguez de la Fuente. It is a branch of the World Wildlife Fund.

ASOCIADO

In the university system, a part-time lecturer who is usually a practitioner in his or her specialised field.

ASTILLEROS

State shipbuilding company. In 1995 INI proposed that its work force be cut by 60%, which was the occasion of violent conflict throughout the summer. A compromise solution was reached in October of that year.

ASTURIAS

ASTURIAS is one of Spain's autonomous regions. It has a population of 1.1 million and covers an area of 10,565 square kilometres. ASTURIAS is in the north of Spain, bordering to the west on GALICIA and to the east on CANTABRIA. Its main agricultural products are apples (cider is an important bi-product), milk and potatoes. The triangle comprising the three cities of Avilés, Gijón and Oviedo is heavily industrialised. Traditionally a coal-mining area, Asturias produces 53% of Spain's coal, but as elsewhere, this industry is in crisis and the area has suffered much industrial unrest. ASTURIAS also accounts for 32% of national steel production. As with plants in other regions, the steel industry has suffered a painful process of modernisation and restructuring. Oviedo is the regional capital.

ASUNCIÓN, ANTONI

Former *Ministro de Interior* in the GONZÁLEZ government.

ATAPUERCA (BURGOS)

In 1995, the remains of a boy, young man and two other adults were found in ATAPUERCA. They are alleged to be the oldest in Europe.

ATENCIÓN PRIMARIA DE SALUD

Primary health care: this term refers to health provision in ambulatorios or health centres and to that given by the general practitioner.

ATENEO
This Madrid club was founded in 1820 and was frequented by literary figures such as Miguel de Unamuno and politicians such as Primo de Rivera and Azaña. It is well known for its library and its cultural activities of a literary nature. Similar institutions exist in other cities: the ATENEO in SEVILLA is particularly well-known.

ATHLÉTIC
BILBAO football club, founded in 1898 and the second oldest in Spain. It is one of the so-called 'historic' clubs, along with REAL MADRID and BARÇA.

ATLÉTICO DE MADRID
Madrid's second football team and arch rival of REAL MADRID. Its home is the Vicente Calderón stadium and its colours are red and white. Its president is JESÚS GIL Y GIL.

ATOCHA
One of the oldest and most beautiful railway stations in Madrid. It serves stations to the south. The AVE or high-speed train departs from here for SEVILLA.

ATS See: *AYUDANTE TÉCNICO SANITARIO*

ATXAGA, BERNARDO (1951–   )
This Basque writer and poet won the *Premio Nacional de la Literatura* in 1989 for a collection of short stories in Basque, *Obabakoak*, whose translation into Spanish became a best-seller. He has since written *El hombre solo* (1993) and *Esos cielos* (1996).

AUDIENCIA NACIONAL
The High Court. This court investigates and pronounces on offences which concern national rather than community interests. Such offences include treachery, forgery, fraud which affects residents in more than one AUTONOMÍA and offences committed outside Spain. It also has powers of extradition.

AUDIENCIA PROVINCIAL

These provincial courts hear oral public proceedings, in single instance, of major offences. They also deal with appeals against decisions, sentences and judgements of lower courts. They are concerned only with civil and criminal matters.

AUDIENCIA TERRITORIAL

Prior to 1980, these were regional courts. They have been replaced by TRIBUNALES SUPERIORES DE JUSTICIA.

AUTOESCUELA

Driving schools which provide practical and theoretical instruction for the driving test.

AUTONOMÍAS (ESTADO DE)

Spain's ESTADO DE AUTONOMÍAS is the organisation of the state according to a federal system, in which all 17 regions of the country are self-governing. The 17 regions are: ANDALUCÍA, ARAGÓN, CANARIAS, CANTABRIA, CASTILLA Y LEÓN, CASTILLA-LA MANCHA, CATALUÑA, EXTREMADURA, GALICIA, BALEARES, MADRID, MURCIA, NAVARRA, PAÍS VASCO, ASTURIAS, LA RIOJA and LA COMUNIDAD VALENCIANA. The two North African enclaves of CEUTA and MELILLA have an ambiguous status: debate still continues as to how much independence they should be accorded.

Not all regional administrations have the same range of powers. The historical autonomous regions (that is, those which were independent in the past) are CATALUÑA, EL PAÍS VASCO and GALICIA; they enjoy more independence than the others. It is hoped, however, that in the future all regions will have the same degree of autonomy. The responsibilities of government departments such as Education, INSERSO (INSTITUTO NACIONALDE SERVICIOS SOCIALES) and Employment have been devolved to the autonomous regions. CATALUÑA and the PAÍS VASCO have their own police forces. NAVARRA and the PAÍS VASCO also have the power to raise their own taxes and thus pay for services received from central government. This federal system was put into place by ADOLFO SUÁREZ in 1978 just after the death of FRANCO. Although it works well in general, it must be said that the system is heavy in administrative costs. For instance, in 1991, the autonomous regions were responsible for 19% of overall spending, but employed 31% of Spain's civil servants.

AUTOPISTA DE LEIZARÁN
Motorway to be built in the PAÍS VASCO and bitterly opposed by left-wing nationalists. It has been the object of numerous acts of sabotage and fire-bombing.

AUTOPISTAS
The Spanish motorway system has been subject to massive expansion in recent years. All motorways are prefixed by the letter A. Some charge a toll – from 225 pesetas from SAN SEBASTIÁN to the French frontier (A8), to 6,940 ptas from BARCELONA to Alicante (A7).

AUTOPISTAS CONCESIONARIA ESPAÑOLA, S.A.
This company promotes and maintains the following regional motorways: La Jonquera-BARCELONA-Tarragona, ZARAGOZA-Mediterránea, and Mongat-Malgrat.

AUTOPISTAS DEL MARE NOSTRUM, S.A.
This company is the state concessionaire for the Tarragona-VALENCIA, VALENCIA-Alicante and SEVILLA-Cádiz motorways. It constructs and maintains the motorways, and operates the tolls.

AVE
The AVE (*Alta Velocidad Española*) is the name of the Spanish high speed train, akin to the French TGV and the Japanese bullet train. The name is doubly significant: besides the literal translation of the acronym (Spanish high speed) AVE also means bird. Currently, there are only two lines, one linking MADRID with SEVILLA and another from MADRID to Huelva via Cádiz. The choice of this line rather than one going north to BARCELONA and France was due to two factors. Firstly, the desire to improve communications with the poorer regions to the south, and secondly, to have a prestigious link with EXPO 92 in SEVILLA. The AVE has cut the length of the journey from MADRID to SEVILLA from six and a quarter hours to two and a half. The line will be extended in the future to cover the MADRID-BARCELONA-French frontier route thus creating a North-South high speed railway link. The AVE has

the international gauge of 1,435 mm rather than the Spanish gauge of 1,668 mm. See also: RENFE.

AVT See: *ASOCIACIÓN DE VÍCTIMAS DEL TERRORISMO*

AVUI

One of the most important CATALÁN newspapers, entirely written in CATALÁN and published in BARCELONA. Along with EL PAÍS, it was the first newspaper to appear after FRANCO's death. It has a circulation of 30,000.

AYUDANTE

In the university system, a junior lecturer, usually a post-graduate student completing a higher degree.

AYUDANTE TÉCNICO SANITARIO

Male or female nurse, usually working in a hospital.

AYUNTAMIENTO

The Town Hall or AYUNTAMIENTO is responsible for its local MUNICIPIO. It is controlled by the ALCALDE or Mayor, together with his CONCEJALES or town councillors.

AZCONA, RAFAEL (1926–   )

Journalist and script-writer. His most fruitful collaborations have been with LUIS BERLANGA, with whom he worked on the scripts of films such as *La escopeta nacional* (1977) and with CARLOS SAURA. He has written over 100 film scripts in the past 35 years.

AZNAR, JOSÉ MARÍA (1953–   )

Leader of the right-wing PP (PARTIDO POPULAR) since January 1989, when he succeeded MANUEL FRAGA. He was a member of parliament for the AP (ALIANZA POPULAR) from 1982 to 1989 and *presidente* of the autonomous region of CASTILLA Y LEÓN from 1987 to 1989. He was the PP candidate for the presidency in 1989 and 1993. AZNAR was the object of an assassination attempt by ETA in April 1995. In 1996, the PARTIDO POPULAR won the general elections and AZNAR became prime minister (PRESIDENTE DEL GOBIERNO) of Spain.

AZOR

AZOR ('goshawk') is the name of the yacht used by both General FRANCO and FELIPE GONZÁLEZ.

BACALAO

Music with a rhythmic beat which originated in the clubs and discothèques outside VALENCIA, equivalent to the British 'techno' or 'house' music. It is very popular in other clubs on the edges of large towns and cities. The motorways which are lined with discotheques of this sort are called *la ruta del* BACALAO.

BACHILLERATO UNIFICADO Y POLIVALENTE

This course (known as BUP) is designed for students from 15 to 17 and prepares them for University entrance or for vocational training. BUP consists of three year-long courses and is academic in character. In the third year, students may choose between Arts or Sciences or opt for a combination of the two. Assessment is continuous but there is a final examination held in June and September. Students are allowed to proceed to the next class if they fail no more than two subjects. This system, introduced in 1970 under the LGE (*Ley General de Educación*) is gradually being replaced by a new one. See also: LOGSE

BAJO ULLOA, JUANMA (1967–   )

A young film-maker whose first film *Alas de mariposa* won considerable acclaim at the FESTIVAL DE SAN SEBASTIÁN. He also directed *La madre muerta* and *Tierra* (1996).

BALCELLS, CARMEN (1936–   )

Doyenne of literary agents and based in BARCELONA, CARMEN BALCELLS handles authors such as Gabriel García Márquez, Mario Vargas Llosa, JUAN MARSÉ and MANUEL VÁZQUEZ MONTALBÁN.

BALLESTEROS, SEVERIANO (1957–   )

BALLESTEROS was born in Pedrera (CANTABRIA) and has been a golf professional since 1974. Known the world over as 'Sevy', he has won three British Opens (1979, 1984, 1988) and the US Masters twice (1980 and 1983). He was the first man to win 50 European golf tournaments. He served as a role model for many young Spanish golfers such as OLAZÁBAL.

BALSERO
Name given to those who attempt to enter Spain illegally by crossing the straits of Gibraltar from North Africa to Spain. The name comes from the Spanish for 'raft' and refers to the danger-ous craft in which immigrants seek to travel to Europe. They are also known as *espaldas mojadas* or wet-backs. See also: PATERA

BANCA CATALANA
Bank, based in CATALUÑA and BALEARES, of which 96% of the cap-ital is held by the BANCO BILBAO VIZCAYA (BBV).

BANCO AZUL
The seats of those DIPUTADOS whose party is in government. They are upholstered in blue, hence the expression, 'blue bench'.

BANCO BILBAO VIZCAYA, S.A.
This bank is engaged in all major aspects of banking and is extremely active in South America, with offices in Argentina, Colombia, Venezuela, Brazil and Mexico. It was formed in 1989 as a result of the merger between the *Banco Bilbao* and the *Banco Vizcaya*.

BANCO CENTRAL HISPANO
This bank has over 4,000 branches throughout Spain as well as branches in Germany, Belgium, France, Gibraltar, Italy, the UK and in South America. It was formed as a result of a merger between the *Banco Central* and the *Banco Hispanoamericano* in 1991.

BANCO DE ESPAÑA
This bank was awarded exclusive rights of issue in 1874, was nationalized in 1962 and is currently completely independent from government control. It is the nation's central bank and is subject to the *Ley de Autonomía del Banco de España*. It is responsible for managing foreign currency reserves and exchange rate policy: it oversees the work of the clearing banks and may impose sanctions on those which do not comply with its

requests. It also issues notes and coins and is the official bank of the state and of the autonomous regions.

BANCO DE FOMENTO
This bank merged in 1995 with *Hispamer*, to form *Hispamer Banco Finanzas*.

BANCO DE LA PEQUEÑA Y MEDIANA EMPRESA
This bank finances small and medium businesses or PYMES (PEQUEÑAS Y MEDIANAS EMPRESAS).

BANCO DE SANTANDER
Large clearing bank, which works closely with the Royal Bank of Scotland and the North American bank, First Fidelity. It has a joint venture with the insurance company *Geminis*. One of the big four Spanish clearing banks, it has 341 branches abroad (many of which are in South America) and 1,481 in Spain.

BANCO DEL COMERCIO
Formerly the *Banco de Financiación Industrial* (*Indubán*), this bank now finances and undertakes industrial promotions.

BANCO EXTERIOR DE ESPAÑA
This bank operates as a private bank but differs from other banks operating in Spain in that it is particularly orientated towards foreign trade transactions and specifically to export credit transactions. It is now part of the ARGENTARIA group.

BANCO GALLEGO
Formerly known as the *Banco de Crédito e Inversiones*, this bank changed its name in 1988.

BANCO INDUSTRIAL DE BILBAO
This bank finances medium-term investments and industrial participants. It is a wholly owned subsidiary of the BANCO BILBAO VIZCAYA.

BANCO POPULAR ESPAÑOL
This bank is involved in all types of banking business and ancillary services. It has branches throughout Spain and also in Germany, Belgium, France, the Netherlands, the UK,

Switzerland and Venezuela. It is controlled by members of the OPUS DEI. It is the smallest of the big four Spanish clearing banks.

BANCO SABADELL
A medium sized clearing bank dealing with individual clients and small and medium sized businesses. It has a network of more than 400 branches throughout Spain.

BANCO ZARAGOZANO
This bank operates through a network of 349 branches and agencies nationwide. It is also involved in leasing, mortgage granting, factoring, capital and money markets, insurance, real estate administration and investment management.

BANDERA
The colours of the Spanish flag are red (at the top), yellow (double width) and red.

BANDERAS, ANTONIO (DOMÍNGUEZ BANDERAS, JOSÉ ANTONIO) (1961–)
ANTONIO BANDERAS began his career with the Spanish National Theatre before moving into the cinema, first with PEDRO ALMODÓVAR and then in Hollywood. He appeared in ALMODÓVAR's *Mujeres al borde de un ataque de nervios* and *Átame*, and made his American debut in *Mambo Kings*, after which he appeared in a number of films, including *Philadelphia*, *Miami Rhapsody*, and *The House of Spirits*. He also starred in *Assassins* opposite Sylvester Stallone, and in *Two Much* with Melanie Griffith. Perhaps his most famous role has been as the narrator *Ché* in the recent film *Evita*, with Madonna. He is considered by some to be the '90s equivalent of Rudolf Valentino.

BANDOS
Edicts issued by the ALCALDE of a town or city on relatively minor matters. The ALCALDE may do this without consulting his councillors.

BANDRÉS, JUAN MARÍA (1932–)
Basque politician, he has been a SENADOR, DIPUTADO and EURODIPUTADO. He was the founder and leader of EUSKADIKO EZKERRA, which was eventually absorbed into the PSOE. During the

transition years, he negotiated the rehabilitation of ex-ETA terrorists. In 1994 he retired from politics and is now *presidente* of the *Comisión de Ayuda al Refugiado*.

BANESTO

BANESTO, the *Banco Español de Crédito*, is Spain's fourth largest bank. In 1995 it was revealed that its assets were worth 605 billion pesetas less than previously thought, and its former chairman, MARIO CONDE, was sued by the bank's shareowners for mismanagement and fraud. It was then amalgamated with the BANCO SANTANDER. The name BANESTO is known internationally for its sponsorship of a cycling team of which MIGUEL INDURÁIN was a member until his retirement from the sport.

BANKINTER

This bank is a private corporation concentrating on banking activities. Founded in 1965, it finances industrial and business deals with medium- and long-term loans and investments.

BAQUEIRA BERET

A well-known and popular ski resort in CATALUÑA, often frequented by the Spanish royal family.

BARAJAS

National and international airport, located in MADRID. At present it has two runways and a third is under construction, but there is serious congestion especially in the summer months. Currently under discussion is whether the present airport should be expanded to accommodate 5 runways or whether to build a second airport to serve MADRID.

BARBACID MONTALBÁN, MARIANO (1950–   )

Biochemist. Latterly, *vicepresidente* of the *Instituto de Investigación Farmacéutica Bristol-Mayers Squibb*, he has spent most of his working life in the United States, in the National Cancer Institute in Bethesda. In 1982 he discovered the first cancer-producing gene, a fundamental discovery for understanding the causes of cancer. He is one of a growing number of Spanish scientists with an international reputation.

BARBERÁ, RITA (1948–   )

Alcaldesa of VALENCIA since 1991, she succeeded Clementina Ródenas in this post. She defines herself as a person working in politics but who is not a politician and is one of a growing number of women mayors in Spain. Currently (1997) she is the *presidenta* of the *Federación Española de Municipios y Provincias* – the association of mayors of Spanish towns and cities. Ideologically, she is close to the PP.

BARBERO, MARINO (1930–   )

Examining magistrate for the CASO FILESA from 1991 to 1995, when he resigned, alleging that he had not been supported by the CGPJ (CONSEJO GENERAL DEL PODER JUDICIAL). Barbero was originally a professor of criminal law.

BARÇA

Popular name for the Barcelona Football Club, housed in the Camp Nou stadium. Its slogan, *el* BARÇA *es mes que un club* (BARÇA is more than a club) sums up the importance of the football team for CATALUÑA. Their supporters are known as the *culés*: their colours are blue and burgundy.

BARCELONA

BARCELONA is Spain's second city and capital of CATALUÑA. It is an ancient and beautiful port on the Mediterranean. In 1992 it was home to the Olympic Games and as a result of 800,000 million pesetas invested by the state, the AUTONOMÍA and private investors, much of BARCELONA (especially the port area) has been refurbished and the city, instead of turning its back on the sea, now looks out towards it. The transport system has been transformed, new sports stadiums built and the *Villa Olímpica del Poblenou* (the Olympic Village) converted into flats and apartments for BARCELONA citizens. BARCELONA is internationally known for its architectural creations by Antoni Gaudí.

BARDEM, JAVIER (1970–   )

Young film actor, member of a famous acting family. His most recent films have been: *Boca a boca* (1995) in which he appeared with JOSEP MARÍA FLOTATS, *Tierra* (ULLOA) which came out in 1996, and in 1997 he appeared in ALMODÓVAR's *Carne trémula* and ALEX

DE LA IGLESIA's *Perdita Durango*. He has worked in three films with BIGAS LUNA and has received the PREMIO GOYA for best actor twice. He was also awarded the CONCHA DE ORO at the SAN SEBASTIÁN film festival. His mother is the actress PILAR BARDEM.

BARDEM, JUAN ANTONIO (1922–   )

Film director who worked extensively throughout the FRANCO years and whose films contrast ideologically with those of the establishment. Among other films, he has directed *Muerte de un ciclista* (1955) and *Calle Mayor* (1956). He has recently produced a television series on the life of Lorca.

BARDEM, PILAR (1939–   )

Mother of JAVIER and Mónica, and sister of JUAN ANTONIO, PILAR BARDEM is a well known actress in her own right, both in the cinema and on stage.

BARRAL, CARLOS (1928–1989)

Writer and editor. Director for many years of *Barral Editores*, one of the leading publishing houses in CATALUÑA. Among his better known works are *Años de penitencia*, *Los años sin excusa* and *Penúltimos castigos*. He discovered and published many of the Latin American authors of the so-called 'boom'.

BARRANCO, MARÍA

Cinema and theatre actress, well known for her comic performances – from Málaga, she has a strong southern accent, which she can use to comic effect. She belongs to the new generation of young Spanish actors who appeared in the 1980s. She was one of the '*chicas* ALMODÓVAR' and appeared in *Mujeres al borde de un ataque de nervios* and *¿Qué he hecho yo para merecer esto?*. In 1996 she won the prize for best actress in the *Festival de Cine Joven* in *Alfaz del Pi* (ALICANTE). Also in 1996 she appeared in *Bwana*, which won the prize for best film at the SAN SEBASTIÁN film festival. This film represented Spain in the 1997 Oscar Awards.

BARRIO CHINO

Red light districts, which are to be found in many Spanish cities.

The largest and least discreet one is in BARCELONA, right next to the RAMBLAS.

BARRIONUEVO PEÑA, JOSÉ (1942–   )

Lawyer, journalist and politician, BARRIONUEVO was *ministro del Interior* from 1982 to 1988 and *ministro de Transporte* from 1988 to 1991. During his time at the MINISTERIO DEL INTERIOR, he applied some harsh policies but also declared his willingness to negotiate with ETA and to reintegrate into society those members of ETA who had renounced violence. In 1995 he was accused by RICARDO GARCÍA DAMBORENEA of helping create GAL and was placed under investigation on suspicion of kidnapping, misuse of public funds and association with an armed gang. In 1996, BARRIONUEVO paid 15 million pesetas bail to ensure his freedom.

BASE

Term used to refer to the rank and file members of Spanish political parties.

BBK See: *BILBAO BIZKAIA KUTXA*

BBV See: *BANCO BILBAO VIZCAYA*

BC NET – COOPERACIÓN ENTRE PYMES

These centres provide information for small and medium-sized businesses. There are 38 centres in all.

BEAUTIFUL

This English term has been used in recent years to refer to members of the jet-set, who appear frequently in the gossip magazines.

BECAS

Scholarships are available to students in need. In 1995, 850,000 scholarships were awarded with a total value of 100.000 million pesetas. ANDALUCÍA was the AUTONOMÍA which received the highest number of scholarships.

BECERRIL, SOLEDAD

Politician: has been *ministro de la Cultura*. Currently (1995) *alcaldesa de Sevilla*. She belongs to the PARTIDO POPULAR.

BEIRAS, XOSÉ MANUEL (1936–   )
Politician and Galician nationalist, founder of the *Partido Socialista Galego* in 1963. He is a professor of economics and leader of the BLOQUE NACIONALISTA GALEGO.

BELÉN, ANA (1950–   )
Singer, song-writer and actress. She has worked in the classical theatre as well as appearing in films such as *Sonámbulos* (1977) and *Demonios en el jardín* (1982). She was especially popular in the television series *Fortunata y Jacinta* (1979), directed by MARIO CAMUS. She has also recorded many albums, together with her husband VICTOR MANUEL. In 1996 she toured Spain with SERRAT, VICTOR MANUEL and MIGUEL RÍOS, in a very successful concert entitled *El gusto es nuestro*.

BELLOCH JUIVE, JUAN ALBERTO (1950–   )
Politician, and jurist. He was formerly a judge and *presidente* of the *Audiencia de* BILBAO in 1988 and member of the CGPJ in 1990. He founded the *Asociación pro Derechos Humanos* in the PAÍS VASCO. He was *ministro de Justicia* under the last GONZALÉZ government. He is currently a DIPUTADO for PSOE (1996) for ZARAGOZA.

BENEGAS, TXIKI
Basque politician, *secretario de Relaciones Políticas e Institucionales* on the PSOE executive until the new executive took office in 1997. He is currently DIPUTADO for Vizcaya.

BENEMÉRITA
Term often applied to the GUARDIA CIVIL. It means 'worthy of merit'.

BENET, JUAN (1927–1993)
Novelist and engineer. *Volverás a Región* was a novel which began a new literary style in the Spanish novel, directly opposed to the neo-realism which was in vogue at the time. Other novels by BENET are *Una meditación* and *La otra casa de Mazón*.

BENIDORM
Originally a small fishing village, this town grew to massive proportions during the tourist boom of the 1960s (80,000 inhabitants

during the winter and over 2 million in the summer). Situated in the province of Alicante, BENIDORM has wonderful beaches and a favourable climate. It is a popular resort for the elderly during the winter months and with young people during the summer.

BENÍTEZ REYES, FELIPE (1961–   )
Poet and author. He won the PREMIO NACIONAL DE POESÍA in 1996 for his collection *Vidas improbables*. Among his other published works are *El equipaje abierto* and *Impares Fila 13*.

BERLANGA, LUIS (1921–   )
Film director and critic, BERLANGA's most important film is *¡Bienvenido míster Marshall!* (1952) which has become one of the classics of the Spanish cinema. His cinema suffered under the dictatorship through a rigorous censorship but in the 1980s he was able to make a series of popular and successful films including a trilogy which recounts the transition from dictatorship to democracy, *La escopeta nacional* (1978), *Patrimonio nacional* (1980) and *Nacional III* (1982). For many years BERLANGA collaborated on scripts with RAFAEL AZCONA. His latest film *Todos a la cárcel* (1993) was co-written with his son, Jorge Berlanga.

BERTA
Nickname for the central computer of the MINISTRO DEL INTERIOR in which files on Spanish citizens are kept.

BETIS
The name of the SEVILLA football club. It comes from the Roman name for the province of ANDALUCÍA.

BIBLIOTECA NACIONAL
Founded in 1712, and situated in MADRID, (Paseo de Recoletos 20), it houses a collection of important historical documents, books, letters, incunabula, engravings and maps. It owns manuscripts by Calderón, Lope de Vega and Borges and drawings by Goya, Durer and Piranesi. The Museo del Libro was created in 1995 and has 7 rooms equipped with interactive multi-media work stations.

BIESCAS
Town in ARAGÓN in which the camp-site La Virgen de las Nieves

is situated. In August 1996 the camp-site was destroyed by an avalanche of mud and rock and 86 people were killed.

BIGAS LUNA, JOSÉ JUAN (1946–   )

Film director. He made a series of low-budget films in the 1970s but has become internationally known through a series of semi-erotic films including *Jamón jamón* (1992), *La teta y la luna* and *Huevos de oro* (1993). *Bambola* was presented in the 1996 Cannes Film Festival, and *La camarera del Titanic* opened in Spain in 1997.

BILBAO

BILBAO, situated on the River Nervión, is one of Spain's largest cities and capital of the province of Guipúzcoa. Although it has always been an important industrial centre, its importance has waned recently, because of its dependence on ship-building and the iron and steel industry. A stunning new art gallery, clad externally in titanium, has just been built on the banks of the Nervión. It was designed by Frank Gehry, and contains works from the Guggenheim collection in New York.

BILBAO BIZKAIA KUTXA

The largest savings bank in the Basque country and the fourth largest in Spain.

BIMBO

Along with *Panrico*, one of the two companies which provide Spain with factory-produced bread and buns.

BLAHNIK MANOLO (1946–   )

Shoe designer with an international reputation. He was born in CANARIAS and currently lives in London. He is known for his exclusive footwear which he sells to the rich and famous.

BLANCO GARRIDO, MIGUEL ÁNGEL (1968–1997)

Young Basque PP councillor who was captured by the Basque terrorist group ETA on July 11th, 1997 and executed on the 13th, 2 days later. ETA had demanded that Basque prisoners held in jails outside the Basque country should be removed to other jails within the territory. When the government of JOSÉ MARÍA AZNAR refused, ETA shot BLANCO. The Spanish people came out onto the streets in massive numbers, to protest against terrorism and the king himself appeared on television to condemn the murder.

BLÁZQUEZ PÉREZ, RICARDO
Formerly Bishop of Palencia, he was appointed by the Pope in September 1995 to be the Bishop of BILBAO. This was an unpopular appointment, as BLÁZQUEZ PÉREZ is a conservative and non-Basque speaker.

BLOQUE NACIONALISTA GALEGO
The BNG is a left-wing group which came third in the 1989 regional elections, winning 5 seats out of 75. In the October 1993 elections it more than doubled its vote (to 18.7%) and won 13 seats out of 75. In late 1991 it amalgamated with the *Partido Nacionalista Galego*, led by Pablo González Mariñas which had split from the CG in 1986. It won 2 seats in the CONGRESO in 1995 and has now become the major nationalist party in GALICIA. Its current leader is XOSÉ MANUEL BEIRAS.

BNG See: *BLOQUE NACIONALISTA GALEGO*

BOADELLA, ALBERT (1943–   )
Theatre director and founder, in 1962, of the CATALÁN theatre troupe, ELS JOGLARS. ELS JOGLARS has always been subversive. Indeed BOADELLA himself was imprisoned for staging *La torna* in 1977. Recent productions of the company have included *Yo tengo un tío en América* (1991), a satire on the 500th anniversary of the discovery of America. In 1996 the company produced *Ubu President*, a political satire.

BODEGAS Y BEBIDAS, S.A.
This company and its subsidiaries buy, sell, manufacture and bottle wines. The group is also involved in the production and sale of liqueurs and other beverages as well as food-stuffs.

BODEGUIYA
Informal bar in the MONCLOA Palace in which FELIPE GONZÁLEZ used to meet close friends and colleagues.

BOE See: *BOLETÍN OFICIAL DEL ESTADO*

BOFILL, RICARDO (1939–   )
Important CATALÁN architect, he has designed a range of prestigious buildings, including the Teatro Nacional de Cataluña and the new BARCELONA airport. In 1963 he created the *Taller de Arquitectura Bofill* whose aim is to produce innovative architectural designs.

BOHIGAS, ORIOL (1925–   )
CATALÁN architect, formerly director of the *Escola Técnica Superior d'Arquitectura de Barcelona* and also the city's director of urban projects. He played a major role in the architectural projects devised for the 1992 Olympic Games.

BOIXOS NOIS
Tribe of skinheads, based in CATALUÑA. They are active at football matches especially those in which BARÇA is playing.

BOLETÍN OFICIAL DE LAS CORTES GENERALES
This publication publishes draft bills at various stages of approval. Only fully-approved Acts of Parliament appear in the BOLETÍN OFICIAL DEL ESTADO.

BOLETÍN OFICIAL DEL ESTADO
This bulletin, published daily, is the official organ of the state and publishes such items as examination dates and the text of new laws and statutes. Indeed, all laws must be published in the BOLETÍN if they are to have official status.

BOLLAÍN, ICÍAR (1968–   )
Basque actress. She was discovered by VICTOR ERICE at the age of 15 and he cast her as *Estrella* in *El sur* (1983). She appeared with her twin sister Marina in *Las dos orillas* (1986) and in 1992 in *Díme una mentira*. In 1995 she played *Maite* in Ken Loach's *Tierra y Libertad*. She also directed her first feature film in 1995, entitled *Hola, ¿estás sola?*

BOLSA
Name for the Stock Exchange. There are four in Spain, in MADRID, VALENCIA, BILBAO and BARCELONA.

BONET, MARÍA DEL MAR (1947–   )

This song-writer and singer from MALLORCA was heavily involved in the *Nova Cançó* (New Song) movement in the 1960s in which music was used as a form of protest against the military régime. Her latest album was released in 1995 and is entitled *Salmaia*. MARIA DEL MAR BONET sings in CATALÁN. See also: RAIMÓN, JOAN MANUEL SERRAT, LLUIS LLACH

BONO

A voucher, pass or special price on items such as museum entry or bus and metro travel.

BONOBUS

A compound word from *bono*, 'voucher', and *bus*, this is a travel card which entitles the holder to ten bus journeys at a reduced rate.

BONOLOTO

State lottery. Players can participate four times in a draw during one week, using the same numbers.

BORAU, JOSÉ LUIS (1929–   )

Film director and teacher at the *Escuela Oficial de Cinematografía*. His most important films are *Furtivos* (1975) a drama which was a great success at the box-office and *Tata mía* (1986), a comedy. Recently he has worked in television where he directed the series *Celia* (1992) based on the children's stories by Elena Fortún. In 1987 he won the *Medalla de Oro de las Bellas Artes*.

BORBÓN Y BATTEMBURG, JUAN DE (1913–1993)

Son of Alfonso XIII and father of the present King, JUAN CARLOS, JUAN DE BORBÓN, or *El Conde de Barcelona*, lived the majority of his life in exile in Portugal. He formally relinquished his claim to the Spanish throne in 1977, in favour of his son.

BORBÓN Y BORBÓN, JUAN CARLOS DE (1938–   )

King of Spain, grandson of King Alfonso XIII and great-great-grandson of Queen Victoria. Educated in Switzerland and at the University of MADRID. Married Sofía of Greece in 1962. One son, FELIPE, and two daughters, ELENA and CRISTINA. Named future king of Spain by FRANCO, instead of his father, JUAN DE BORBÓN. Ascended to the throne in November 1975. He played an important role during the transition from dictatorship to democracy, especially on the night of the 23rd of February 1981 when MILANS DEL BOSCH attempted a coup d'état. The King appeared that night on Spanish television and ordered those soldiers implicated in the plot to lay down their arms. His words on that occasion have become legendary. '*La corona, símbolo de permanencia y unidad de la Patria, no puede tolerar acciones o actitudes que pretenden interrumpir por la fuerza el proceso democrático que la Constitución, votada por el pueblo español, determinó en su día a través de referéndum*'. In August 1995, the King again hit the headlines when it was disclosed that there had been an attempt against his life by the Basque terrorist group ETA.

The King of Spain has three major functions. Firstly, he is the supreme representative of the state, most obviously in the area of international relations. Secondly, he is a symbol of Spanish unity, recognised as Head of State by the 17 AUTONOMÍAS or regional governments. Thirdly, he represents continuity, as embodied in the principle of succession.

BORBÓN Y GRECIA, CRISTINA DE (1965–   )
Second daughter of the King and Queen of Spain. Currently lives in BARCELONA where she works as a cultural adviser to the CAIXA. In 1997 she married the international handball player, Iñaki Urdangarín, in BARCELONA.

BORBÓN Y GRECIA, ELENA DE (1963–   )
Eldest daughter of the King and Queen of Spain. She married JAIME DE MARICHALAR on 18th of March 1995 in Seville. It was the first royal wedding in Spain since 1906. After their marriage, the couple acquired the title of *Duques de Lugo*.

BORBÓN Y GRECIA, FELIPE DE (1968–   )
Also known as the *Príncipe de Asturias, don* FELIPE is the only son of the King and Queen of Spain and heir to the Spanish throne. Born in 1968, he has been educated extensively abroad, recently completing a master's degree in international relations in Georgetown in the United States. His secondary education

was in Madrid and Toronto: he later completed a law degree in Madrid and has also completed courses in the army, air force and naval academies.

BORRELL FONTELLES, JOSÉ (1947–   )

University professor of mathematics and member of the PSOE. He has been director of the *Secretaría de Estado de Hacienda* and was *ministro de Obras Públicas, Transportes y Medio Ambiente* in the last GONZÁLEZ government.

BOSÉ LUCÍA (1931–   )

Originally an Italian film actress and former Miss Italy, LUCÍA BOSÉ has worked extensively in the Spanish film industry with directors such as JOSÉ ANTONIO BARDEM and JAIME CHÁVARRI. She is the mother of the actor and singer MIGUEL BOSÉ.

BOSÉ, MIGUEL (1956–   )

Singer, director and actor, BOSÉ belongs to a well-known Spanish family, his father being the bull-fighter LUIS MIGUEL DOMINGUÍN, and his mother LUCÍA BOSÉ, cinema actress.

BOTELLA, ANA (1953–   )

Wife of JOSÉ MARÍA AZNAR, leader of the PARTIDO POPULAR. She is a member of the PP and supports her husband in his political ambitions in much the same style as the American first ladies. As a civil servant, she has worked in the MINISTERIO DEL INTERIOR, in the MINISTERIO DE OBRAS PÚBLICAS and in the tax department in RIOJA.

BOTÍN, EMILIO (1934–   )

Presidente of the BANCO SANTANDER since 1986. BANCO SANTANDER is now the biggest bank in Spain having acquired BANESTO in 1994.

BOYER SALVADOR, MIGUEL (1939–   )

Formerly *ministro de la Economía* in the GONZÁLEZ government (1982–85) and *presidente* of the BANCO EXTERIOR DE ESPAÑA (1985–88), BOYER was a key figure in the first years of the socialist government. Among other things, he devalued the peseta, reduced the working week to 40 hours and reformed the tax system. On the 23rd of February 1983, he expropriated RUMASA, the group of companies created by JOSÉ MARÍA RUIZ MATEOS. In 1996 he formally broke off his affiliation with the Socialist party. He is married to ISABEL PREYSLER.

BP OIL ESPAÑA, S.A.
This company imports and refines crude oil and sells petroleum products at its main plant in Castellón de la Plana.

BRIGADA DE ESTUPEFACIENTES
The Spanish Drug squad.

BUÑUEL, LUIS (1900–1983)
Born in Calanda, Teruel, BUÑUEL is one of the great directors of the cinema. His first film, *Le chien andalou* (1928), was made in collaboration with SALVADOR DALÍ and is a film classic. Much of his work was shot outside Spain: he made *Nazarín*, *Los olvidados* and *El ángel exterminador* in Mexico and *Diario de una camarera*, *Belle de jour* and *El encanto discreto de la burguesía* in France. Two of his great films, *Viridiana* and *Tristana* were made in Spain.

BUP See: *BACHILLERATO UNIFICADO Y POLIVALENTE*

CAA See: *COMANDOS AUTÓNOMOS ANTI-CAPITALISTAS*

CABALLÉ FOLCH, MONTSERRAT (1934–)

Internationally celebrated CATALÁN mezzo-soprano, CABALLÉ made her operatic debut in Basle in 1956 having studied at the LICEU in BARCELONA. In the 38 years of her career, she has appeared on the operatic stage no fewer than 3,800 times and has starred in 130 different roles. She has worked with most of the famous conductors, including Karajan, Bernstein, Solti and Guilini. She specialises in operas by Verdi and Donizetti.

CABAÑEROS

Area of outstanding ecological importance in the provinces of Ciudad Real and Toledo. It was the subject of a fierce ideological battle between the army and ecologists who campaigned for 12 years to prevent the region from being used as a firing range. In 1995, CABAÑEROS was declared a national park.

CABILDO Y CONSEJOS INSULARES

The MUNICIPIOS in the Spanish islands come under a CABILDO or CONSEJO rather than a DIPUTACIÓN. In the CANARIAS there exists the *Mancomunidad de Cabildos* and in the BALEARES, a *Consejo General Interinsular*, which bring the different CABILDOS together in a joint body.

CABLEVISIÓN

Cable company, in which the television company CANAL+ and the telephone company TELEFÓNICA both collaborate. Other cable companies are *Cableuropa* and *Multivisión*.

CABRALES (QUESO DE)

One of the best of Spanish cheeses; made in ASTURIAS. It is a blue, strongly favoured cheese, wrapped in leaves.

EL CABRIL

Storage site in the Sierra Morena (Hornachuelos) in which all the radio-active materials in Spain are buried. It is administered by ENRESA (EMPRESA NACIONAL DE RESIDUOS RADIOACTIVOS). It was opened in 1992 in the midst of much local opposition.

CACHO, FERMÍN (1969–   )

Gold medal winner in the Barcelona Olympic Games in 1992 in the 1,500 metres. He became European champion over the same distance in 1994 and won the silver medal in the World Championships in Stuttgart in 1993.

CADAQUÉS

Originally a fishing village on the COSTA BRAVA, CADAQUÉS is now a tourist resort, made famous by the surrealist painter, SALVADOR DALÍ.

CADENA DE ONDAS POPULARES ESPAÑOLAS

COPE is a radio network with 111 stations. It is the second most popular radio network after CADENA SER with over 3 million listeners. It also has interests in the commercial television networks. The Roman Catholic Church has an 80% holding in the network which is managed by the CONFERENCIA EPISCOPAL.

CADENA SER

The most popular radio network in Spain with over 4 million listeners. HOY POR HOY, the programme hosted by IÑAKI GABILONDO on SER is the radio programme with most listeners in Spain (almost 2 million).

CAE See: *CONSEJO ASESOR DE EXPORTACIÓN*

CAFÉ GIJÓN

Café in the Paseo del Prado in MADRID, famous in the past for its literary *tertulias*, or gatherings of poets and novelists.

CAFÉ PARA TODOS

'Coffee for everyone' – a saying coined at the time of the

creation of the AUTONOMÍAS. It was felt that if certain COMPETEN-
CIAS, or powers, were devolved to one or more AUTONOMÍA, the
others would want them too.

CAIXA
BARCELONA-based bank which originally started life as a
Savings Bank but is now one of Spain's largest financial institu-
tions. It was formed in 1989 as a result of a merger between the
*CAIXA de Pensions per a la Vellesa i d'Estalvis de Catalunya i
Balears* and the *CAIXA de BARCELONA*.

CAJA LABORAL POPULAR
This bank lends money to the cooperatives at MONDRAGÓN, as
well as being the commercial headquarters of the cooperative
movement and responsible for research and planning. There are
currently 93 branches throughout the PAÍS VASCO.

CAJA RURAL
The CAJAS RURALES are mutual savings banks originally founded
to help finance small farmers. Many of them now form part of
the *Asociación Española de Cajas Rurales* and the *Banco de
Crédito Cooperativo*. Others are allied to the *Banco de Crédito
Agrícola* (now part of the *Caja Postal*)

CAJAS DE AHORRO
The CAJAS DE AHORRO or savings banks, began life as mutual savings banks, but as in other similar institutions throughout
Europe and America, they have gradually adopted the procedures of mainstream banking institutions. There has also been a
steady process of mergers which has reduced their number from
78 in 1990 to 57 in 1991. This number is still falling. The three
most important CAJAS are the *Caja de Madrid*, *La* CAIXA and BIL-
BAO BIZKAIA KUTXA. The CAJAS enjoy certain tax benefits.

CAJERO AUTÓMATICO
Also known as the *cajero permanente*, these are automatic cash
dispensers. They are usually shared by several banks.

CALATRAVA, SANTIAGO (1951–   )
Important architect, designer of the TELEFÓNICA tower which
overlooks BARCELONA and the Bac de Roda-Felip 2 bridge.

LA CALDERA DE TABURIENTE

Important national park in La Palma (CANARIAS). Famous for its volcanic landscape. It was declared a national park in 1954 in order to conserve some of the original pine forests in the Canary Islands. It is sited in a huge bowl (or *caldera*) formed by the flow of water and by land-slides.

CALENDARIO ESCOLAR

The school calendar differs in Spain according to whether a pupil attends primary or secondary school. Normally primary school children begin the school year in the middle of September and finish in the last week of June. Secondary school pupils start in the second half of September and finish in the last week of June also. University students start their term at the beginning of October and finish at the beginning of June. At all levels of education, there are two weeks holiday at Christmas and one week at Easter.

CALVIÑO, JOSÉ MARÍA (1943–   )

Director-General of RTVE from 1982 to 1986, he was the first post-FRANCO director and the first who tried to make the television company self-financing.

CALVO SOTELO, LEOPOLDO (1926–   )

CALVO SOTELO was *ministro de Comercio* in the first post-FRANCO government under Carlos Arias Navarro (1975–1977). He was subsequently *ministro de Obras Públicas* in SUÁREZ' first government, *Presidente* of the government from 1981 to 1982 and leader of the UCD after SUÁREZ' resignation. The attempted coup d'etat of 23rd of February took place during the investiture of CALVO SOTELO.

CAMACHO, MARCELINO (1918–   )

Leader and guiding light of the trade union COMISIONES OBRERAS from its inception in 1964. He was *secretario general* from 1976 to 1987 when he was succeeded by ANTONIO GUTIÉRREZ. He was sentenced to 6 years imprisonment under the FRANCO régime when trade unionism was illegal. He was released at the time of the amnesty declared by ADOLFO SUAREZ's government in 1976.

CÁMARA ALTA
The higher chamber of the CORTES, also known as the SENADO. It is housed in the *Palacio del Senado*.

CÁMARA BAJA
The lower chamber of the CORTES, also known as the CONGRESO and housed in the *Palacio del Congreso*.

CÁMARA DE COMERCIO, INDUSTRIA Y NAVEGACIÓN
Chambers of Commerce in Spain are responsible to the *Ministerio de Industria y Energía*. Membership is obligatory: all those involved in those activities covered by the CÁMARA must be affiliated. The CÁMARA defends the interests of its members and provides a variety of services such as legal, economic and financial advice. It also helps with export promotion, documentation and trade missions.

CAMARÓN DE LA ISLA (1950–1992)
Flamenco singer, who sang with PACO DE LUCÍA and latterly, with TOMATITO. He died of lung cancer in 1992. He was one of the great influences on younger singers and musicians.

CAMBIO 16
One of the most popular of the weekly news and current affairs magazines, with a circulation of 110,000. Its name 'Change 16' comes from the number of people who founded the magazine in 1972.

CAMF See: *CENTROS DE ATENCIÓN A MINUSVÁLIDOS FÍSICOS*

EL CAMINO DE SANTIAGO
EL CAMINO DE SANTIAGO is the original Pilgrim's Way through northern Spain to SANTIAGO, home of the shrine of St. James. It leads through a series of pilgrim towns and cities, with churches, roads, bridges and hospices of historical and cultural importance. 1993 was the year of St. James or the *Año Compostelano*. Projects initiated recently to improve and enhance the status of the pilgrims' route have included better signposting and restora-

tion of sections of the route and of monuments of historical significance.

CAMP See: *CENTROS DE ATENCIÓN A MINUSVÁLIDOS PSÍQUICOS*

CAMPSA See: *COMPAÑIA ARRENDATARIA DE MONOPOLIO DE PETRÓLEOS, S.A.*

CANAL 9
Local television station in the COMUNIDAD VALENCIANA. With a 19.9% share of the audience, it is the largest and most successful of the local channels. It produces a large number of its own programmes.

CANAL 33
Television station which broadcasts entirely in CATALÁN. Together with TV3, it forms part of TELEVISIÓ DE CATALUNYA, controlled by the *Corporació Catalana de Radio i Televisió*.

CANAL+
A pay television channel. It specialises in showing new films, sports programmes and documentaries. It costs three thousand pesetas a month to subscribe and requires a decoder to receive pictures. Among its share-holders are EL CORTE INGLÉS and CADENA SER.

CANAL SATÉLITE DIGITAL
Digital satellite television channel used, to date, by a million viewers. It offers a 'pay per view' service for first division football matches.

CANAL SUR
Regional television channel in ANDALUCÍA.

CANARIAS See: *ISLAS CANARIAS*

CANDANCHÚ
Ski resort in the Pyrenees in ARAGÓN. It is very popular with the Spanish royal family.

LA CANDELARIA
The Feast of the Purification of Our Lady and the Presentation

of Jesus. An important feast day in Spain, it takes place on the 2nd of February. A number of towns have special processions commemorating the offering of the two doves in the temple.

CANO, CARLOS
Andalusian singer and songwriter, his first album *A duras penas* appeared in 1976. He writes *coplas* and *habaneras* which tell simple stories about ordinary people. Among his most popular compositions are *Alacena de las monjas*, *Sevillanas de Chamberí* and *Mari-María*.

CANO, LOURDES
Popular TV actress, she currently appears in the hugely successful TV series, *Farmacia de guardia* which is shown by the private TV company ANTENA 3.

CANÓN SINDICAL
Contribution paid to trades' unions. It is paid by non-members in the workplace, as well as by union members.

CANTABRIA
This AUTONOMÍA is situated in the north of Spain, to the east of ASTURIAS and to the west of the PAÍS VASCO. It is a mountainous region, with its major industries based in SANTANDER, Torrelavega and Reinosa. SANTANDER is an important port with a mixed economy comprising tourism, steel making, shipbuilding, and the manufacture of marine equipment, heavy capital goods and household appliances. It is also a large fishing port with a ferry service to Plymouth in the United Kingdom. Tourism on the coast and in the mountains is an important service industry and the region is famous for its dairy products. SANTANDER is the regional capital.

CAP See: *CERTIFICADO DE APTITUD PEDAGÓGICA*

CAR See: *CENTROS DE ACOGIDA A REFUGIADOS*

CARA AL SOL
Song sung by members of the *Falange*, the fascist movement founded in 1933 by José Antonio Primo de Rivera.

CARABANCHEL
Large prison in MADRID.

CÁRITAS
Charitable institution, affiliated to the Roman Catholic Church, which works on social projects within the community. One of its current projects is with illegal immigrants from North Africa (BALSEROS).

CARLES, RICARD MARÍA
Archbishop of BARCELONA, he was accused in 1996 of money laundering by tax officials in Italy.

JUAN CARLOS See: *BORBÓN Y BORBÓN, JUAN CARLOS DE*

CARRERAS I COLL, JOSÉ (1945–   )
Internationally known tenor. CARRERAS made his début in the LICEU in BARCELONA in 1971 but his career really took off in 1974 at the Metropolitan Opera House in New York. He also had a very successful season with Karajan in 1976 at the Salzburg Festival. He has achieved great popular appeal through having sung with Pavarotti and DOMINGO in huge concerts, often in the open air. He suffered from leukaemia during the1980s but has now overcome this illness and is back on the operatic stage. He specialises in the Italian repertoire. He received the gold medal of the *Academia de Bellas Artes* in 1985.

CARRERO BLANCO, LUIS (1903–1973)
Politician and member of the armed forces. He was a *consejero nacional* and *subsecretario* in FRANCO's government. In 1973 he became PRESIDENTE DEL GOBIERNO. On the 20th of December of the same year he was killed as a result of a car bomb placed by the terrorist group ETA.

CARRILLO SOLARES, SANTIAGO (1915–   )
Communist politician. *Secretario general* of the *Junta Socialista Unida* from 1936 to 1939. He spent many years in exile. He became the leader of the PARTIDO COMUNISTA in 1960 and was elected to the CONGRESO in 1977, 1979, and 1982. After the defeat of the Communist party in the 1982 elections, he resigned as

leader of the party in favour of GERARDO IGLESIAS. He left the Communist Party in 1985 and founded the *Partido de los Trabajadores*. This party eventually amalgamated with the PSOE.

CARTUJA 93, S.A.
This company was established in 1991 to administer the World Fair in SEVILLA in 1992, and afterwards, to attempt to use the site, pavilions and infrastructure to commercial advantage. It is jointly financed by the state, by the region and by the city itself.

CARVAJAL Y URQUIJO, JAIME (1939–   )
Managing Director of the Ford Company in Spain. He was appointed to the SENADO by the King in 1979.

CAS See: *CENTRO DE AYUDA Y SEGUIMIENTO*

CASA DE CAMPO
Large park (1,700 hectares) to the west of MADRID. Until 1931 it was a royal hunting park, closed to the public, but is now one of the most popular open spaces within the city. It also has a *Parque Zoólogico* or zoo, a *Parque de Atracciones* (funfair) and a *Teleférico* or cablecar.

CASA DE LA VILLA
Name by which the AYUNTAMIENTO *de* MADRID is popularly known.

CASA DEL PUEBLO
The local branches of the PSOE are housed in premises called the CASA DEL PUEBLO.

CASA REAL
The Royal Household. It consists of four departments under the control of the *jefe de la Casa Real* (usually a personal friend of the king). Three of these departments are military and include the aides-de-camp and security services.

CASA See: *CONSTRUCCIONES AERONÁUTICAS*

CASAS ADOSADAS
Semi-detached or terraced chalets. They are now much in evidence on the outskirts of Spanish cities and on the coasts. They contrast strongly with the traditional type of living accommoda-

tion in Spain, the block of flats which are generally situated in the city centre or on estates in newer suburbs.

CASAS DE OFICIOS
These training centres are usually located in towns and cities. Their aim is to teach the young unemployed traditional Spanish arts and crafts, though with the aid of modern technology. Students are expected to help improve the environment and facilities within the town.

CASCOS AZULES
The 'blue berets' or 'blue helmets' – those soldiers who work abroad on UN missions.

CASERÍO
Farm-stead in the Basque country. The name applies both to the large family farm-house and to the land which is farmed. CASERÍOS are typically about 6 hectares in size and worked by members of the family. In recent years, these small farms have not been able to support the whole family and income is supplemented by family members who work in nearby towns.

CASO ALCÀSSER
On Wednesday, 27th of January, 1993, the bodies of three young girls, Desirée Hernández, Miriam García and Antonia Gómez were found, having been missing since November of the previous year. Nine hours later, Miguel Ricart was arrested: he confessed to rape but accused a friend, ANTONIO ANGLÉS of murder. ANGLÉS was pursued throughout Spain but eventually gave the police the slip and has still not been traced.

EL CASO AMEDO
JOSÉ AMEDO and MICHEL DOMÍNGUEZ, two ex-policemen, were convicted of working for the illegal right-wing organisation, GAL, allegedly financed by the Spanish government. They have been accused, among other crimes, of having masterminded the attack against the Monbar Hotel, in which four members of the left-wing terrorist organisation ETA were killed. They follow an open prison régime because of their role in the terrorist attacks against two bars in France, Batzoki and Consolation.

CASO, ÁNGELES (1959–   )

ÁNGELES CASO was born in Gijón (ASTURIAS) in 1959 and has worked in the media as a television and radio presenter and programme director. In 1990 she received the *Premio Antena de Oro de la Federación de Asociaciones de Radio*. She was a finalist in the *Premio Planeta* 1994 with her novel *El peso de las sombras*.

CASO ARNY

In 1996, allegations of homosexual prostitution were made against the ARNY nightclub in Seville by some of the underage boys who worked there. A number of celebrities as well as local politicians and dignitaries have been implicated in the affair as clients of the nightclub and the prostitution service. The trial ended in December 1997 with the acquittal of the principal defendants.

CASO FILESA

A political scandal concerning illegal contributions to the PSOE especially for its electoral campaigns. It is alleged that money was paid through a holding company (FILESA) by the party, to so-called consultants for fictitious reports and technical studies. These fees were then returned to the party in the form of donations. Former party officials are implicated including Josep María Sala (ex-senator), Carlos Navarro (ex-member of parliament) and the *ex-secretario de finanzas* of the PSOE, GUILLERMO GALEOTE.

CASO GARCÍA GOENA

GARCÍA GOENA was murdered in Hendaye in 1987. The case is being investigated by BALTASAR GARZÓN as part of the wider investigations into the GAL affair. As such, personalities like RAFAEL VERA and LUIS ROLDÁN are implicated.

CASO IBERCORP

In this affair, which broke in 1992, 11 people were accused of insider trading and illegal use of contacts, including the *ex-gobernador* of the BANCO DE ESPAÑA, MARIANO RUBIO and an ex-trustee of the BOLSA *de Madrid*, Manuel de la Concha. It transpired that the *Banco* IBERCORP was a front organisation for many illegal financial operations. In 1992, IBERCORP suspended payments and was bought, for one peseta, by *Caja Cantabria*.

CASO LASA Y ZABALA See: *LASA AND ZABALA*.

CASO LEYBA
Investigation into the death of a French citizen, LEYBA, allegedly killed by the GAL commandoes during the GUERRA SUCIA (dirty war).

CASO MATALAZ
3 Basque terrorists belonging to the COMANDO *Matalaz* have disappeared, having been held in custody for four years without being brought to trial. The subsequent investigation has been called the CASO MATALAZ and has raised questions about the unreasonable delays in bringing such cases to trial.

CASO MONBAR
Criminal case in which the murder of four members of ETA in France is under investigation. The judge in charge of this case is BALTASAR GARZÓN and it forms part of a group of cases in which the illegal organisation GAL is implicated and, by extension, figures such as MANGLANO and PEROTE.

CASO OÑEDERRA
Ramon Oñederra (Kattu) was murdered in Bayonne, France in 1983. The case is being investigated by BALTASAR GARZÓN as part of the general case against GAL. As such, well-known figures such as CORCUERA, VERA, ROLDÁN, Galindo and PEROTE are all implicated.

CASO SÓLLER
A court case in which a former president of the ISLAS BALEARES is accused of receiving kickbacks for awarding the contract for the building of the SÓLLER tunnel to a personal friend. The friend and two former *consejeros* are also implicated in the affair.

CASO TOUS
The TOUS affair concerns the rupture of the TOUS dam in VALENCIA in 1982. Three engineers were tried for negligence in 1995 but were aquitted. The inhabitants of the area have been seeking

compensation since the dam burst, and in 1996 the first payments were made.

CASTELLANO

CASTELLANO (or *español*) is the official language of the Spanish state. The other languages spoken in Spain (VASCO, GALLEGO and CATALÁN) are also official within their respective autonomous communities. Spanish is the fourth language in the world based on numbers of speakers. There are over 330 million people who speak Spanish as their first language.

CASTELLERS

Builders of CATALUÑA's famous human towers which can reach up to nine stories. These form part of the revival of Catalán culture which took place after the death of FRANCO and which seeks to re-assert Catalán national identity. See also: SARDANA

CASTELLETS

Human towers which are constructed by groups of men in national dress on important festive days in CATALUÑA. They sometimes reach the height of six metres.

CASTILLA Y LEÓN

One of Spain's AUTONOMÍAS. It has a population of 2.6 million and covers an area of 94,193 square kilometres. The region capital is VALLADOLID. It is geographically the largest region in Spain and its highland plateaux are suitable for cereal and vegetable production and for sheep farming. Coal mining and energy production are important for the region's economy, as well as car manufacture, pharmaceuticals and armaments. VALLADOLID is the headquarters of the FASA-RENAULT car manufacturing plant. FASA has another production plant at Palencia, 40 miles to the north of VALLADOLID. Palencia province is important for its food industries, especially sugar and chocolate, and is the largest biscuit production centre in Spain. The cities of Burgós and León have magnificent mediaeval cathedrals with spectacular stained glass windows. Both have light engineering and chemical industries also.

CATALÁN

CATALÁN is spoken by nine million people in CATALUÑA, the BALEARES and the COMUNIDAD VALENCIANA. It is a Romance language with a literary tradition dating back to 1140. Both CASTELLANO and CATALÁN are the official languages of CATALUÑA and the BALEARES. Valenciano, felt by most linguists to be a dialect of CATALÁN is spoken in the COMUNIDAD VALENCIANA and has been its official language since 1982. CATALÁN is also spoken in some areas of ARAGÓN and outside Spain, in the Roussillon region of France, Andorra and in the Sardinian city of Algher.

CATALUÑA

CATALUÑA, along with GALICIA and the PAÍS VASCO, is one of the three historical AUTONOMÍAS. It has a population of six million and covers an area of 31,930 square kilometres in the north-east of Spain, with ARAGÓN to the west and the French border to the north. It is the richest and most highly developed area in Spain, with good links with France and Europe and an outward and forward-looking spirit. Because of this, it has been the focal point for large waves of immigration from other parts of Spain, especially from ANDALUCÍA. There is an important nationalist movement in CATALUÑA and a strong sense of identity and tradition. It has its own Parliament, the GENERALITAT and its own language, CATALÁN, which is widely spoken throughout the region and is the official working language of the autonomous government. BARCELONA is the capital of the region and one of Spain's major container ports with a free port zone alongside. (See also: ZONA FRANCA). It is an important tourist centre and the heart of the wine-producing region. Its industries include textiles, paints, plastics, fertilisers, food-processing, machinery and tanning. It is made up of four provinces, BARCELONA, Gerona, Lérida and Tarragona, of which BARCELONA is by far the biggest, with a population of over 4 million. CATALUÑA first achieved prominence in the Middle Ages, (the GENERALITAT dates from the 13th century) under the sway of the *Condes* of BARCELONA. It later became part of the Kingdom of ARAGÓN and became increasingly dominant in the commercial and political life of those countries bordering on the Mediterranean. It was at that time that the middle classes first rose to prominence. Their influence has been predominant ever since in promoting Catalán life, culture and enterprise.

CATEDRÁTICO
Full professor at a university, or head of a department in a secondary school. At a university, it is from the body of CATEDRÁTICOS that the RECTOR, or vice-chancellor is chosen.

CAVA
Champagne-style sparkling wine, produced in CATALUÑA and especially popular in Spain during the Christmas festivities. CAVA is served chilled, at 7 to 9 degrees centigrade and is either medium-dry, dry, brut or brut extra. A good CAVA is light in colour with yellowish or greenish reflections. It is made from the traditional white grapes of CATALUÑA, Macabeo, Xareló and Perellada. CAVAS have a very large export market: FREIXENET sells more than Moet Chandon in the United States and they are market leaders in Europe and in the UK.

CBE See: *CORPORACIÓN BANCARIA DE ESPAÑA*

CC See: *CENTRISTAS DE CATALUÑA*

CC RTV See: *CORPORACIÓ CATALANA DE RADIO I TELEVISIÓ*

CCOO See: *COMISIONES OBRERAS*

CDC See: *CONVERGENCIA DEMOCRÁTICA DE CATALUNYA*

CDG See: *CENTRO DRAMÁTICO GALEGO*

CDGC See: *CENTRE DRAMATIC DE LA GENERALITAT DE CATALUNYA*

CDGV See: *CENTRE DRAMATIC DE LA GENERALITAT VALENCIANA*

CDMC See: *CENTRO PARA LA DIFUSIÓN DE LA MÚSICA CONTEMPORÁNEA*

CDN See: *CONVERGENCIA DE DEMÓCRATAS NAVARROS*

CDS See: *CENTRO DEMOCRÁTICO Y SOCIAL*

CEAPA See: *CONFEDERACIÓN ESPAÑOLA DE ASOCIACIONES DE PADRES DE ALUMNOS*

CEBRIÁN, JUAN LUIS (1944–   )

Journalist and novelist. He was a founder member of the intellectual magazine *Cuadernos para el diálogo*. He also worked for *El Pueblo* and *Informaciones*. Founder and first editor of the MADRID newspaper EL PAÍS, the first major newspaper to appear after the death of FRANCO. He edited the paper for 13 years in which time it became the largest and most influencial in the country. He is now on the board of PRISA (PROMOTORA DE INFORMACIONES, S.A.) and received the *Premio Nacional del Periodismo* in 1983.

CECA See: *CONFEDERACIÓN ESPAÑOLA DE CAJAS DE AHORROS*

CEDEX See: *CENTRO DE ESTUDIOS DE EXPERIMENTACIÓN DE OBRAS PÚBLICAS*

CEE See: *CONFERENCIA EPISCOPAL ESPAÑOLA*

CEE See: *CONSEJO ESCOLAR DEL ESTADO*

CELA TRULOCK, CAMILO JOSÉ (1916–   )

Born in Iria Flavia, Padrón (La Coruña), CELA is the author of novels, short stories, poetry and travel books. He was awarded the Nobel Prize for Literature in 1989. His first novel, *La familia de Pascual Duarte* (1942), was made into a film in 1976. Other important works are *La colmena* (1951), *Viaje a la Alcarria* (1948), *El gallego y su cuadrilla* and *Mazurca para dos muertos* (for which he won the *Premio Nacional de Literatura* in 1985). He is considered one of the most important and influential writers of the Spanish *posguerra* (post-war period). He was awarded the most important Spanish literary prize, the PREMIO CERVANTES in 1995.

CELAYA, GABRIEL (1911–1991)

Prolific poet and author of over fifty books. He is considered to belong to a poetic tendency called *poesía social*. Among his most important collections are *Lo demás es silencio* and *Cantos íberos*. *Memorias inmemoriales* is felt to be the synthesis of his entire work.

CENTRE DRÀMATIC DE LA GENERALITAT DE CATALUNYA
Theatre company founded by the *Departamento de Cultura* of the CATALÁN regional government in 1981 with the intention of promoting and producing plays in CATALÁN. Their first play was *Nit de Sant Joan*, produced by the *Dragoll Dagom* group. Its first director was H. Bonnin: its current director is D. Reixach. The Centre is based at the *Teatro Romea* in BARCELONA.

CENTRE DRÀMATIC DE LA GENERALITAT VALENCIANA
Theatre company created in 1988 by the regional government of VALENCIA to promote and produce classical theatre. Its first director was A. Díaz: he was succeeded by Tordera. The centre is based at the *Teatro Rialto* in VALENCIA.

CENTRISTAS DE CATALUÑA
The CC is a political group which occupies the centre ground in CATALÁN regional politics. It failed to secure representation in the 1992 regional assembly elections.

CENTRO CONCERTADO
Private schools which are funded by the state are known as CENTROS CONCERTADOS. These schools are either fully funded, in which case their pupils do not pay fees, or they are partially funded and receive top-up fees from students. CENTROS CONCERTADOS are not allowed to select their students except by giving priority to children of poorer families and those living closest to the school. 90% of schools in Spain are supported by public funds.

CENTRO DE ALTA SEGURIDAD
High-security prison. There is only one in Spain, in Herrera de la Mancha.

CENTRO DE EDUCACIÓN ESPECIAL
Schools for children with special needs. Where possible, children are integrated into normal schooling, but where this is not possi-

ble, handicapped children attend special schools. In rural areas there are sometimes special classes available for these children in mainstream schools.

CENTRO DE EDUCACIÓN PERMANENTE DE ADULTOS

These are adult education centres, funded by education departments and the local authorities.

CENTRO DE ESTUDIOS DE EXPERIMENTACIÓN DE OBRAS PÚBLICAS

This research organisation is responsible to the MINISTERIO DE FOMENTO and works in the development of engineering techniques, design and technology especially in the construction and transport industries. CEDEX has 850 people working for it in a number of laboratories in Spain and in Europe.

CENTRO DE ESTUDIOS JURÍDICOS DE LA ADMINISTRACIÓN DE LA JUSTICIA

This institute is an autonomous body whose function is to select and train members of the public prosecution corps and other personnel active in the administration of justice.

CENTRO DE INVESTIGACIÓN Y DOCUMENTACIÓN EDUCATIVA

This centre coordinates research into education as laid down in the 1990 *Plan Nacional de Investigación Educativa*. Founded in 1983, it exists to improve educational standards within Spain by disseminating the results of research undertaken in universities or by international bodies.

CENTRO DE INVESTIGACIONES ENERGÉTICAS MEDIOAMBIENTALES Y TECNOLÓGICAS

This research organisation answers directly to the MINISTERIO DE INDUSTRIA Y ENERGÍA. It aims to find alternative energy sources, to improve the efficiency of those already in use and to research into the effect of the consumption of certain types of energy on the environment. It has research centres in MADRID (MONCLOA), Soria (Ceder) and Almería.

CENTRO DE INVESTIGACIONES SOCIOLÓGICAS

Body which conducts surveys into contemporary social problems and attitudes in Spain. Known as the CIS, it comes under the aegis of the MINISTERIO DE LA PRESIDENCIA. It dates from 1977 (its immediate predecessor was the IOP or *Instituto de la Opinión Pública*). The CIS has undertaken more than 1,200 surveys of Spanish society.

CENTRO DE PUBLICACIONES

Most ministries now have a publications office whose role is to inform the public of the work undertaken by the ministry and of related issues.

CENTRO DEMOCRÁTICO Y SOCIAL

This party had been founded prior to the 1982 elections by ADOLFO SUÁREZ who had stepped down as UCD president after resigning as prime minister in 1981. In 1989 the CDS concluded a regional pact with the PP. In 1991, SUÁREZ resigned as its president. In 1993 it suffered almost total collapse in the elections and was disbanded.

CENTRO DRAMÁTICO GALEGO

Theatre company founded in 1984 by the regional government of GALICIA in order to promote and produce classical and Galician theatre. Its director is M. Guede.

CENTRO DRAMÁTICO NACIONAL DE ESPAÑA

State theatre company which aims to produce and promote the repertory of the classical theatre, created in 1987 by the *Ministerio de Cultura*. It is based in MADRID at the *Teatro María Guerrero*. Its first director was ADOLFO MARSILLACH. Subsequent directors have been NURIA ESPERT, José Luis Gómez and José Tamayo. The current director is Juan Carlos Plaza who was appointed in 1989.

CENTRO NACIONAL DE NUEVAS TENDENCIAS ESCÉNICAS

Arts Centre set up in 1984 by the *Instituto Nacional de las Artes Escénicas y de la Música*. Its aim is to promote and produce works of art of an avant-garde nature.

CENTRO PARA LA DIFUSIÓN DE LA MÚSICA CONTEMPORÁNEA

This organisation was established in 1985 to promote the composition of modern music. It has a laboratory with full electronic and computer facilities, housed in the MUSEO NACIONAL CENTRO DE ARTE REINA SOFÍA. The CDMC is part of the MINISTERIO DE EDUCACIÓN Y CULTURA.

CENTRO SUPERIOR DE INFORMACIÓN DE LA DEFENSA

Known colloquially as *La casa*, this organisation is the Spanish Secret Service. It is a branch of the military: the head of service is always a top-ranking army officer. Its former boss, general MANGLANO, along with colonel PEROTE, is under investigation for illegal telephone tapping of influential figures in Spain, including the King himself.

CENTROS BASE PARA LOS MINUSVÁLIDOS

In recent years Spain has set up a number of centres to help the disabled, both physically and mentally, under the aegis of INSERSO. There is also much cooperation with international agencies in this field, including the European Community and the OECD.

CENTROS DE ACOGIDA A REFUGIADOS

These centres care for refugees or those seeking asylum in Spain, together with their families. They are allowed to remain in these refuges for up to 6 months. Private centres also exist and these are eligible for state grants.

CENTROS DE ATENCIÓN A MINUSVÁLIDOS FÍSICOS

Small care units for the physically disabled.

CENTROS DE ATENCIÓN A MINUSVÁLIDOS PSÍQUICOS

Small care units for the severely mentally disabled.

CENTROS DE DÍA PARA LA TERCERA EDAD

These day centres provide many services for the elderly, including canteen facilities, leisure activities, home helps, heath care, hairdressing and chiropody services.

CENTROS DE DOCUMENTACIÓN EUROPEA

These centres exist to produce and distribute information about the European Union. There are 31 in Spain, 7 of which are in MADRID. They are each headed by a director and are usually based on university premises.

CENTROS DE ENCUENTRO DE PROFESORES

Teachers' centres which provide in-service training and which will in future, deliver the CAP or teacher's certificate.

CENTROS DE INFORMACIÓN EMPRESARIAL – EUROVENTANILLAS

These documentation centres exist to provide businessmen with information about Europe. There are centres in MADRID, BARCELONA, SEVILLA, BILBAO and Málaga.

CENTROS DE RECUPERACIÓN DE MINUSVÁLIDOS FÍSICOS

Rehabilitation centres for the physically disabled.

CENTROS RESIDENCIALES PARA LA TERCERA EDAD

These are old people's homes for those Spaniards over 60 who are unable to care for themselves. There are several different types, ranging from those whose residents are in good health to those more akin to nursing homes. Some are run by the Health Service, others by non-profit making charities.

CEOE See: *CONFEDERACIÓN ESPAÑOLA DE ORGANIZACIONES EMPRESARIALES*

CEPA See: *CENTRO DE EDUCACIÓN PERMANENTE DE ADULTOS*

CEPSA

Petroleum company which, in 1991, expanded into acrylic production and founded the manufacturing company, *Induquímica*. In that same year, the French group *Elf Aquitaine* acquired 30% of its capital.

CEPYME See: *CONFEDERACIÓN ESPAÑOLA DE PEQUEÑAS Y MEDIANAS EMPRESAS*

CERTIFICADO DE APTITUD PEDAGÓGICA
Teaching certificate, required for teachers of vocational subjects who only have a diploma at technician level. The CAP is now also required for those graduates wishing to enter the OPOSICIONES examinations for teaching posts.

CERVANTES, S.A.
This insurance company was founded in 1931 and specialises in motor-related insurance and also in fire and accident insurance.

CERVERA, CARMEN
Formerly a Spanish beauty queen, Carmen (Tita) Cervera, married the Baron Hugo Thyssen-Bornemisza and became a patroness of the arts. Together with her husband, she founded the MUSEO THYSSEN-BORNEMISZA which houses a collection of spectacular paintings dating from the fourteenth century.

CESID See: *CENTRO SUPERIOR DE INFORMACIÓN DE LA DEFENSA*

CEUTA
A Spanish enclave on the North African coast which is both a free port and a garrison town. It is administered as an integral part of Spain. It has a population of about 75,000 people and an area of 18 square kms. See also: MELILLA.

CG See: *COALICIÓN GALEGA*

CGPJ See: *CONSEJO GENERAL DEL PODER JUDICIAL*

CHACEL, ROSA (1898–1994)
Doyenne of Spanish letters, CHACEL is a survivor of the so-called *Generación of '27*. Together with her husband, the painter Timoteo Pérez Rubio, she lived in exile from 1937 to 1977. Among her most important works are her first novel *Estación, ida y vuelta* (1930), *Memorias de Leticia Valle* (1946) and *Barrio de maravillas* (1976). In 1987 she was awarded the *Premio Nacional de las Letras Españolas*.

CHAMARTÍN
Important railway station, located in the CHAMARTÍN area of MADRID. Services to the north of Spain depart from here.

CHAMBERÍ
Working-class district in the heart of MADRID. Many of the ZARZUELAS or light operas are set in this area.

CHAQUETEO
Term used to describe people (especially politicians) who switch from one political party to another, as circumstances change.

CHARNEGO
Derogatory term applied by native Cataláns to immigrants from the rest of Spain who now live in CATALUÑA.

CHÁVARRI, JAIME (1943–   )
Film director. He has worked extensively with the producer ELÍAS QUEREJETA. His best known films are *Las bicicletas son para el verano* (1983) – an adaptation of FERNANDO FERNÁN-GÓMEZ' stage play – and a musical, *Las cosas del querer* (1989).

CHAVES GONZÁLEZ, MANUEL (1945–   )
Socialist politician, he was spokesman for the *Comisión de política social y empleo* in the first socialist term of office. He was *ministro de Trabajo y Seguridad Social* from 1986 to 1990 and has been *presidente* of the JUNTA DE ANDALUCÍA since 1990. In the regional elections of 1996, CHAVES won the majority of seats for the PSOE in the JUNTA.

CHELI
Originally the language of the gypsies. Many words have been borrowed from CHELI by young people and have entered standard Spanish.

CHILLIDA EDUARDO (1924–   )
Sculptor, born in the PAÍS VASCO. Much of his work is monumental in scale (such as his works in iron and steel *Peine del viento* and *Consejo al espacio y al tiempo*) and are placed in the countryside and overlooking the sea. In 1997 he was at the centre of a controversy for wishing to place one of his sculptures on TINDAYA, a mountain on FUERTEVENTURA.

CHINCHÓN
Alcoholic drink, similar to the French pastis. Its name comes

from the city of Chinchón, in the province of MADRID. It is normally drunk with coffee after a meal.

CHOCOLATE CON CHURROS
Typical breakfast or snack usually eaten in bars on Sundays or special occasions. The chocolate drink is served very thick, together with long strips of fried batter (CHURROS).

CHUPA
Slang term for leather jackets, usually black in colour.

CHUPA CHUPS
International firm, owned by the Bernat family, which specialises in sweets and confectionery.

CIDE See: *CENTRO DE INVESTIGACIÓN Y DOCUMENTACIÓN EDUCATIVA*

CIEMAT See: *CENTRO DE INVESTIGACIONES ENERGÉTICAS MEDIOAMBIENTALES Y TECNOLÓGICOS*

112
It is intended to introduce this number for emergency telephone calls. Currently, the emergency services (police, firemen, hospitals) use a variety of numbers.

CIG See: *CONVERXENCIA INTERSINDICAL GALEGA*

CINCO DÍAS
Newspaper specialising in business and the economy and founded in MADRID in 1978. It has a circulation of about 40,000 and produces two supplements, Investigación y Desarrollo and Invertir.

CÍRCULO DE EMPRESARIOS
Institute of Directors, which comprises a group of 150 senior executives.

CIRCUNSCRIPCIONES
The electoral constituencies or CIRCUNSCRIPCIONES are the 50 Spanish provinces, plus CEUTA and MELILLA. Each CIRCUNSCRIPCIÓN returns different numbers of DIPUTADOS according to the number

of electors. Rural provinces proportionally return considerably more DIPUTADOS than do urban constituencies.

CIS See: *CENTRO DE INVESTIGACIONES SOCIOLÓGICAS*

CISCAR CASABÁN, CIPRIÀ (1947–   )

Diputado for VALENCIA, currently head of the *Secretaría de Organización* in the PSOE executive and previously spokesman for the GONZÁLEZ government.

CITROËN HISPANIA, S.A.

This company manufactures, assembles and distributes Citroën cars and trucks, makes spare parts and accessories and provides after-sales service. It also rents out vehicles and sells related products to the car industry. It is almost wholly owned by *Automobiles Citroën*.

CiU See: *CONVERGENCIA i UNIÓ*

CIUDAD CONDAL

Name by which the city of BARCELONA is often referred to. It receives this name from the *Condes de* BARCELONA.

CJE See: *CONSEJO DE LA JUVENTUD DE ESPAÑA*

CLAUSTRO DE PROFESORES

Body of teaching staff within a school, with the head teacher as chairperson. This body is responsible for planning, coordinating and administering all areas which are directly related to education.

CLÁUSULAS NORMATIVAS

These clauses in employment contracts stipulate that provisions in earlier, expired contracts continue to apply until a new contract is agreed upon. The clauses appertain to salary, work schedules and work conditions and lead to a lack of flexibility within the company. They are gradually being phased out.

CLEMENTE, JAVIER (1950–   )

Manager of the Spanish national football team since 1992. His early career as a footballer was cut short by injury. Since 1992 the national team has played 39 international matches, won 24 and lost three.

CLH See: *COMPAÑIA LOGÍSTICA DE HIDROCARBUROS*

CNC See: *CONGRESO NACIONAL DE CANARIAS*

CNES See: *COMISIÓN NACIONAL DE ELECCIONES SINDICALES*

CNMV See: *COMISIÓN NACIONAL DEL MERCADO DE VALORES*

CNNTE See: *CENTRO NACIONAL DE NUEVAS TENDENCIAS ESCÉNICAS*

CNP See: *CUERPO NACIONAL DE POLICÍA*

CNT See: *CONFEDERACIÓN NACIONAL DE TRABAJO*

COALICIÓN CANARIA

Coalition of nationalist parties in the Canary Islands. It gained four parliamentary seats in the 1996 elections. It was formed prior to the 1993 general elections by 5 smaller nationalist parties including the *Partido Nacionalista Canario* and the *Centro Canario Independiente*. These parties represent all facets of the political spectrum. The major party in the coalition is the *Agrupación de Independientes de Canarias* (AIC) which holds 18 out of the 60 seats in the regional parliament and controls the island councils of TENERIFE and LANZAROTE.

COALICIÓN GALEGA

Third ranked in the Galician assembly in 1985, CG won one seat in the national elections of 1986. It won only two seats in the 1989 elections, due to internal friction and failed to retain them in 1993.

COALICIÓN POPULAR

This group was formed in 1979 by members of ALIANZA POPULAR, when it became clear that a loose alliance of right-wing parties was unattractive to the electorate. In this form, the right fared better in the elections of 1982 and 1986 but was still unable to equal the PSOE in popularity. Finally, this grouping formed a much tighter, unitary party which took the name PARTIDO POPULAR.

COBI
COBI, the mascot of the 1992 Barcelona Olympic Games, was created by the designer JAVIER MARISCAL.

CODA See: *COORDINADORA DE ORGANIZACIONES DE DEFENSA DEL MEDIO AMBIENTE*

CÓDIGO CIVIL
The civil code: that is, those laws which deal with civil justice and law.

CÓDIGO DE JUSTICIA MILITAR
The code or laws of military justice which may only be applied to members of the Armed Forces.

CÓDIGO PENAL DE LA DEMOCRACIA
Penal code approved by the PARTIDO POPULAR in 1995, the most important clause of which is the raising of the age of criminal liability from 16 to 18. Length of sentences were also adjusted and prisoners freed in accordance with these shorter sentences. A new category of offence was introduced (*delitos societarios*) intended to discourage white-collar crime.

CODORNIÚ
The biggest producer of *cava* or champagne-style wine. It is a family-run firm, based in CATALUÑA and founded in 1872 by José Raventós. The company also owns vine-yards in California.

COFRENTES
Nuclear power station, situated in COFRENTES, in the province of VALENCIA.

COIXET, ISABEL (1962–   )
Young film-director. She has made two feature films, *Demasiado viejo para morir joven* (1990) and *Cosas que nunca te dije* (1996) which was a great box-office success. *Cosas* won the *Ondas* prize for best director and the prize for the best film at the Prague Film Festival.

COLCHONERO
Adjective used in connection with the ATLÉTICO football club and used to describe its fans also.

COLEGIO
This term can either refer to state primary schools (up to 14 years of age) or to private schools teaching students up to the age of 18.

COLEGIO UNIVERSITARIO
These higher education institutions prepare students for the first stage (or ciclo) of higher education and are attached to universities. Students may then continue to the next stage at the relevant faculty.

COLEGIOS PROFESIONALES
These are professional associations such as the *Colegio de Abogados* or the *Colegio de Médicos*. In order to exercise a particular profession, one is required to belong to the local branch of the relevant professional assocation. These bodies act to protect the interest of their members, act as advisors and safeguard professional standards of behaviour. They run training courses and are required to inform members of any change in legislation of relevance to their profession.

COLOMO, FERNANDO (1946–   )
Film director. COLOMO specialises in comedies such as *La línea del cielo* (1983) and *¿Qué hace una chica como tú en un sitio como éste?* (1978) with CARMEN MAURA. His most recent films are *Rosa, rosae* (1993), *Alegre ma non troppo* and *El efecto mariposa*.

COLZA SCANDAL
In 1981, it was discovered that industrial rape seed oil had been sold for domestic consumption. More than 1,000 people died from eating food cooked in the oil and 25,000 were disabled. Despite complicated litigation, none of the victims has yet received compensation. Victims' associations have brought private actions against former civil servants, accusing them of negligence. The government itself has established a system of grants to enable sufferers to return to work.

COMANDO
Name given to small terrorist units (usually belonging to the Basque group ETA) who carry out their activities independently.

COMANDOS AUTÓNOMOS ANTI-CAPITALISTAS
A small left-wing group, originally part of ETA-*militar* but now operating independently.

COMARCA
A type of regional organisation which includes the MUNICIPIOS. Those areas which prefer to work at COMARCA level within their regions may do so and some MUNCIPIOS come together to bid for and distribute EU monies under the aegis of the COMARCA.

COMERCIANTES
These are persons who work for themselves in 'one man businesses'. This is the most common form of business organisation in Spain. These people work mainly in the retail sectors (food, drink, crafts, etc.) They are automatically members of their local CÁMARA DE COMERCIO and are supported by various organisations such as IMPI (the INSTITUTO DE LA PEQUEÑA Y MEDIANA EMPRESA INDUSTRIAL) and the INSTITUTO DE LA EMPRESA FAMILIAR.

COMISARIOS
Currently, Spain has two commissioners or COMISARIOS on the College of Commisioners in the European Union, MARCELINO OREJA of the PP and MANUEL MARÍN of the PSOE.

COMISIÓN DEL SISTEMA ELÉCTRICO NACIONAL
Independent regulatory body for the electricity industry. It exists to ensure transparency in the production and distribution of electricity.

COMISIÓN ESPECIAL DE CUENTAS
Each local authority in Spain has an audit commission which inspects its accounts each year. The commission is composed of members of the DIPUTACIÓN with representatives from all political parties.

COMISIÓN INFORMATIVA
These advisory bodies are found in some of the larger MUNICIPIOS.

Their function is to advise specific departments in those areas in which their members have specialised knowledge.

COMISIÓN NACIONAL DE ELECCIONES SINDICALES
This body is responsible for administering union elections and recording results.

COMISIÓN NACIONAL DEL MERCADO DE VALORES
Created in 1988, this body acts as a watchdog for the Spanish Stock Exchange. It arranges audits, authorises and monitors broking companies and agencies and admits and suspends listed companies and securities. It attempts to safeguard the investor by ensuring that insider dealing does not take place.

COMISIÓN PROVINCIAL DE GOBIERNO
This commission works at province level and is composed of a president, vice-president and other DIPUTADOS. The task of the COMISIÓN is to help the president in his duties and to carry out any tasks delegated to it by central or regional government.

COMISIONES DE CONGRESO
These committees are composed of representatives of the political parties in the CONGRESO. Their role is to examine amendments to laws and to prepare resolutions which will be presented to the CONGRESO.

COMISIONES DELEGADAS DEL GOBIERNO
Inter-departmental governmental committees composed of the ministers concerned. There are five in number: the *Comisión de Política Exterior*, the *Comisión para la Seguridad del Estado*, the *Comisión de Asuntos Económicos*, the *Comisión de Política Autonómica* and the *Comisión para Política Educativa, Cultural y Científica*. Their function is to debate, discuss and advise.

COMISIONES OBRERAS
Trades' Union which began life with a majority of communist members. Founded in ASTURIAS in 1962 as a result of the miners' strikes, it remained illegal until 1977. It has about 2 million members, for the most part in MADRID and ANDALUCÍA. Its current leader is ANTONIO GUTIÉRREZ. It supports a federal Spain and

independence for the PAÍS VASCO and CATALUÑA. See also:
MARCELINO CAMACHO

COMITÉ DE EMPRESA

Under Spanish law, all medium and large firms must have an elected Workers' Council of *delegados* or shop stewards. They are elected on a 'list' system from the trades unions and other groups within the workplace. In order to have such a COMITÉ, the firm must have at least 50 employees. Management is obliged to inform and consult with this body.

COMITÉ ORGANIZADOR OLÍMPICO BARCELONA '92

This committee organised the BARCELONA Olympic Games of 1992. It was set up in 1987 and chaired by the mayor of BARCELONA, PASQUAL MARAGALL with Josep Miquel as chief executive. The committee had three areas of responsibility – operations, resources and sport.

COMPAÑIA ARRENDATARIA DE MONOPOLIO DE PETRÓLEOS, S.A.

For many years this state petroleum company had a monopoly on all sales of petrol throughout Spain. In recent years it has undergone many changes: in 1987 it became part of the REPSOL group. Then in 1991 it was split into two companies and the retail outlets were bought by REPSOL, CEPSA, and PETROMED. In 1993, CAMPSA ceased to fix the prices of petrol and changed its name to CLH (COMPAÑIA LOGÍSTICA DE HIDROCARBUROS).

COMPAÑIA DE RADIOFUSIÓN INTERCONTINENTAL

This radio network (also known as INTER) has stations in MADRID, CÓRDOBA, Linares and Onteniente.

COMPAÑIA LOGÍSTICA DE HIDROCARBUROS

A company created in 1993 which assumed some of the former responsibilities of CAMPSA, including storage, transport and distribution of petrol products. It is responsible for the logistical services of REPSOL, including the oil pipe lines and the 1,300 service stations. It is a conglomerate which includes REPSOL, ELF, BP and CEPSA.

COMPAÑIA NACIONAL DE LA DANZA

Originally founded in 1979 as the *Ballet Nacional de España Clásico*. Its first director was Víctor Ullate. María de Ávila, his successor, introduced contemporary works by choreographers such as Georges Balanchine and Anthony Tudor. NACHO DUATO became director in 1990. Since its inception the company has travelled widely, visiting countries such as Japan, Russia and the United States.

COMPAÑIA TRANSMEDITERRÁNEA, S.A.

Oldest company to belong to the DIRECCIÓN GENERAL DEL PATRIMONIO DEL ESTADO holding group. It is a shipping company involved in all activities in this sector such as transportation, ship construction and repair, insurance and package tours. It operates between Algeciras and North Africa and between other ports and the BALEARES and CANARIAS.

COMPAÑIA VALENCIANA DE CEMENTOS PORTLAND, S.A.

This company manufactures and sells cement, and is involved in the marketing, acquisition, holding and disposal of securities and shareholdings. Other activities include the manufacture of ceramic tiles and paving, dry mortar, cement and concrete.

COMPETENCIAS

Term used for the powers which were devolved from central government to the regions. Not all regions have the same number of COMPETENCIAS – indeed each region was allowed to decide how much autonomy it wished to enjoy and the time scale in which these responsibilities would be devolved.

COMPLUTENSE

The name of the largest university in Spain, which has over 100,000 students. (The *Facultad de Derecho* or Law Faculty alone has 20,000 students). It was founded in 1293 by the King of Castille, Sancho IV. It was originally located in Alcalá de Henares (whose Roman name was Compluto) but was transferred to Madrid in 1836. Most of its buildings are in the *Ciudad Universitaria* (Moncloa): there is another campus in Somosaguas.

COMUNIDAD AUTÓNOMA DE CASTILLA-LA MANCHA

This AUTONOMÍA lies in the centre of Spain, between EXTREMADURA in the west and the COMUNIDAD DE VALENCIA in the east. It has a population of one and a half million people and covers 79,130 square km. Its capital, Toledo, is an important tourist centre. It also has a number of small industries such as light engineering and also pharmaceuticals and electronic components. Otherwise, CASTILLA-LA MANCHA is predominantly agricultural: sheep farming, wine and vegetable production are its chief source of income.

COMUNIDAD AUTÓNOMA DE MURCIA

MURCIA is one of the Spanish AUTONOMÍAS, situated in the south-eastern corner of Spain between the COMUNIDAD VALENCIANA and ANDALUCÍA. It has a population of one million and covers an area of 11,317 square km. Its main industries are agriculture and tourism. The capital of the region is Murcia but Cartagena is more important both historically and economically. The largest oil refinery in Europe is to be found on the small island of Escombreras.

COMUNIDAD AUTÓNOMA VASCA

The Basque autonomous community was created under the 1978 Spanish CONSTITUCIÓN. NAVARRA was excluded from the community, despite its historical roots as a Basque province.

COMUNIDAD ECÓNOMICA EUROPEA

Spain joined the European Economic Community of EU in June 1985.

COMUNIDAD VALENCIANA

The COMUNIDAD VALENCIANA is one of the AUTONOMÍAS and is located on the east coast of Spain, south of CATALUÑA and north of MURCIA. Its capital is VALENCIA. The region is fertile and famous for its citrus fruits and rice. It is also an important tourist centre and has recently invested to produce an infrastructure of a high standard to support tourist developments such as hotels, apartments, retirement complexes and leisure facilities. VALENCIA itself is a centre for the furniture and ceramic industry. Ford's

Spanish headquarters is located here, as well as their car and engine manufacturing plant. Alicante is a centre for the shoe and carpet industries. This autonomous region has had responsibilities for Education, Health and Law devolved to it.

CONCEJAL/ES

The CONCEJAL is a town or city councillor, elected by universal suffrage on a proportional representation system. Voters elect a list nominated by each party. Nominees are ranked in order and the number of councillors elected for a particular party depends on the number of votes cast for that party. Councillors serve for four years with an unlimited number of terms of office.

CONCEJO ABIERTO

This 'open assembly' operates in MUNICIPIOS of less than 100 inhabitants, if the inhabitants so request it. The ALCALDE is elected by the *Asamblea Vecinal* (neighbourhood assembly) and all those of voting age have the right to take decisions on local matters.

CONCERTACIÓN SOCIAL

Government policy of consulting interested parties (e.g. workers and employees) on specific issues and then reaching an agreement. Examples of this policy are the PACTOS DE LA MONCLOA and the ACUERDO MARCO INTERCONFEDERAL. This policy of 'social contracts' lasted from 1977 to 1984.

LA CONCHA

Name of the largest beach in SAN SEBASTIÁN, so-called because of its shell-like shape. It has a famous decorated railing which separates it from the promenade.

LA CONCHA DE ORO

The most prestigious prize awarded at the annual FESTIVAL *Internacional de Cine de* SAN SEBASTIÁN.

CONCIERTO ECONÓMICO

In 1981, the PAÍS VASCO came to an agreement with central government to recover its former economic privileges, principally in the area of raising taxes. NAVARRA is the only other region which has similar privileges.

CONCURSO INTERNACIONAL DE PIANO JOSÉ ITURBI

Biennial piano competition open to pianists of any nationality under the age of 32. The first prize is worth one million pesetas, the second 750,000 and the third 50,000.

CONCURSO INTERNACIONAL DE PIANO PREMIO JAÉN

Annual piano competition open to pianists of all nationalities. The first prize is worth 2 million pesetas and the winner is awarded a gold medal and offered numerous musical engagements.

CONDE, CARMEN (1907–   )

Novelist, first woman to enter the REAL ACADEMIA ESPAÑOLA in 1978. She was awarded the *Premio Ateneo Sevilla* in 1980 and the *Premio Nacional de Literatura Infantil y Juvenil* in 1978. Among her better known works are *Júbilos* and *Las oscuras raíces*.

CONDE, MARIO (1948–   )

Presidente of BANESTO from 1987 to 1993, MARIO CONDE seemed the 'golden boy' of Spanish business and banking until the bank collapsed in 1993. It was discovered that 605,000 million pesetas were missing and the bank was eventually taken over by the BANCO DE ESPAÑA. CONDE underwent a trial, accused of mismanagement, incompetence and fraud and was condemned to six years' imprisonment.

CONFEDERACIÓN DE SINDICATOS INDEPENDIENTES Y SINDICAL DE FUNCIONARIOS

The two unions of the title amalgamated in 1991 to bring together over 180 union groups. It had a membership of 116,000 in 1994.

CONFEDERACIÓN ESPAÑOLA DE ASOCIACIONES DE PADRES DE ALUMNOS

Parents' association whose objective is to improve state schooling in Spain. It is made up of 47 separate federations which work towards free lay schooling from 3 to 18, the provision of free school meals, transport and books.

CONFEDERACIÓN ESPAÑOLA DE CAJAS DE AHORROS

A savings bank which itself has important accounts such as the UNED (UNIVERSIDAD NACIONAL DE EDUCACIÓN A DISTANCIA) but which also represents, advises and keeps statistical data for its constituent savings' banks. It is involved in research and training as well as coordinating the network of cash distributors belonging to the savings banks. It deals on the London Stock Exchange.

CONFEDERACIÓN ESPAÑOLA DE ORGANIZACIONES EMPRESARIALES

Employers' association, currently headed by José María Cuevas. It was formed in 1977 and replaced three earlier organisations. It has 184 employers' federations which total more than 1 million members. Its fundamental role is to represent employers in trades union negotiations with the Government and international bodies.

CONFEDERACIÓN ESPAÑOLA DE PEQUEÑAS Y MEDIANAS EMPRESAS

This is a federation of small and medium-sized firms. It is made up of 73 associations and is a constituent member of the CEOE.

CONFEDERACIÓN ESTATAL DE ASOCIACIONES DE ESTUDIANTES

This body is also known as the *Unión de Estudiantes* (UDE) and is the equivalent of a national union of students. It has over 47,000 members in 21 universities and school unions. It provides various services to its members, such as legal and financial advice and counselling: it also publishes the *Boletín Unión de Estudiantes*. Its declared aim is to promote an open and pluralistic state education system.

CONFEDERACIÓN ESTATAL DE SINDICATOS MÉDICOS

The joint body of medical trades' unions.

CONFEDERACIÓN GENERAL DEL TRABAJO

Trade union formed in 1979, following a split in the CNT. It has 50,000 members and is anarchist in tendency.

CONFEDERACIÓN NACIONAL DE TRABAJADORES
Anarchist trade union particularly strong in the 1930s. Important in CATALUÑA. It was legalised in 1977. Among its most important leaders were Federica Montseny and Durruti.

CONFEDERACIÓN SINDICAL DE CATALUNYA
Small, but active trade union in CATALUÑA.

CONFERENCIA EPISCOPAL ESPAÑOLA
The Conference of Spanish Bishops, an assembly which represents the views of the Spanish hierarchy.

CONFERENCIAS IBEROAMERICANAS
A series of conferences which take place between Spain and the Latin American countries. The first was held in 1991 in Guadalajara, Mexico.

CONGRESO DE LA REFUNDACIÓN
Name given to the IXth party conference of the former ALIANZA POPULAR. It was at this conference that ALIANZA became a single party rather than a loose coalition of seven right-wing groups and took the name PARTIDO POPULAR.

CONGRESO DE LOS DIPUTADOS
The CONGRESO or Lower House has between 300 and 400 DIPUTADOS or Members of Parliament. Elections are universal, free and secret and all Spaniards are eligible to vote. Votes are not cast for individuals but for a party list in which the candidates appear in an order established by the parties concerned. Elections take place in the 52 provinces every four years, unless Parliament is dissolved earlier.

CONGRESO FEDERAL
Principal assembly of the PARTIDO SOCIALISTA OBRERO ESPAÑOL. It formulates policies which will be implemented by the PSOE when in office: it meets every two years and is composed of delegates elected by proportional representation by the provincial assemblies.

CONGRESO NACIONAL
Supreme assembly of the PARTIDO POPULAR, which meets every

three years. Delegates come from each region; numbers vary according to local membership levels. Among other functions, the CONGRESO NACIONAL shapes basic party policy, approves the accounts and debates all questions relating to strategy, the electoral programme and party management.

CONGRESO NACIONAL DE CANARIAS
This party was founded in 1986 to campaign for the independence of the Canary Islands. It rejects membership of the EU.

CONSEJERÍAS
Term used for the regional ministries of most AUTONOMÍAS. They are known as *departamentos* in ARAGÓN, PAÍS VASCO and NAVARRA (*departments* in CATALUÑA) and *consellerías* in VALENCIA. They work like the ministries in central government.

CONSEJO ASESOR DE EXPORTACIÓN
Government agency within the MINISTERIO DE ECONOMÍA and responsible for the promotion of exports.

CONSEJO ASESOR DE SANIDAD
Health Advisory Council. This council, composed of up to 25 members who are health professionals, advises the Minister of Health on scientific, ethical and professional questions.

CONSEJO DE ESTADO
A major organ of state, whose role is to advise the government on questions of legal importance. It is made up of lawyers and other representatives of administration and government. As opposed to the French *Conseil d'État* it does not act as a final appeal court in administrative cases.

CONSEJO DE GOBIERNO
Each AUTONOMÍA has a president, elected from the members of the ASAMBLEA LEGISLATIVA. He, in turn, nominates a CONSEJO DE GOBIERNO, a body with executive and administrative powers. One of its major functions is to issue decrees and resolutions which are not required to go through the ASAMBLEA. Members of this body are empowered to issue orders or *órdenes* concerning minor matters relating to their own department.

CONSEJO DE LA JUVENTUD DE ESPAÑA
Government body whose purpose is to encourage young people to participate in youth associations: it also organises seminars and activities for young people.

CONSEJO DE MINISTROS
The cabinet of ministers in government.

CONSEJO DE SEGURIDAD NUCLEAR
This state body is answerable directly to Parliament and is responsible for citizen protection in case of nuclear emergency.

CONSEJO DE UNIVERSIDADES
Universities' Council, part of the MINISTERIO DE EDUCACIÓN Y CULTURA and whose role is to coordinate the university system in general. Despite university autonomy, many decisions taken at local level must be referred to the CONSEJO.

CONSEJO ECONÓMICO Y SOCIAL
A body created in 1991 to advise the Spanish government on economic planning and on social and labour issues.

CONSEJO ESCOLAR
Each school must have a governing body known as the CONSEJO ESCOLAR, which is made up of teachers, parents, pupils and a non-teaching member of staff. Among other rights and duties, the CONSEJO ESCOLAR appoints (and dismisses) the head teacher and staff, decides on matters of discipline and sets and implements school budgets.

CONSEJO ESCOLAR DEL ESTADO
The national confederation of CONSEJOS ESCOLARES or school councils. It has 80 members and is composed of the same interest groups as the CONSEJOS – that is, of staff, parents and pupils, and private school operators.

CONSEJO GENERAL DEL PODER JUDICIAL
This body is the highest judicial body in Spain and is composed of 21 members of the judiciary. The president is elected by the other 20 of whom 12 are nominated by members of the legal profession and 8 by Parliament. The CGPJ is responsible for appoint-

ments, promotions, inspection and discipline within the legal profession. It was established as a result of the 1978 Constitution with a view to making the judiciary independent from the government in power.

CONSEJO INTERTERRITORIAL DEL SISTEMA NACIONAL DE SALUD

Joint Health Council. Since devolution, many regions have their own health services: this council was established in 1987 to introduce cohesion and coordination within the health system.

CONSEJO NACIONAL DE AGUAS

National Water Board whose responsibility is the use and condition of the national water supply.

CONSEJO NACIONAL DE MAYORES

This council was founded in 1986 to bring together those associations which deal with the elderly and the retired. It provides for the exchange of experiences and coordinates and plans joint programmes. It undertakes research projects and training and provides information on topics concerning the elderly.

CONSEJO SOCIAL

Instead of a union, those firms in Spain which are managed as cooperatives may have a CONSEJO SOCIAL which undertakes some union functions but is not allied to them. These councils are important in the MONDRAGÓN system of cooperatives. Within the university system, the CONSEJO SOCIAL is a University Court. 60% of its members are members of unions or employers' associations.

CONSEJO SUPERIOR BANCARIO

National Banking Authority. This authority has a statutory right to be consulted on matters such as interest rate policy.

CONSEJO SUPERIOR DE DEPORTES

The Sports Council is attached to the MINISTERIO DE EDUCACIÓN Y CULTURA.

CONSEJO SUPERIOR DE INVESTIGACIONES CIENTÍFICAS

A new body created in 1996 to integrate all organisations which carry out scientific research – many of which are within the university system. The CSIC works out of the MINISTERIO DE EDUCACIÓN Y CULTURA. Its current director is César Nombela.

CONSELL NACIONAL DE LA JOVENTUT CATALUNYA

This body represents 70 youth organisations in CATALUÑA. It was founded in 1979 to promote exchanges, to provide educational opportunities and to organise seminars and conferences for young people throughout CATALUÑA. It publishes a magazine called *Debat Juvenil*.

CONSELLER

A minister in the autonomous governments of CATALUÑA, the COMUNIDAD VALENCIANA and in the BALEARES.

CONSERVERA CAMPOFRÍO, S.A.

This company produces sausages, hot dogs, cured and uncured hams and other cooked meats, including paté, turkey products and animal feed.

CONSORCIO DE COMPENSACIÓN DE SEGUROS

A commercial body responsible for all sectors of public administration in the event of accidents or losses. It provides cover in road accidents where the insurance company has collapsed or where accidents have been caused by unknown persons. It also provides cover in the case of forest fires and floods.

CONSTITUCIÓN

The Spanish Constitution of 1978 (the 7th in the history of Spain) consists of 169 articles which lay the foundation of the modern Spanish state. Of prime importance are those articles which deal with the PODERES FÁCTICOS (the Church and the Armed Forces). The Constitution states that ultimate responsibility for defence lies with the democratically elected government and not with the Armed Forces and also establishes religious freedom and the absence of a state religion (Article 16).

CONSTRUCCIONES AERONÁUTICAS
Aeronautical engineering company, builder of the prototype of the Eurofighter-2000. It also has a share in the consortium which is producing the Airbus, also a joint European venture.

CONSTRUCCIONES Y AUXILIAR DE FERROCARRILES, S.A.
This company is involved in the manufacture of components, rolling materials and equipment for the transport industry. It also manufactures products for the metallurgical, plastic, boiler-making and carpentry industries, as well as machine tools and industrial machinery.

CONTINENTE
Second largest chain of hypermarkets in Spain. In 1995, it had 45 stores, 12,076 employees and a turnover of 448,100 million pesetas.

CONTRATO A TIEMPO PARCIAL
Part-time work contracts were first introduced into Spain in the employment legislation of 1994.

CONTRATO BASURA
Literally 'rubbish contract' – a slang term used to describe any short-term work contract.

CONTRATO DE APRENDIZAJE
Apprenticeships were first introduced into Spain in the employment legislation of 1994.

CONTRATO DE INTERINIDAD
Temporary contract given to a worker who covers for another who has taken leave of absence.

CONTRATO DE RELEVO
These contracts are available to those unemployed persons who are substituting for workers about to take retirement and who have opted to work shorter hours.

CONTRATO EN PRÁCTICAS
These contracts are for qualified workers or graduates who wish to obtain practical experience in their area of expertise. They last

for a period of 6 months to 2 years and must be undertaken within four years of having obtained the professional qualification.

CONTRATO INDEFINIDO
Long-term, full-time contract. There are special economic incentives available for employers in professional areas in which women are under-represented. There are similar incentives for employers to take on younger workers, up to the age of 25 and for employing older workers (over 45) who have been unemployed for more than a year.

CONTRATO TEMPORAL
Fixed-term work contracts, first introduced in 1984.

CONVALIDACIÓN
This term refers to the validation or recognition of academic qualifications obtained in other countries. CONVALIDACIÓN must be acquired for entry to certain courses wihin the university system.

CONVENIO ECÓNOMICO
The equivalent of the Basque CONCIERTO ECONÓMICO, it is the agreement by which NAVARRA enjoys the right to levy and collect taxes within its region. Customs duties and taxes on petrol and tobacco are excluded.

CONVERGENCIA DE DEMÓCRATAS NAVARROS
The CDN was launched in 1995 by a group which broke away from the PP affiliated UPN. It won ten of 50 regional assembly seats in 1995.

CONVERGENCIA DEMOCRÁTICA DE CATALUNYA
Main partner of the CIU coalition, founded by JORDI PUJOL in 1974 and still led by him.

CONVERGENCIA i UNIÓ
CONVERGENCIA i UNIÓ (a coalition between CONVERGENCIA DEMOCRÁTICA DE CATALUNYA and UNIÓ DEMOCRÁTICA DE CATALUNYA) is the ruling party of CATALUÑA. Headed by JORDI PUJOL, it has governed the region since 1980. JOSÉ MARÍA AZNAR has had to

negotiate with the party in order to form his 1996 government and the party has thus become powerful in national as well as local affairs. It holds 16 seats in the CORTES.

CONVERXENCIA INTERSINDICAL GALEGA
Regional trade union with enough support to qualify for negotiating status. In 1990 it obtained 23% of the regional vote. It is based in Vigo.

COOB 92 See: *COMITÉ ORGANIZADOR OLÍMPICO BARCELONA '92*

COOPERATIVAS
Cooperatives are an important form of business organisation in Spain, especially in the agricultural sector. They are regulated by the *Ley General de Cooperativas* (1987). The autonomous governments have been instrumental in encouraging their development.

COORDINADORA DE ORGANIZACIONES DE DEFENSA AMBIENTAL
Founded in 1978, CODA is an ecological pressure group with over 35,000 members throughout Spain. Since 1986, it has fought over 500 ecological battles and has won a large number of them. It has 16 offices open to the public. Its officers are frequently consulted on environmental issues.

COPA DEL REY, LA
Football competition in which the 1st and 2nd division teams all compete. It is a knock-out competition in which each team plays its opponent twice, once at home and once away. The winner of this competition is then entered for the UEFA Cup. In 1997 this was the BARCELONA football team.

COPE See: *CADENA DE ONDAS POPULARES ESPAÑOLAS*

CORCUERA CUESTA, JOSÉ LUIS (1945–   )
Politician, at one time *ministro del Interior* (1988–93). He has been implicated in scandals involving misuse of public funds. He started life as an electrician and first entered politics through the

UGT (UNIÓN GENERAL DE TRABAJADORES). He resigned his government post when the TRIBUNAL CONSTITUCIONAL revoked the LEY CORCUERA. This article in the law on *Protección de la Seguridad Ciudadana* allowed the police to enter a citizen's home on suspicion of misconduct, without permission from the *juez* or local magistrate.

CÓRDOBA

Capital of the province of CÓRDOBA, originally capital of Moorish Spain. It has many buildings dating from the time of the Moors including the famous mosque of Abd-er-Rahman 1, now a world heritage site. Its Jewish quarter and *Álcazar* (fortress) are also famous.

CORDÓN MUNILLA, PUBLIO

Owner of an insurance company, *Previasa*, PUBLIO CORDÓN was kidnapped in 1996 by GRAPO, the right-wing terrorist organisation.

CORPORACIÓ CATALANA DE RADIO I TELEVISIÓ

The Catalán Broadcasting Corporation. It manages both TV-3 and CANAL 33.

CORPORACIÓN BANCARIA DE ESPAÑA

This corporation was set up in 1991 to replace the ICO (*Instituto de Crédito Oficial*). It is composed of a number of banks, such as the BANCO EXTERIOR DE ESPAÑA and the *Caja Postal de Ahorros* (The Post Office Savings Bank). Its function is to coordinate financial activities in the banking and other financial sectors. It trades under the name ARGENTARIA.

CORPORACIÓN FINANCIERA ALBA

A holding company with interests in firms which are active in securities, real-estate investment and banking. It is also involved in the development and acquisition of real estate for leasing.

CORPORACIÓN SIDERÚRGICA INTEGRAL

Publicly-owned iron and steel company based in ASTURIAS. The government plans to privatise the company in 1997. Currently the AGENCIA INDUSTRIAL DEL ESTADO is the only share-holder.

CORREFOCS

CATALÁN word for groups of people in disguise who run through the crowds on festive days, hurling firecrackers. This custom has experienced a revival in recent years, due to the reassertion of CATALÁN national values and identity.

EL CORREO CATALÁN

Evening newspaper, published in BARCELONA.

CORTE CONSTITUCIONAL

This body is made up of 12 members, approved by the reigning monarch. 4 members are nominated by the CONGRESO, 4 by the SENADO, 2 by the government in power and 2 by the CONSEJO GENERAL DEL PODER JUDICIAL. It has 3 major responsibilities: firstly, to examine and pronounce on the constitutionality of the laws; secondly, to pronounce on conflicts in jurisdiction between central and autonomous governments and thirdly, to pronounce on individual cases when all other legal resources have been exhausted. The CORTE CONSTITUCIONAL has played a vital role in ensuring the autonomy of the regions and in establishing the basic rights and freedoms of Spanish citizens.

EL CORTE INGLÉS

Largest chain of department stores in Spain. In 1995 it increased its size by buying out the rival company, GALERÍAS PRECIADOS. The CORTE INGLÉS chain has interests in the media also (CADENA SER and CANAL+).

CORTES

The Spanish Parliament, composed of two assemblies, the CONGRESO or lower house and the SENADO, the upper house. As in other democracies, the lower house or CÁMARA BAJA takes precedence. The CONGRESO meets in the *Palacio del Congreso* or *Palacio de las Cortes* and the SENADO assembles in the *Palacio del Senado*. See also: CONGRESO and SENADO

CORTES CONSTITUYENTES

Name given to the parliament elected in 1977 whose function was to draw up the new 1978 constitution.

CORTES GENERALES
This term is given to both chambers of parliament when they act in consort, such as on state occasions.

CORTÉS, JOAQUIN (1969–   )
Flamenco dancer, who suddenly shot to fame after his appearance in ALMODÓVAR's *Tacones lejanos*. He was trained as a classical dancer and was a member of the Ballet Nacional de España for a number of years. He left the company in 1990 to develop his career as a solo artiste. He has appeared both in pop videos and on the catwalk. In 1992 he founded his own company, the *Joaquín Cortes Ballet Flamenco* and has since toured Europe with his flamenco shows. In 1997 he had a great success with *Pasión Gitana* ('Gypsy Passion')

CORTIJO
Large estate in the south of Spain (especially in ANDALUCÍA and EXTREMADURA).

COSTA BLANCA
The coastal resort regions of MURCIA, ALICANTE and part of the province of Almería, from Cabo San Antonio to Punto Almerimar. The name means 'white coast'.

COSTA BRAVA
The coastal resort region of CATALUÑA on the Mediterranean, between BARCELONA and the French border. Its name means 'wild coast'.

COSTA DE LA LUZ
Coastal resort region on the Atlantic coastline of Huelva and Cádiz provinces. It stretches from the Portuguese border to the southernmost tip of Spain at Tarifa. The name means 'coast of light'.

COSTA DEL AZAHAR
Mediterranean coastal region in the provinces of Castellón de la Plana and VALENCIA, between the COSTA DORADA and the COSTA BLANCA. Its name means 'orange-blossom coast'.

COSTA DEL SOL
Mediterranean coastal resort region in ANDALUCÍA, stretching from Punto Almerimar to Tarifa. The name means 'coast of the sun'.

COSTA DORADA
Mediterranean coastal resort region south of the COSTA BRAVA, in the provinces of BARCELONA and TARRAGONA. The name means 'golden coast'

COTO DOÑANA
This is the most important National Park in Spain and of immense ecological importance. It has been classified by UNESCO as a Biosphere Reserve. Situated at the mouth of the River GUADALQUIVIR, south of SEVILLA, it is located in an area of *marismas* or marshland which is the home of huge numbers of wintering birds such as godwits, coots, pintails and shovellers. Several rare species in danger of extinction breed at Doñana, including the imperial eagle, the bittern and the marbled teal. The park is also home to mammals such as the Spanish lynx and deer. Doñana is currently under threat from the developers who wish to promote tourism on the nearby coast and from farmers, keen to drain the land and use harmful pesticides and fertilizers.

COU See: *CURSO DE ORIENTACIÓN UNIVERSITARIA*

COVADONGA
The first national park to be created in Spain, COVADONGA was founded in 1918 on the twelve hundredth anniversary of the beginning of the Reconquest of Spain by Don Pelayo. It is in the heart of the Pyrenees, in ASTURIAS.

CRISOL
Chain of multi-media shops selling books, records and videos.

CRIVILLÉ, ALEX (1970–)
Motocyclist, Spanish champion in the 125cc category. He now rides in 500cc races and is second in the world in this category.

CRMF See: *CENTROS DE RECUPERACIÓN DE MINUSVÁLIDOS FÍSICOS*

CRUZ ROJA ESPAÑOLA
The Spanish Red Cross. The CRUZ ROJA team is a common sight on beaches and on the road, and provides first aid in case of accident. Until recently it was a government organisation, but in 1997 it became independent.

CRUZ, PENÉLOPE
Film actress, her most famous role to date has been that of the Virgin Mary in the Italian film *Pero amore e solo per amore*, directed by Giovani Veronese. She has also appeared in *La rebelde* (Marco Grimaldi), *Talk of Angels* (Nick Hamm), *La belle époque*, *Carne trémula*, *Jamón, jamón*, and in 1997, AMENÁBAR's *Abre los ojos*.

CRUZCAMPO
Largest beer manufacturer in Spain. It is owned by the Irish company Guinness. It was originally owned by the Anglo-Spanish family, Osborne.

CSC See: *CONFEDERACIÓN SINDICAL DE CATALUNYA*

CSI See: *CORPORACIÓN SIDERÚRGICA INTEGRAL*

CSIC See: *CONSEJO SUPERIOR DE INVESTIGACIONES CIENTÍFICAS*

CSI–CSIF See: *CONFEDERACIÓN DE SINDICATOS INDEPENDIENTES Y SINDICAL DE FUNCIONARIOS.*

CSN See: *CONSEJO DE SEGURIDAD NUCLEAR*

CTC
CATALÁN cable company with rights to lay cables throughout CATALUÑA. Its principal share-holder is ENDESA. Other share-holders are LA VANGUARDIA, *Cableuropa* and GAS NATURAL.

CUADERNOS PARA EL DIÁLOGO
First current affairs magazine to be published in Spain of a combative nature, it was founded in 1963 and covered news items, features and articles on society and culture. It has since closed, but was important and influential in its day.

CUADRA, LA

Spanish theatre group founded in 1971 in SEVILLA. It gains much of its inspiration from Andalucían popular culture and is especially famous for its set design. The director is Salvador Tavora, who is best known for his production of *El Quejido*.

CUARENTA PRINCIPALES

Spanish radio station, owned by CADENA SER. It has more than 60 studios throughout Spain and specialises in broadcasting the top forty. It is the most widely listened to of the popular music stations.

CUBIERTAS-ENTRECANALES

Third largest building company in Spain, formed in 1996 from the merger of CUBIERTAS and ENTRECANALES. It has a turnover of 325,000 million pesetas per year.

CUERDA, JOSÉ LUIS (1947–   )

Film director and television producer. His most successful films have been *El bosque animado* (1987) on which he collaborated with RAFAEL AZCONA and *Amanece, que no es poco* (1988).

CUERPO DE INSPECTORES DE EDUCACIÓN

Education Inspectorate. It is open to those members of the teaching profession who have passed the competitive examination or OPOSICIÓN. Inspectors work in the private as well as in the public sector.

CUERPO NACIONAL DE POLICÍA

The Spanish police form was created in 1986 by amalgamating the *Cuerpo General* and the POLICÍA NACIONAL. It has succeeded in throwing off the unsavoury reputation of the latter force.

CUEVAS, JOSÉ MARÍA (1935–   )

Business-man, *ex-secretario* of the CEOE (CONFEDERACIÓN ESPAÑOLA DE ORGANIZACIONES EMPRESARIALES) and currently *presidente* of the same association. He plays an influential role in deciding economic policy with JOSÉ MARÍA AZNAR.

CULEBRÓN

Name given to the *telenovelas* or soap operas which are usually shown after lunch on Spanish television. They are bought in, principally from Brazil, Mexico and Venezuela and are enormously popular. *Cristal* and *La dama de rosa* are examples of recent soaps with a mass following.

CUOTAS EMPRESARIALES
Employers' social security contributions. Currently, they are higher than others in the European Community.

CUPONAZO
Name given to the lottery tickets sold by the ONCE (ORGANIZACIÓN NACIONAL DE CIEGOS ESPAÑOLES) and which have a pay-out of up to 200 million pesetas.

CÚPULA
Term used to refer to the leaders of political parties. It is also used with reference to ETA.

CURSO DE ORIENTACIÓN UNIVERSITARIA
The last year at school, which is devoted to preparing students for university entrance. Students have a choice of four options: scientific-technological, biomedical, arts and social sciences. It is essential to have passed COU to enter university as well as to have passed the entrance examination (SELECTIVIDAD). Acceptance at University is determined by marks at COU and BUP levels, and by the final mark in the SELECTIVIDAD. This course will cease to be taught in 1999–2000. See also: BUP and LOGSE.

DAGOLL-DAGOM

Theatre group founded in 1973 in BARCELONA. It opened with a play based on a work by Rafael Alberti, *Yo era un tonto* (1974).

DALÍ, SALVADOR (1904–1989)

Spanish surrealist painter from CATALUÑA. For much of his life he painted strange objects and events based on dream imagery and symbolism. In 1940 he moved to the United States where he became a Catholic and began to paint religious subjects. He collaborated with LUIS BUÑUEL in the surrealist films *Un chien andalou* (1928) and *L'Age d'or* (1930). He returned to Spain and died in his birth-place, Figueras.

DE LA IGLESIA, ÁLEX (1966–   )

Young Basque film director who has, to date, made two feature films, *Acción mutante* and *El día de la bestia*. This latter film was one of the most popular films of 1995. In 1997, he directed *Perdita Durango*.

DE LA ROSA MARTÍ, JAVIER (1947–   )

International financier and Catalán business man. Vice-president of the GRUPO TORRAS, a holding company in which KIO (Kuwait Investment Office) invested 5 billion dollars. He was accused by his Arab colleagues of fraud and misappropriation of funds to the tune of 100,000 million pesetas. He is currently undergoing a criminal trial as a result of his activities both in Spain and in the United Kingdom.

DE LA SOTA, ALEJANDRO (1913–1996)

The most important Spanish architect of the second half of the twentieth century. His most accomplished works are the building of the GOBIERNO CIVIL in Tarragona and the gymnasium of the Colegio Maravillas in MADRID. He received the gold medal of the

Academia de Bellas Artes in 1986 and that of the *Academia de Arquitectura* in 1988.

DE LOS ÁNGELES, VICTORIA (1923–   )

Born in BARCELONA, this international opera star specialises in Puccini, Massenet and the Spanish repertoire. She made her debut in MADRID in 1944 and has had a career spanning fifty years.

DE LUCÍA, PACO (1948–   )

Flamenco guitarrist who combines jazz and rock with traditional flamenco rhythms. In 1961 he joined José Greco's flamenco group and by 1967 he had cut his first record *La guitarra fabulosa de Paco de Lucía*. In 1969 he produced *Fantasía flamenca*. He also starred in SAURA's *Bodas de sangre*. He accompanied the great flamenco singer CAMARÓN DE LA ISLA.

DE MARICHALAR, JAIME (1965–   )

Spanish aristocrat. He married ELENA DE BORBÓN (the eldest daughter of the Spanish royal family) in March 1995 and was made *Duque de Lugo*. He works in the banking sector.

DE PALACIO, LOYOLA (1950–   )

Lawyer and politician. She was SENADORA from 1987 to 1989. For several years she was *diputada* for Segovia. She is currently *ministra de Agricultura*, *Pesca y Alimentación*. At the age of 27, she became leader of NUEVAS GENERACIONES, (the youth group for AP). In the last two legislatures she was spokeswoman for PP.

DE PAULA, RAFAEL

Bull fighter from Jerez, he has recently been sentenced to a term in prison for breaking and entering.

DEDICACIÓN EXCLUSIVA

In the past many professionals (including doctors and politicians) have held several posts simultaneously (PLURIEMPLEO). This term refers to the new arrangements by which professionals in a number of sectors are allowed to hold one post only.

DEFENSOR DEL PUEBLO

The post of DEFENSOR DEL PUEBLO or ombudsman was established by the 1978 CONSTITUCIÓN. His role is to regulate the activities of ministers, the administration and the civil service with regard to the individual rights of citizens. He is elected by the members of parliament.

DEFENSORES ALTRUISTAS DE LOS DERECHOS DE LA TERCERA EDAD (DATE)

This association was founded in 1985 to defend the rights and interests of the elderly. It aims to help the elderly defend their civil, political and economic rights and does so through giving legal advice, obtaining documents, presenting papers and organising appeals. It also has a programme of holidays for older people.

DEHESA

Type of man-made landscape in EXTREMADURA which is covered thinly with oak trees: it is used for extensive agricultural activities such as pig-farming and cork-collecting. It is also the term used for those farms/ranches specialising in the breeding of bulls for bullfights (*toros de lidia*).

DEIA

Basque newspaper, published in SAN SEBASTIÁN and partly written in the Basque language. It represents the moderate wing of Basque nationalism and is linked to the PNV.

DELCLAUX, COSME (1963–   )

Son of a wealthy Basque industrialist, COSME DELCLAUX was captured by the Basque terrorist group ETA in 1996. He was released on the 1st of July 1997 after 233 days in captivity. His parents were alleged to have paid a ransom of 4 million pounds.

DELEGACIÓN

The DELEGACIÓN is a municipal department which deals with public services such as security, education, and traffic and transport. The members of staff in these departments are not political appointees.

DELEGACIÓN DE SANIDAD

Local health authority.

DELIBES, MIGUEL (1920–   )

DELIBES was born in VALLADOLID where he has lived all his life. His novels recount the life of the people from this area (CASTILLA). His most famous works are *El camino*, *Las ratas*, *Cinco horas con Mario*, *La mortaja* and *Viejas historias de Castilla la Vieja*. In 1982 he won the PREMIO PRÍNCIPE DE ASTURIAS and in 1991, the *Premio Nacional de las Letras Españolas*.

DELITOS CULPOSOS

In accordance with the 1995 CÓDIGO PENAL, the public may claim compensation for the errors of public bodies even if these errors were unintentional (DELITOS CULPOSOS). See also: DELITOS DOLOSOS

DELITOS DOLOSOS

These are intentional errors or omissions committed by members of any public body. Individuals may claim compensation where these errors have been detrimental to them in any way.

DEMOCRACIA SOCIALISTA

The DS was launched as a separate party by a group of PSOE dissidents in 1990.

DEMOSCOPIA

Organisation which conducts opinion polls.

DENOMINACIÓN DE ORIGEN

The DENOMINACIÓN DE ORIGEN arose to protect the identity and purity of regional foods. Each DENOMINACIÓN has its own regulatory boards, administered by the regional governments. Many of the foods covered by these regulations are produced in small quantities using cottage industry methods. A DENOMINACIÓN DE ORIGEN ensures that the food is produced and prepared in a particular geographical area, whereas a DENOMINACIÓN *específica* refers to a special method of preparation of a product whose ingredients may come from elsewhere. DENOMINACIONES include wine (there are 43 wine regions so classified in Spain) and foods such as apples, cheese, eggs, prawns, saffron, ham, olive oil and hazelnuts.

DEPORTES NUEVOS

Many unusual sports are now practised in Spain including *bar-*

ranquismo (descending rivers in canyons), *benji* (bungee-jumping), *building* (climbing up the outside of high-rise buildings) and *rafting* (white-water canoeing).

DESERTIZACIÓN
Term used for the process of soil erosion and desertification currently taking place in certain areas in the south of Spain, such as MURCIA and ANDALUCÍA. It is the worst environmental problem which Spain will have to face in future years and is due, in great part, to over-use of water in intensive agriculture as well as climatic changes.

DEUSTO
Private university in BILBAO (PAÍS VASCO), run by the Jesuits.

DÍA DE LA CONSTITUCIÓN
This national holiday falls on the 6th of December and celebrates the proclamation of the 1978 CONSTITUCIÓN.

DÍA DE LAS FUERZAS ARMADAS
6th of January, the day on which military personnel and equipment parade before the King and Queen of Spain.

DIADA
This term refers to the feast-days celebrated in CATALUÑA – the 11th of September, the 23rd of April (*Sant Jordi*), the DIADA *de Sant Esteve* and the DIADA *de la Sardana*.

DIARIO 16
Daily newspaper, rather more populist in approach than EL PAÍS and influential in the 1980s.

DÍAS AZULES
Days on which the members of the public may receive reduced rates on train tickets.

DÍAZ MERCHAN, GABINO (1926–   )
Presidente of the CONFERENCIA EPISCOPAL ESPAÑOLA (that is chairperson and spokesman for the Spanish bishops) from 1981 to 1987, succeeding VICENTE ENRIQUE Y TARANCÓN. He did much to smooth the relationship between the Church and the Socialist government.

DÍAZ YANES, AGUSTÍN (1951–   )

Film director, his first film *Nadie hablará de nosotras cuando hayamos muerto* (1996) was an instant success, winning eight of the ten PREMIOS GOYA for which it was nominated, including best script, best picture and best new director. Previously he specialised in film scripts, including those for *Baton Rouge*, *A solas contigo* and *Belmonte*.

DICCIONARIO DE CUERVO

This dictionary, comprising 9,500 words, was published in 1995. It had been begun by the Colombian philologist José Cuervo in 1870 and was continued after his death by the *Instituto Caro y Cuervo* in Bogotá. Its full title is the *Diccionario de construcción y régimen de la lengua castellana*.

DICCIONARIO DE LA REAL ACADEMIA ESPAÑOLA

Official dictionary of the Spanish language, compiled by members of the REAL ACADEMIA. The first edition appeared in 1741 and was called the *Diccionario de Ortografía*. There have been 21 editions. The last one appeared in 1992.

DIEGO, GABINO (1966–   )

GABINO DIEGO's first cinema role was that of *Luisito* in *Las bicicletas son para el verano* (1983) and since then he has appeared in a variety of pictures such as *¡Ay Carmela!* (1990), *El rey pasmado* (1991) and *La noche más larga* (1991). One of his latest films is *Los peores años de nuestra vida*, directed by Emilio Martinez-Lázaro.

DIEGO, JUAN (1942–   )

Film and television actor. He first rose to fame in MARIO CAMUS' *Los santos inocentes* (1983) and since then has appeared in a number of successful pictures such as *La corte de Faraón* (1985) and *La noche oscura* (1988). He was the first Spanish actor to play the role of General FRANCO in *Dragon Rapide* (1986).

DIEZ MINUTOS

One of the so-called REVISTAS DEL CORAZÓN and perhaps the most scandalous. It was founded in 1951 and has a readership of almost two million. It specialises in features on television personalities and the *folklóricas* (singers often of gypsy extraction who sing traditional Spanish and Latin-American ballads).

DINERO NEGRO

Money which is obtained illegally (through drug trafficking or on the black market) and which is therefore not taxed.

DIPLOMAS OFICIALES DE ESPAÑOL

These diplomas in Spanish as a foreign language are awarded by the MINISTERIO DE EDUCACIÓN Y CULTURA. There are 3 levels, the *Certificado Inicial de Español*, the *Diploma Básico de Español* and the *Diploma Superior de Español*.

DIPUTACIÓN FORAL VASCA

The term for the local government in each Basque province.

DIPUTACIÓN PERMANENTE

This body exists to ensure the continuity of government when both parliamentary chambers are in recess. It is composed of 21 members who represent the parliamentary groups in proportion to their numerical importance. It is a singularly Spanish institution whose original role was to prevent anti-democratic activities when parliament was not sitting. Similar bodies exist for each of the regional governments.

DIPUTACIÓN PROVINCIAL

The DIPUTACIÓN is responsible for the govenment and administration of the 50 Spanish PROVINCIAS. The members of the DIPUTACIÓN or DIPUTADOS are elected by the CONCEJALES.

DIPUTADOS

There are between 300 and 400 DIPUTADOS in the CONGRESO. Each province has at least three DIPUTADOS plus one extra for each 144,000 inhabitants over the base number of 60,000. The provinces with least DIPUTADOS are Ávila and Soria, with three each. Those with most are BARCELONA with 33 and MADRID with 32.

DIRECCIÓN GENERAL DE CATASTROS

A government department answering to the MINISTERIO DE

ECONOMÍA Y HACIENDA and which is responsible for the administration, collection and evaluation of property taxes (*catastro*).

DIRECCIÓN GENERAL DE COMERCIO EXTERIOR

Government department accountable to the MINISTERIO DE ECONOMÍA Y HACIENDA and responsible for import and export licences and customs and excise, in accordance with national and EU law.

DIRECCIÓN GENERAL DE INSTITUCIONES PENITENCIARIAS

This body is responsible for the prison service in Spain and forms part of the MINISTERIO DEL INTERIOR.

DIRECCIÓN GENERAL DE SALUD PÚBLICA

This division of the MINISTERIO DE SANIDAD is responsible for public health, including health education, food hygiene, vaccination programmes and epidemiology.

DIRECCIÓN GENERAL DE SEGUROS

This department, which is part of the MINISTERIO DE ECONOMÍA Y HACIENDA, is responsible for the control and coordination of the insurance and pension sector. All companies in this sector must be officially registered with the department and they are obliged to submit their annual financial statements for inspection.

DIRECCIÓN GENERAL DE TRÁFICO

Government department responsible for traffic; it forms part of the MINISTERIO DEL INTERIOR. Among other things, it publishes information about traffic flow, hold-ups and *puntos negros* – accident black spots.

DIRECCIÓN GENERAL DE TRIBUTOS

Department of taxes (Tax Office), which reports directly to the MINISTERIO DE ECONOMÍA Y HACIENDA. It is responsible for tax policy and design, research and evaluation of fiscal policy.

DIRECCIÓN GENERAL DEL PATRIMONIO DEL ESTADO

This is a state holding company for different industrial enterprises, including financial, industrial, commercial and service industries. The holding is now known as the *Grupo Patrimonio*. It includes companies such as TABACALERA, the *Empresa Nacional de Autopistas* and *Paradores de Turismo de España*.

DIRECCIÓN GENERAL DEL SERVICIO JURÍDICO DEL ESTADO

The highest legal consultative body for central public administration. It reports to the MINISTERIO DE JUSTICIA. It advises all bodies, at state, regional and provincial level.

DIRECCIÓN GENERAL DEL TESORO Y POLÍTICA FINANCIERA

This is a department of the MINISTERIO DE ECONOMÍA Y HACIENDA and has responsibilities in the management of the national debt and oversight of the records of financial institutions.

DIRECTOR (DE CENTRO PÚBLICO)

The headteacher of a public school is elected by the governing body (the CONSEJO ESCOLAR) and is responsible for the management of the school. He or she is assisted by the *jefe de estudios* who has control over academic matters and who acts for the director, when necessary. The appointment lasts 3 years.

DNI See: *DOCUMENTO NACIONAL DE IDENTIDAD*

DO See: *DENOMINACIÓN DE ORIGEN*

DOCE DE OCTUBRE

This is an important date in the Spanish calendar as it is the feast day of the Virgen del Pilar, patron of ZARAGOZA. It has since been designated *Día de la Hispanidad* because this was the date on which Christopher Columbus first discovered America in 1492. It is also known as *el Día de la Raza*.

DOCUMENTO NACIONAL DE IDENTIDAD

National Identity Card, sometimes known as the *carné*. The card has a number which is used for identification purposes, in those circumstances in which proof of identity is needed. Technically, it is an offence for all Spaniards over 14 years old not to carry their DNI with them. A DNI is valid for 5 years for persons up to 30 years old and for 10 years for those from 30 to 70.

DOMINGO EMBIL, PLÁCIDO (1941–   )

One of the world's leading lyric dramatic tenors. Born in MADRID, he started his career in the ZARZUELA or Spanish light opera tradition, with his family in Mexico. In 1959 he made his debut as a baritone, took his first tenor role in 1960 and sang first in New York in 1966. His repertoire is enormous, consisting of over 90 roles. He appears not only on the opera stage but increasingly as a conductor. DOMINGO specialises in works by Puccini and Verdi but in recent years he has released a number of records which include arias from light opera and popular Italian and Spanish songs.

DOMÍNGUEZ MARTÍNEZ, MICHEL (1958–   )

Implicated in the GAL affair, with his police colleague JOSÉ AMEDO. He was originally recruited because of his knowledge of French which he used to communicate with a Frenchman who had been kidnapped by the Spanish police. Later he accompanied Portuguese mercenaries who had been hired by the police to place bombs in the Batzoki and Consolation bars in the French Basque country. DOMÍNGUEZ and AMEDO were imprisoned in 1988. DOMÍNGUEZ has recently been implicated, by LUIS ROLDÁN, in the murder of Juan Carlos Garcìa Goena, in 1987, the last victim in the GAL affair.

DOMÍNGUEZ, ADOLFO (1944–   )

Internationally acclaimed clothes designer. Born in Orense, GALICIA, he is identified with the slogan *la arruga es bella* (creases are beautiful) which symbolized a reaction against the conventional middle-class fashions of the FRANCO era.

DOMINGUÍN, LUIS MIGUEL (1926–1996)

DOMINGUÍN was one of the most famous bullfighters in Spanish history. He was admired by such disparate figures as General FRANCO, Pablo Picasso and RAFAEL ALBERTI: indeed one of his *traje de luces* was designed by Picasso himself. He was also famed as a great lover: in 1954 he married LUCÍA BOSÉ (with whom he had three children, MIGUEL, Lucia and Paola). His second wife was Rosario Primo de Rivera, a descendent of the Falangist leader and he also had a much publicised affaire with his neice, Mariví

Dominguín. He was known as *Número Uno* because of his prowess in the bullring as well as in the bedroom.

DON ALGODÓN
A chain of over 133 clothes shops, founded by Pepe Barroso in 1980. This company has now expanded into other commercial areas, including the media and leisure industry.

DONOSTIA
Basque name for the city of SAN SEBASTIÁN.

DRAE See: *DICCIONARIO DE LA REAL ACADEMIA ESPAÑOLA*

DRAGADOS Y CONSTRUCCIONES, S.A.
Building company which expanded in the 90s with its acquisition of *Bermarmol* (a marble production company) and *Control y aplicaciones* (an electronics group). In 1992 it reorganised into six divisions – construction, industrial, real estate, urban services, motorways and international. Of special interest has been the company's involvement in the building of the metro in Toulouse.

DROVE, ANTONIO (1942–   )
Film director. His best films are adaptations of well-known novels: *La verdad sobre el caso Savolta* (1978) by Eduardo Mendoza and and *El túnel* (1987) by the Argentinian novelist Ernesto Sábato.

DS See: *DEMOCRACIA SOCIALISTA*

DUATO, NACHO (1956–   )
Classical dancer, born in VALENCIA and currently director of the COMPAÑIA NACIONAL DE LA DANZA. He trained with the *Ballet Rambert* in London and with Maurice Béjart. He joined the *Nederland Dans Theatre* and became their leading choreographer. In 1990 he became the artistic director of the COMPAÑÍA NACIONAL DE LA DANZA. In 1995 he was awarded the title of *Caballero de la Orden de las Artes y las Letras*, given by the French Embassy in Spain. Recently he has moved into film and television work.

DUCADOS
Spanish brand of cigarettes. The tobacco used is dark (*tabaco negro*) as opposed to the more common *tabaco rubio* or Virginian tobacco.

DUERO
The river DUERO is one of the longest rivers in the Iberian peninsula (895 kilometres). It rises on the Castilian plain near Soria and flows into the Atlantic in Portugal. The drop of nearly 400 metres from Soria to Oporto has created a landscape of impressive gorges.

DURÁN I LLEIDA, JOSEP (1952–)
Politician and CATALÁN nationalist, currently leader of UNIÓ DEMOCRÁTICA DE CATALUNYA and *vicepresidente* of the *Internacional de la Democracia Cristiana*.

DURÁN, MIGUEL (1955–)
Director-general of ONCE from 1986 to 1993. In 1990 he was appointed president of *Publicaciones de Barcelona, S.A.* and *Gestevisión-Tele 5, S.A.* He worked with the Italian entrepreneur Silvio Berlusconi on this latter project.

DÚRCAL, ROCÍO (1945–)
Singer and actress. Her early career in the 1960s was in the cinema where she was very successful in films such as *Canción de juventud* (1962) and *Rocío de la Mancha* (1962). Since the late 1970s she has worked principally as a singer and entertainer, mainly in Latin America.

EA See: *EUSKO ALKARTASUNA*

EBRO
Important Spanish river, 910 km. in length, which rises in CANTABRIA but which flows south east into the Mediterranean. It flows through ZARAGOZA.

EBRO AGRÍCOLAS, S.A.
This company manufactures, markets, exports and imports sugar and products used in agriculture, human and animal food of all types. It is also involved in the rental, purchase and sale of property.

ECAOL See: *ENTIDADES DE CRÉDITO DE ÁMBITO OPERATIVO LIMITADO*

ECHANOVE, JUAN (1961–)
Film and television actor, he first came to fame in a successful television series *Turno de oficio* (1985). He later appeared in *Divinas palabras* (1987), *Bajarse al moro* (1988) and *La noche más larga* (1991). In 1993 in *Madre Gilda* he was the third Spanish actor to interpret the role of General FRANCO. His most recent appearance was in PEDRO ALMODOVAR's *La flor de mi secreto*.

ECONOMÍA SUMERGIDA
The black economy – that is, all economic activity which is carried out informally or illegally. The main culprits are the construction and footwear industries. Although it is difficult to estimate how important the informal Spanish economy is, some experts have calculated it at 20% of GDP.

EDAD PENAL
The age of criminal liability: this was recently raised from 16 to 18.

EDITORIAL TUSQUETS
Important CATALÁN publishing house, managed by Beatriz de Moura. It is now part of the PLANETA group.

EDUCACIÓN COMPENSATORIA
Compensatory education – that is, education provided on an ad hoc basis to disadvantaged students such as drug addicts, ex-offenders and those who for whatever reason have been unable to continue with mainstream education.

EDUCACIÓN GENERAL BÁSICA
This was the old educational programme for children from 6 to 14. It comprised three cycles, the first from 6 to 7 (*primer ciclo*), 8 to 10 (*segundo ciclo*) and 11 to 14 (*tercer ciclo*). It took place in a COLEGIO. Those who were successful at this level could either opt for FORMACIÓN PROFESIONAL or for BUP. Those who were unsuccessful could opt for FORMACIÓN PROFESIONAL or leave school. This system was gradually phased out by the new educational reform act, the LOGSE and by 1997 was completely replaced by the system of EDUCACIÓN PRIMARIA and EDUCACIÓN SECONDARIA OBLIGATORIA. See also: LOGSE

EDUCACIÓN INFANTIL
According to the 1990 Education Act (LOGSE), children may attend school before the age of 6. There are two cycles available: the *jardín de infancia* or kindergarten up to the age of 4 and the *centro de párvulos* or nursery school for children up to 6.

EDUCACIÓN PRIMARIA
Primary education under LOGSE lasts from the age of 6 to 12 and comprises 3 cycles of 2 years each. The teaching of a foreign language starts in the second cycle: the language of the AUTONOMÍA is also taught alongside CASTELLANO. In the COMUNIDAD VALENCIANA for instance, *Valenciano* is taught throughout the 6 years. Teachers must have the teaching qualification of MAESTRO.

EDUCACIÓN SECUNDARIA OBLIGATORIA

According to the new education acts (LOGSE), schooling in Spain is obligatory from the age of 6 to 16. EDUCACIÓN PRIMARIA consists of three cycles, each of which lasts 2 years. At 12, children move into EDUCACIÓN SECUNDARIA. This comprises two cycles, both lasting two years. Assessment is continuous. Those who pass are awarded the certificate GRADUADO EN EDUCACIÓN SECUNDARIA.

EE See: *EUSKADIKO EZKERRA*

EFE

Spain's premier news agency, the fifth largest in the world after AP, UPI, Reuters and AFP and the largest agency to work in Spanish. It was founded in 1938 in FRANCO's Spain and has since become a huge international communications network. It has journalists in 102 countries and a work force of 1,145. It is still controlled by the government.

EGB See: *EDUCACIÓN GENERAL BÁSICA*

EGIN

Daily newspaper sympathetic to the Basque separatist movement, first published in 1977. ETA often publishes its communiqués here. Some of its copy is in the Basque language. It has a circulation of about 50,000.

EGM See: *ESTUDIO GENERAL DE MEDIOS*

EGPGC See: *EXÉRCITO GUERRILLEIRO DE POBO GALLEGO*

ELA-STV

Trade Union, very strong both in the PAÍS VASCO and in NAVARRA. Its present *secretario general* is José Elorrieta. Currently it has 90,000 members but faces fierce opposition from the UGT.

ELECCIÓN DE LOS DIPUTADOS

The DIPUTADOS are elected according to a proportional representation system. A party or coalition puts forward a list of candidates and each elector must vote for the whole list. The number of candidates elected depends on the number of votes cast for the party as a whole: those who appear at the head of the list get priority over those who appear lower down.

ELECCIONES ANTICIPADAS
Early general elections. Only the PRIMER MINISTRO can decide to dissolve parliament and call an early election.

ELECCIONES MUNICIPALES
The elections to the AYUNTAMIENTO are held according to a proportional representation system in which electors vote for a party list.

ELECTRA DE VIESGO, S.A.
This company operates hydraulic, thermal and nuclear power stations supplying electricity to industrial and domestic customers in the north of Spain.

ELKARRI
Basque movement in favour of dialogue and consensus in the PAÍS VASCO.

ELOSÚA, S.A.
Food manufacturing company founded in León in 1927. It began life as a producer of olive oils and gradually expanded until in 1985, it took over *Aceites Carbonell* and thus became the largest producer of olive oils in the country. It also produces and markets vegetables.

ELS COMEDIANTS
Experimental theatre group, founded in 1971. It works often in the open air, in public spaces, with fireworks and with the public taking part in the performance. This troupe produced the closing ceremony for the Olympic Games in Barcelona in 1992.

ELS VERDS
Small party, representing the Greens in CATALUÑA. In 1996, they stood together with the Catalán branch of IU and won 8% of the vote in CATALUÑA.

EMPRESA NACIONAL DE AUTOCAMIONES, S.A.
State-owned truck manufacturer, it used to produce the *Pegaso* truck. The *Pegaso* is now produced by an Italian company.

EMPRESA NACIONAL DE CELULOSAS

This company, working in the packaging, paper and printing sector, operates in the areas of forestry, pulp production and environmental protection.

EMPRESA NACIONAL DE ELECTRICIDAD, S.A.

State electricity company which was partially privatised in 1988 when 25% of its shares were released on the stock exchange. In 1993 it became part of the public holding company TENEO.

EMPRESA NACIONAL DE RESIDUOS RADIOACTIVOS, S.A.

A state company whose function is to deal with radioactive waste and to decommission nuclear power stations where necessary. It was created in 1984 and is both a public service and a commercial operation.

EMPRESA NACIONAL DE SEGUROS AGRARIOS

This commercial company provides insurance cover for the farming sector which has always proved difficult to insure because of the high risk factor. It is nominally under the jurisdiction of the *Ministerio de Agricultura, Pesca y Alimentación* and it coordinates, underwrites and draws up formal agreements with private insurers.

EMPRESA NACIONAL DEL URANIO

This company is involved in the production of uranium concentrates and the procurement of nuclear fuel.

EMPRESA NACIONAL SIDERÚRGICA, S.A.

Originally the state iron and steel industry. In line with other such companies throughout Europe, it has undergone a series of rationalisation programmes. In 1992 it became the *Corporación de la Siderurgia Integral* as a result of the fusion between it and ALTOS HORNOS DE VIZCAYA.

EMPRESAS DE TRABAJO TEMPORAL

Employment agencies created in 1995 to help the unemployed find temporary work. Their creation effectively breaks the monopoly of INEM (INSTITUTO NACIONAL DE EMPLEO) in this sector.

ENAGAS
State company, originally owned entirely by the INI, which provides gas and has developed an ambitious programme to construct gas pipelines.

ENASA See: *EMPRESA NACIONAL DE AUTOCAMIONES, S.A.*

ENCHUFISMO
Informal system by which jobs, contracts and so on are given to individuals on the basis of contacts rather than personal merit.

ENCUESTA DE POBLACIÓN ACTIVA
Survey which annually calculates the number of unemployed. In 1996 this was 22% of the labour force. However, most commentators believe that the true rate is about 13%. The higher figure comes from the answer to the question asked: would you accept a job if one was offered?

ENDESA See: *EMPRESA NACIONAL DE ELECTRICIDAD, S.A.*

ENDESA See: *EMPRESA NACIONAL DE RESIDUOS RADIOACTIVOS*

ENESA See: *EMPRESA NACIONAL DE SEGUROS AGRARIOS*

ENP See: *ESPACIOS NATURALES PROTEGIDOS*

ENRESA See: *EMPRESA NACIONAL DE RESIDUOS RADIOACTIVOS, S.A.*

ENRIQUE Y TARANCÓN, VICENTE (1907–1994)
Appointed primate of Spain in 1969 and in 1971 Archbishop of Madrid, he was *presidente* of the CONFERENCIA EPISCOPAL DE ESPAÑA from 1972 to 1981. He upheld the view that the Church should support the transition to democracy, maintaining that the Vatican should disassociate itself from the FRANCO régime and that the Church in Spain should be disestablished.

ENSIDESA See: *EMPRESA NACIONAL SIDERÚRGICA S.A.*

ENTIDADES DE CRÉDITO DE ÁMBITO OPERATIVO LIMITADO

Credit companies which have had to harmonize with recent EU regulations. Examples of these companies are the finance companies (*entidades de financiación*) which provided hire-purchase finance for the sale and purchase of a wide variety of goods: and leasing companies (*entidades de arrendamiento financiero*) which lease capital equipment.

ENUSA   See: *EMPRESA NACIONAL DEL URANIO*

ERCROS

This company is active in agrochemicals, chemicals, explosives and the defence industry. It also has interests in the treatment of waste materials and environmentally friendly goods.

ERICE, VICTOR (1940–   )

A very highly regarded film-maker, despite having directed only three major films: *El espiritú de la colmena* (1971), *El sur* (1983) and *El sol del membrillo* (1992). *El sol del membrillo* was a prize winner at the Cannes Film Festival in 1992.

EROSKI

A chain of supermarkets, and one of the largest companies in Spain. It is part of the MONDRAGÓN cooperative.

ERTZAINTZA

The police force of the PAÍS VASCO, created when the region was awarded its autonomy. They are a controversial body because they are seen by Basque nationalists as colluding with the ruling PNV and obstructing revolutionary change.

ESCAMILLA, TEO (1940–   )

Film photographer. He has worked with most of the major Spanish directors including CARLOS SAURA in *Cría cuervos* (1975) and *Elisa vida mía* (1977): with JAIME CHÁVARRI in *A un dios desconocido* (1977) and with JOSÉ LUIS BORAU in *Tata mía* (1986). In 1980 he founded his own production company with Jaime de Armiñán.

ESCAÑO
Seat in the CORTES. Spain has a proportional representation system of elections. Each party list of candidates wins varying numbers of seats, according to the number of votes it obtains.

ESCUELA DE TAUROMAQUIA
Bullfighting school, set up in MADRID in the seventies, from which several new and interesting young bullfighters have graduated.

ESCUELA OFICIAL DE IDIOMAS
These are official schools of languages which run their own examinations and are attended by those students who wish to learn a range of modern languages. A small fee is charged. To obtain the official diploma one must pass each level of the course which extends over a period of five years. One can enter at the age of 16. The teaching staff must belong to the body known as the *Profesores de Escuelas Oficiales de Idiomas*.

ESCUELA PRIVADA
Since 1985, there have been two types of private school; the *escuela concertada* which is financed by the state for educational activities which are compulsory and the ESCUELA PRIVADA which receives no aid from the state whatsoever.

ESCUELA TÉCNICA SUPERIOR
Technical universities which award students engineering and architecture degrees. Entry is strictly limited and demand for places is very competitive.

ESCUELA UNIVERSITARIA
Institutes of higher education which award degrees lasting 3 years, to students specializing in vocational education, such as nursing, technical engineering, primary education and management.

ESO See: *EDUCACIÓN SECUNDARIA OBLIGATORIA*

ESPACIOS NATURALES PROTEGIDOS
These are areas of outstanding natural beauty which are to some extent protected from harmful agricultural practices and from the pressure of tourism.

ESPAÑA ECONÓMICA
Monthly business magazine, published as a supplement to CAMBIO 16.

ESPANYOL
Second football team in BARCELONA and arch-rival to BARÇA. Its fans tend to be long established Cataláns, whereas the immigrant population prefers to support the BARÇA team. Their home is in the Sarria stadium and their strip is blue and white.

ESPASA CALPE
Publishing house. In 1992 it was taken over by the PLANETA group and a French group, *le Groupe de la Cité*. Since that date it has expanded its production of dictionaries, encyclopaedias and reference books.

ESPERT, NURIA (1935–)
Internationally-known actress and director, NURIA ESPERT is especially known for her roles in the plays of Federico García Lorca. She has worked at both Covent Garden and at the Edinburgh Festival and in 1997 she appeared in her first film, *Actrices*.

ESQUERRA REPUBLICANA DE CATALUNYA
Nationalist Catalán political party. It is the third most important party in CATALUÑA and is left-wing in orientation. It was founded in 1931 by Francesc Macia and though historically important has been overtaken by JORDI PUJOL's CIU. However it has recently gained in popularity at the polls through having adopted a policy of complete independence for the region. See also: CONVERGENCIA i UNIÓ.

ESTANCO
State-owned kiosks which sell newspapers, stamps and tobacco. Until recently, tobacco was only available through these outlets which led to a flourishing black market in cigarettes.

ESTATUTO DE LOS TRABAJADORES
Workers' Charter, modified in 1980 and which established terms and conditions of employment in the workplace. Changing these terms was extremely problematic and thus employers found it difficult to adapt to changing circumstances.

LA ESTRELLA, S.A.
Insurance company founded in 1901 and principally selling life insurance. Other important lines are motor insurance, multi-risk and fire.

ESTUDIO GENERAL DE MEDIOS
Body which researches into audience share in Spanish radio and television.

ETA See: *EUSKADI TA ASKATASUNA*

ETARRA
Name given to members of the Basque terrorist group ETA. The *arra* ending in Basque means 'from'.

ETXEBESTE, EUGENIO (ANTXON) (1951–   )
One of the leaders of the Basque terrorist group ETA, he was deported to Santo Domingo in 1988. He has remained there ever since, together with other members of the group, under police custody. He has acted as a spokesman for ETA in negotiations with the Spanish government. It is alleged that he directs terrorist operations from his base in the Dominican Republic.

EURÓCRATAS
Technocrats working for the European Commission.

EURODIPUTADOS
Spain has 64 EURODIPUTADOS or euro-MPs, of whom 21 are women: almost half the women belong to the IU grouping.

EUROPA PRESS
Press agency founded in 1957. At the outset it was a book distribution agency but gradually became a press agency in response to the need for an alternative source of news to that produced by EFE.

EUROPISTAS CONCESIONARIA ESPAÑOLA
This company runs the concession for the construction and maintainance of the BILBAO-Behobia motorway. Its major shareholders are *Ferrorial S.A.* and *John Laing Holdings*.

EUSKADI

The Basque name for the PAÍS VASCO.

EUSKADI TA ASKTASUNA (ETA)

EUSKADI TA ASKTASUNA (Basque Homeland and Freedom) is the
name of the terrorist group formed in 1959 to engage in violent
struggle against the Spanish state so as to win independence for
the PAÍS VASCO. Its political wing is HERRI BATASUNA. Since General
FRANCO's death in 1975 over 600 people have died in the armed
struggle, despite many attempts to negotiate for peace. This
struggle has spilled over into France as the PAÍS VASCO straddles
the French-Spanish frontier. Relations between the two police
forces have not always been cordial and this has, on occasions,
allowed ETA to operate with impunity. One of the movement's
favourite ways of financing its activities, is to kidnap prominent
Basque business-men and hold them to ransom: it also claims a
'terrorist tax' from local businesses, threatening reprisals to
those which refuse to pay.

EUSKADIKO EZKERRA

One of the smaller Basque nationalist parties, which emerged
from ETA in the early 1980s. By 1992 it had split into two and
later disappeared as a separate force, having merged with the
Basque Socialist Party, the PSE-PSOE.

EUSKAL HERRIA

Expression used in Basque to refer to all the Basque territories
in France and in Spain. There are 7 Basque provinces of which
three (about 20% of the total area) are in France.

EUSKAL TELEBISTA – ETB

This television company broadcasts in the Basque language in
the PAÍS VASCO. It is the oldest of the regional television stations
and first started broadcasting in 1983.

EUSKALDUNIZACIÓN

Campaign to teach EUSKERA or the Basque language to both children and adults, in and out of schools. This was a consequence of
the adoption of Basque as one of the official languages in the
PAÍS VASCO in 1978 under the new CONSTITUCIÓN.

EUSKALTEL

Basque telecommunications company owned partly by the Basque Government and partly by the Basque savings banks BBK and *Kutxa y Vital*. In 1997 it signed an agreement with RETEVISIÓN, the largest private telephone company in Spain, taking responsibility for operations within the PAÍS VASCO.

EUSKERA

EUSKERA or Basque is the official language (together with CASTELLANO) of the PAÍS VASCO. It is a non Indo-European language and thus presents considerable difficulties for non-native speakers. It is spoken by over half a million people, predominantly in the Vizcaya and Guipúzcoa provinces of the PAÍS VASCO.

EUSKO ALKARTASUNA

One of the Basque nationalist parties, founded by CARLOS GARAIKOETXEA in 1986, as a result of frictions within the PNV. It is strongest in NAVARRA, but is only the fifth party in terms of seats and percentage of the popular vote. It pursues more radical policies than the PNV.

EUSKO GUDARIAK

Hymn to the Basque soldier, sung and played on Basque nationalist occasions.

EUSKO LANGILLEEN ALKARTASUNA

Basque workers' trade union. It has over 100,000 members and is represented on official negotiation bodies, having gained more than 15% of votes at regional level. At times it has captured more than 37% of the regional vote.

EUSKO TRENDIBEAK

Basque railways. It has 202 kilometres of 1,000 mm gauge track and is controlled by the Basque regional government.

EVALUACIÓN

The Spanish marking scheme within the educational system is as follows: *matrícula de honor* (distinction), *sobresaliente* (outstanding), *notable* (good), *aprobado* (satisfactory) and *suspenso* (fail). For the doctorate, *apto* means that the degree of doctor has been awarded, and *no apto* that it has not. *Cum laude* means that the thesis has been judged excellent.

EXCEDENCIAS
These are leaves of absence from paid employment. In order to qualify for leave of absence one must have worked for the company for at least one year. Leave of absence can last from two to five years and although one can not demand re-employment, the ex-worker is guaranteed a post when a vacancy arises. Leave of absence is typically granted in order to look after a child or to go to another post abroad.

EXÉRCITO GUERRILLEIRO DE POBO GALLEGO
Left-wing group working for Galician independence and which claimed responsibility for a number of bomb attacks throughout GALICIA and the killing of a civil guard in February 1989.

EXPANSIÓN
Daily newspaper, specialising in financial affairs and covering all aspects of business, commercial news, share prices and so on.

EXPOSICIÓN UNIVERSAL DE SEVILLA
From April to October 1992, SEVILLA hosted EXPO '92, the largest international exhibition ever. This event brought the AVE or high speed train to SEVILLA: the island of La Cartuja in the GUADALQUIVIR was reclaimed and became the site of the fair. Much of the city itself was refurbished.

EXTREMADURA
EXTREMADURA is situated in the west of Spain and borders on Portugal. It is one of the AUTONOMÍAS; it has one million inhabitants and covers an area of 41,602 square kilometres. It is one of the poorest areas of Spain and is almost entirely dependent on agricultural production. Its capital is Mérida, a fine town of Roman origin.

EXTREMADURA UNIDA
Local political party: it won one seat in the EXTREMADURA regional assembly elected in 1995.

EX-U See: *EXTREMADURA UNIDA*

FÁBRICA NACIONAL DE MONEDA Y TIMBRE

Spain's Royal Mint, also known as the *Casa de la Moneda*. It has recently commercialized its activities and now exports high quality paper for official purposes such as passports, banknotes and identity documents. Its principal clients are Mexico, Nigeria, Portugal and Morocco.

FABRICACIÓN DE AUTOMÓVILES RENAULT DE ESPAÑA See: *FASA-RENAULT*

LAS FALLAS DE VALENCIA

The annual fiesta held in the week of the 19th of March (*el día de San José*) in VALENCIA Throughout the year, the *comisiones* (local groups) organise and make enormous set pieces from wood and plaster which are humorous or satirical in character. These impressive pieces are displayed during the third week in March: on the last night of the fiesta, the *cremá* is celebrated in which all the effigies are burned, except those judged to be the best (the *ninots indultats*).

FAMILIA NUMEROSA

Families with 3 or more children have the right to certain benefits such as reduced travel costs.

FARINA, RAFAEL (1923–1995)

Flamenco singer, born into a gypsy family near Salamanca. Although he started his career as a classic *cantaor* (flamenco artist), he came to fame in the sixties through television variety shows in which he sang with Concha Piquer. He was very popular throughout the Hispanic world, both in the theatre and in film.

FARMACIA DE GUARDIA

Hugely successful comedy programme shown on the private TV channel ANTENA 3. It first began to run in March 1991 and has achieved audiences of up to 8 million people. Produced by Antonio Mercero, the series has won a number of prizes including one for best actress, awarded to Concha Cuetos.

FARMACIAS

The number of Spanish chemist shops are strictly regulated. Under the goverment of FELIPE GONZÁLEZ, there were 4,000 inhabitants per pharmacy: this number was reduced in 1996 to 2,800. This led to almost 50,000 people requesting to open chemist shops. Even so, Spain has the largest number of pharmacies within the OECD. Pharmacies have the exclusive rights to sell all prescription drugs as well as a wide range of over the counter products. The cost of drugs is high, as a margin of 40% is allowed to pharmacies on all drugs.

LA FAROLA

Newspaper sold by the homeless.

EL FARRUCO (1936–   )

Antonio Montoya Flores is a flamenco dancer, more usually known as EL FARRUCO. He is the head of a large clan of gypsy singers and dancers which includes his daughters, La Farruquita and Pilar.

FASA-RENAULT

This company manufactures a wide range of cars and vans and also offers services such as vehicle recovery and weekend patrols. It has 10 plants where it produces models such as the Clio, the Renault 4 and the Espace. Its major shareholder is *Renault, S.A.* (France).

FBAE See: *FUNDACIÓN BANCO DE ALIMENTOS DE ESPAÑA*

FCC See: *FOMENTO DE CONSTRUCCIONES Y CONTRATAS*

FCI See: *FONDO DE COMPENSACIÓN INTERTERRITORIAL*

FECSA See: *FUERZAS ELÉCTRICAS DE CATALUÑA, S.A.*

FEDER See: *FONDO EUROPEO DE DESARROLLO REGIONAL*

FEDERACIÓN DE COOPERATIVAS DE TRABAJO ASOCIADO DE EUSKADI

This association brings together 40 cooperatives working throughout the PAÍS VASCO: its function is to raise more capital for further enterprises.

FEDERACIÓN DE MUNICIPIOS Y PROVINCIAS

This association groups together all local government bodies and acts as a pressure group in relation to central government, in both financial and legal matters.

FEDERACIÓN SOCIALISTA MADRILEÑA

A leftish political party, based in MADRID but which has not yet secured representation in the regional assembly in its own right.

FELIPISMO

Term coined to describe the cult of FELIPE GONZÁLEZ. FELIPE GONZÁLEZ won four general elections in succession and had been in office for fourteen years: he had thus acquired a faithful and admiring following (known as *felipistas*). FELIPISMO implied a pragmatic approach to problems as well as strict control over the PSOE.

FEMP See: *FEDERACIÓN DE MUNICIPIOS Y PROVINCIAS*

FENOSA See: *FUERZAS ELÉCTRICAS DEL NOROESTE SOCIEDAD ANÓNIMA*

FEOGA See: *FONDO EUROPEO DE ORIENTACIÓN Y GARANTÍA AGRÍCOLA*

FERIA DE SAN ISIDRO

Madrid's patronal festival which is held in the second week of May. Bull fights are an important part of the week of festivities which also includes concerts and open-air dances.

FERIA INTERNACIONAL DE ARTE CONTEMPORÁNEO

International Fair of Contemporary Art, held annually in MADRID. Both private collectors and buyers from museums attend this event which is held in the Parque Ferial Juan Carlos I. Prices for works of art vary from 10,000 to 25 million pesetas: it is a showcase for both new and more established artists.

FERNÁN-GÓMEZ, FERNANDO (1921–   )

One of the most famous of Spanish actors, he has worked with many directors and appeared in many important films. These include *Ana y los lobos* (1972) by CARLOS SAURA, *El espíritu de la colmena* (1973) by VÍCTOR ERICE and *Belle époque* (1992) by FERNANDO TRUEBA. FERNÁN-GOMEZ is also a director and dramatist, his most famous play being *Las bicicletas son para el verano*.

FERNÁNDEZ OCHOA, PACO (1950–   )

Oldest of a large skiing family, PACO OCHOA has been an Olympic ski champion and 39 times champion of Spain.

FERNÁNDEZ ORDOÑEZ, FRANCISCO (1930–1992)

Ministro de Hacienda from 1977 to 1979 and *ministro de Justicia* from 1980 to 1981 under ADOLFO SUÁREZ and LEOPOLDO CALVO SOTELO. He resigned on the 31st of August 1981 to create a new party, PAD, the *Partido de Acción Democrática* which later became incorporated into the PSOE. He became *ministro de Asuntos Exteriores* under FELIPE GONZÁLEZ from 1982 to 1992.

FERNÁNDEZ, MATILDE (1950–   )

Ministro de Asuntos Sociales in the FELIPE GONZÁLEZ legislature of 1990, she first entered government as part of the quota system for women entering politics. She took an extremely liberal line in the debates on sexuality, AIDS and abortion. As a result she became unpopular with OPUS DEI, the Church and the right.

FERRER, ANA (1959–   )

Judge charged with investigating the ROLDÁN affair and that of CARMEN SALANUEVA.

FERRER SALAT, CARLOS (1931–   )

Businessman. In 1978 he was elected *presidente* of the CEOE (CONFEDERACIÓN ESPAÑOLA DE ORGANIZACIONES EMPRESARIALES) and re-elected in 1981 for another three years. In 1985 he became a member of the *Comité Olímpico Internacional*. He played a key role in the 1992 Olympic Games in BARCELONA.

FERRERO, JESÚS
Novelist, author of *Bélver Yin* and *El secreto de los dioses*.

FERROCARRILES DE VÍA ESTRECHA
This company (FEVE) operates the narrow gauge railway system. These lines operate between the suburbs of large cities such as MADRID and BARCELONA. Long distance services on this gauge are gradually being phased out. See also: RENFE

FESTIVAL DE MÉRIDA
An important arts festival, held each summer in Mérida (EXTREMADURA). Its theatre programme is especially distinguished.

FESTIVAL DE SAN SEBASTIÁN
Important film festival in which prizes are awarded for best photography, best actress (the *Concha de Plata*) and best film (*Premio Especial de Jurado*). It takes place annually in September in the Hotel María Cristina.

FESTIVAL INTERNACIONAL DE TEATRO CLÁSICO DE ALMAGRO
Annual festival held in the province of Ciudad Real to encourage productions of classical plays. The festival was inaugurated in 1978 and includes lectures, courses and exhibitions. It takes place in the first week of July.

FEVE See: *FERROCARRILES DE VÍA ESTRECHA*

FIESTA DE SAN JUAN
St. John's Day (24th of June) is of especial importance in Spain as it is also the saint's day of the monarch JUAN CARLOS.

FIESTA DEL LIBRO
The FIESTA DEL LIBRO is celebrated throughout Spain on April 23rd (the anniversary of the death of Miguel de Cervantes). Besides numerous literary events, bookshops usually give a small discount on books bought on that day. The festival is especially

important in BARCELONA, because April 23rd is also the feast of the patron saint of CATALUÑA, Sant Jordi. The people of BARCELONA give each other two presents, a book and a rose, to celebrate the fiesta.

LA FIESTA NACIONAL
The Spanish bullfight. Recently, it has been regaining the popularity it lost in the 1970s and 1980s. There has been a rise in young bullfighters joining the profession.

FIESTAS LABORALES
Bank holidays. Workers may not take more than 14 of these holidays per year, two of which may be local holidays. Holidays always taken are Christmas Day, New Year's Day, 1 of May (Labour Day) and 12th of October.

FIGUEIRÓ FREIRIA, CARMEN (1884–1997)
The oldest woman in Spain, Carmen was born on the 28th of October 1884. A few days after her son-in-law died of cancer in early 1997, Carmen followed him, declaring that it was not right that a mother should outlive her children. She was 113 and in perfectly good health.

FIGUERAS
Small town in CATALUÑA, famous for the MUSEO DALÍ. SALVADOR DALÍ was born there in 1904.

FINANZAUTO, S.A.
This company operates as a dealer for the Caterpillar Tractor Co. and as a supplier of diesel engines and a wide range of industrial and agricultural vehicles. It also operates an after-sales service and spare parts division.

FINCA
Type of farm in the two CASTILLAS. In CASTILLA LA MANCHA these farms are hundreds or thousands of hectares in size and nowadays some are owned by companies rather than individual landowners. In CASTILLA Y LEÓN, the farms are much smaller in size and worked by family members. Many both own and rent property.

FINIQUITO
Sum of money sometimes given to an employee when he or she finishes a short-term contract.

FISCAL
Legal term. The FISCAL, or public prosecutor, acts for the prosecution in criminal cases but also pleads in defence of the law, the civil rights of individuals and in the public interest. The FISCAL is not allowed to work in any other capacity while in office and must not belong to a political party or trade union.

FISCAL GENERAL DEL ESTADO
Attorney-general or state public prosecutor. He is in charge of all *fiscales* and for the entire working of the prosecution system. He is assisted by the *consejo fiscal* and the *junta de fiscales de sala*.

FISCALÍA
This body is composed of *fiscales* or public prosecutors.

FIZ, MARTÍN (1963–   )
Marathon runner. He won this race in the World Championships in Gotenberg in 1995 with a time of 2 hours 11 minutes 41 seconds: he also won the marathon in the European Championships in Helsinki. Of the six marathons he has entered, he has won five.

FLORES, ANTONIO (1961–1995)
Son of LOLA FLORES and brother of ROSARIO, FLORES had a successful career as a singer and songwriter until his death from a drug overdose in 1995 His last album, *Cosas mías*, sold over 200,000 copies.

FLORES, LOLA (1923–1995)
Known variously as *Lola de España* and *La Faraona*, LOLA FLORES was a very popular entertainer. Born in Jerez of gypsy stock, she had a long-standing relationship with flamenco singer and guitarist Manolo Caracol. She starred in a number of popular films, including *La Faraona* and *Pena, Penita, Pena*; she travelled extensively abroad where she amassed a considerable fortune. She enjoyed a stormy emotional life, and appeared regularly in

the gossip magazines. In 1957 she married Antonio González (*El Pescailla*) and had three children, Lolita, ANTONIO and ROSARIO, all of whom have followed their mother into show business. A friend of General FRANCO, she was felt by some to be the incarnation of the true Spain and by others to be a throwback to the Spain of castanets and tambourines which has been relegated to history. Notwithstanding, she received recognition from the PSOE in 1994 with the awarding of an official state medal. She died from breast cancer in 1995 at the age of 72.

FLORES, ROSARIO (1964–)

Daughter of LOLA FLORES and sister of ANTONIO, ROSARIO is a singer and song writer. Among her albums are *Mucho por vivir*, *De ley* and *Siento*.

FLOTATS, JOSEP MARÍA (1939–)

Catalán actor and director. First Spanish member of the *Comédie Française*. He is currently director of the *Teatro Nacional de Cataluña*.

FN See: *FRENTE NACIONAL*

FNMT See: *FÁBRICA NACIONAL DE MONEDA Y TIMBRE*

FNPT See: *FONDO NACIONAL DE PROTECCIÓN AL TRABAJO*

FOMENTO DE CONSTRUCCIONES Y CONTRATAS

Second largest construction company in Spain with a turnover in 1995 of 419,800 million pesetas.

FOMENTO DEL TRABAJO NACIONAL

Catalán employers' organisation, founded towards the end of the 19th century and powerful in local politics.

FONAS See: *FONDO NACIONAL DE ASISTENCIA SOCIAL*

FONDO DE COHESIÓN

Cohesion fund set up as a result of the 1992 Edinburgh summit and designed to help the poorer EU countries meet the

Maastricht criteria for joining the Economic and Monetary Union. Spain was to be one of its chief beneficiaries.

FONDO DE COMPENSACIÓN INTERTERRITORIAL
This fund was established in 1984 and was intended to redress the economic balance within the 17 AUTONOMÍAS. Although this policy seemed successful at the outset, it later became clear that it was working more to the benefit of the more developed areas. The law governing this fund was therefore amended in 1990 and help was targeted at the poorer regions.

FONDO DE FORMACIÓN CONTINUA DE LAS EMPRESAS
Body created in 1992 by employers and trades unions to administer funds for professional training and to run training programmes. In 1996 it was accused by the European Union of having misused community grants.

FONDO DE GARANTÍA DE DEPÓSITOS
A fund of compulsory deposits from each bank in the Spanish system: this fund exists to protect the public against the collapse of individual banks.

FONDO DE GARANTÍA SOCIAL
This fund protects workers' salaries in the event of bankruptcy or closure. It is funded by employers' contributions. It is an autonomous body on which both workers and employers are represented.

FONDO DE ORDENACIÓN Y REGULACIÓN DE PRODUCCIONES Y PRECIOS AGRARIOS
This body comes under the aegis of the MINISTERIO DE AGRICULTURA and regulates the prices of agricultural products.

FONDO EUROPEO DE DESARROLLO REGIONAL
The Spanish name for the European Regional Development Fund which has played a key role in modernising the infrastructure in the Spanish regions.

FONDO EUROPEO DE ORIENTACIÓN Y GARANTÍA AGRÍCOLA
European Community Agricultural Guidance and Guarantee

Fund. Spanish farmers have greatly benefited from the advice on farm management which this fund provides.

FONDO NACIONAL DE ASISTENCIA SOCIAL
A national fund from which invalidity benefits and pensions are paid.

FONDO NACIONAL DE PROTECCIÓN AL TRABAJO
This body existed to lend money to workers intending to set up their own businesses or to those wishing to invest in their own companies. Loans were paid back over a period from 8 to 10 years at very low rates of interest. Since 1985, these loans are made through the banks.

FONDOS DE PENSIONES
Pension funds have until recently been unimportant in Spain, given the high state pension available to workers (up to 90% of wages on retirement). However, in the 1990s it became clear that this level of payment was no longer sustainable and pension funds have sprung up to provide private pensions for individuals. These funds are mostly managed by the banks, saving banks and insurance companies.

FORMACIÓN PROFESIONAL
A course of vocational training available to students who have completed the BACHILLERATO. Students can obtain the qualification of *técnico* or of *técnico superior*. Normally students enter this programme at 16 or 18. Assessment is continuous. This system replaces the 1970 Education Act programme in which vocational training was divided into two cycles, FP1 and FP2. FP1 was an alternative to BUP, as FP2 was an alternative to COU and university entrance. This programme is now being phased out.

FORMACIÓN PROFESIONAL OCUPACIONAL
Training courses are provided for unemployed workers by the INEM or by individual AUTONOMÍAS. There is always an element of work experience: employers are paid per hour per student to cover extra costs such as accident insurance. Students are also given a grant to cover costs and transport.

FORMENTERA
Small island to the south of IBIZA. The largest town is San Francisco Javier. It has a population of about 3,500 and the bulk of its inhabitants are engaged in farming or fishing.

FORPPA See: *FONDO DE ORDENACIÓN Y REGULACIÓN DE PRODUCCIONES Y PRECIOS AGRARIOS*

FORQUÉ, VERÓNICA (1955–   )
Daughter of the film director and producer José María Forqué, Verónica started her acting career with small parts in her father's films. She became famous through her collaboration with PEDRO ALMÓDOVAR in films such as *¿Qué he hecho yo para merecer esto?* (1983), *Matador* (1985) and *Kika* (1993) but she has also made films with FERNANDO TRUEBA, FERNANDO COLOMO and BASILIO PATINO. She appears frequently on Spanish television.

FORTUNA
Spanish brand of cigarettes. It uses *tabaco rubio* or Virginia tobacco, as opposed to the other famous Spanish brand, DUCADOS.

FORTUNA
Spanish royal yacht, given to the King and Queen of Spain by the King of Saudi Arabia in 1979. When first commissioned, It was considered to be at the forefront of naval technology but has since had a history of breakdowns.

FOTOGRAMAS
Monthly cinema magazine founded in BARCELONA in 1946. It was originally published weekly by *Ediciones* NADAL but was bought in 1988 by *Comunicación y Publicaciones, S.A.* At the present moment it is published under the name of FOTOGRAMAS *y Vídeo*. It has a circulation of about 177,000.

FP See: *FORMACIÓN PROFESIONAL*

FRAGA IRIBARNE, MANUEL (1922–   )
The leader of the Spanish right-wing for many years (first of ALIANZA POPULAR and then of PARTIDO POPULAR, before handing

over to JOSE MARÍA AZNAR). He was a former minister under FRANCO and Ambassador to London from 1973 to 1975. Elected to the CONGRESO in 1977, he has been *Presidente* of the XUNTA DE GALICIA since 1989.

FRANCO BAHAMONDE, FRANCISCO (1892–1875)

Spanish general and dictator, born in El Ferrol (GALICIA). He gained much combat experience in Morocco as a young man and by 1926 was Spain's youngest general. In 1936 he joined the conspiracy against the Popular Front Government and became leader of the rebel forces. Having led these forces to victory, he presided over the Spanish state until his death in 1975. During the Second World War his sympathies lay with Germany and Italy, but he successfully kept Spain out of the war with his policy of neutrality. The 1950s was a period of isolation and misery within the country but in the 1960s FRANCO opened up Spain to tourism and the outside world. In 1969 he declared that, upon his death Spain would once again become a monarchy and that JUAN CARLOS (grandson of Alfonso XIII) would succeed to the throne. The values which FRANCO upheld were those of the monarchy, Roman Catholicism, national unity and patriotism. He died on the 20th of November, 1975.

FRANCO POLO, CARMEN (1926–   )

General FRANCO's only daughter. She married the *Marqués de Villaverde* in 1950 and had seven children. She was awarded the title *Duquesa de Franco* in 1975 by the king.

FREIXENET

An important producer of *cava* or champagne-type wine, typical of CATALUÑA. The company is still owned by the family which founded it, the Ferrers.

FRENTE NACIONAL

The FRENTE NACIONAL or National Front is an extremely right-wing organisation. From 1966 to 1983 FN was known as FUERZA NUEVA or New Force.

FSM See: *FEDERACIÓN SOCIALISTA MADRILEÑA*

FTN See: *FOMENTO DEL TRABAJO NACIONAL*

FUEROS

These were ancient rights or privileges enjoyed principally by the PAÍS VASCO and NAVARRA. The PAÍS VASCO was able to recuperate some of these via the 1981 CONCIERTO ECONÓMICO when it negotiated the right to levy taxes once more. The situation is similar for NAVARRA.

FUERTES, GLORIA (1918–)

Writer specialising in poetry for children. Among her most important collections are *Sola en la sala*, *Canciones para niños* and *La pirata mofeta y la jirafa coqueta*.

FUERTEVENTURA

Island in the CANARIAS archipelago (50,000 inhabitants). Its capital is Puerto del Rosario. Its relief and vegetation are similar to those found on the African coast.

FUERZA NUEVA

Extreme right-wing party founded in 1976. Blas Piñar was a leading figure. It changed its name to FRENTE NACIONAL in 1983.

LAS FUERZAS ARMADAS

The armed forces, composed of the *ejército de tierra* (army), the *armada* (navy) and the *ejército del aire* (airforce). Their mission is to guarantee the sovereignty and independence of Spain, to defend its territory and its constitution. The monarch is the supreme commander of the FUERZAS ARMADAS. The CONSTITUCIÓN of 1978 establishes that the army is subject to civil authority.

FUERZAS ELÉCTRICAS DE CATALUÑA, S.A.

This company's principal activity is the generation and distribution of electricity. It also has interests in open-cast mining and the repair of transformers and machinery.

FUERZAS ELÉCTRICAS DEL NOROESTE, S.A.

Hydroelectric company based in GALICIA.

FUNCIONARIO
A FUNCIONARIO is a government employee. All FUNCIONARIOS must pass the OPOSICIÓN or competitive examination for his or her particular post. In Spain, teachers, lawyers, post-office and railway employees are all FUNCIONARIOS.

15–J
Shorthand form which refers to the 15th of June 1977, the date of the first democratic elections in Spain since the Republic.

FUNDACIÓN BANCO DE ALIMENTOS DE ESPAÑA
Independent body which collects unwanted food and donates it to charity. There are centres in many large cities in Spain, including BARCELONA, Burgos, CÓRDOBA and Granada.

FUNDACIONES
Foundations are set up by individuals, companies or associations as a vehicle for charitable, cultural, educational or medical activities. They are regulated by the *Ley de Fundaciones y de Incentivos Fiscales a la Participación Privada en Actividades de Interés General*. They enjoy very advantageous tax benefits.

LA FURA DEL BAUS
Experimental theatre company from CATALUÑA. The actors work in warehouses and in the open air as well as in conventional spaces. Their performances are physical rather than verbal and revolve around basic, universal themes such as food, water, human sexuality, fertility, rivalry and ritual. Their latest spectacle, entitled *Simbiosis* has played in Germany and Holland as well as throughout Spain.

GABILONDO, IÑAKI (1942–   )
Journalist and radio and television presenter. He was head of the *Servicios Informativos* (News Broadcasting) at RTVE on the 23rd of February 1981 (the day of the failed coup d'état) and brought the news of that event to the Spanish public. The failed coup was recorded on video and he and his companions were obliged to conceal the tape in case of repercussions. Today, he presents the most popular radio programme on CADENA SER, entitled HOY POR HOY.

GABINETE DEL MINISTRO
The private office of a minister of the government. Ministers are permitted to appoint a number of advisers who belong to the same party and who are obliged to resign when their minister leaves office.

GABINETE DEL PRESIDENTE
A group of political advisers which is chosen personally by the PRIMER MINISTRO.

GADES, ANTONIO (1936–   )
Flamenco dancer whose company achieved international fame through films made with CARLOS SAURA, such as *Carmen* and *Bodas de sangre*.

GAL See: *GRUPOS ANTITERRORISTAS DE LIBERACIÓN*

GALA, ANTONIO (1936–   )
Writer and playwright. He was awarded the *Premio Adonais* for *Enemigo íntimo* and the *Premio Planeta* in 1990 for *El manuscrito carmesí*. Among his better-known plays are *Anillos para una dama* and *Petra regalada*. His articles appear weekly in EL

PAÍS. His latest novel, *La regla de tres*, was published in 1996, and a collection of poetry, *Poemas de amor*, appeared in 1997.

GALAXIA

The GALAXIA affair concerned a plot to overthrow the new Spanish democracy. It takes its name from the café in which the conspirators met.

GALEOTE, GUILLERMO (1941–   )

Secretario de Administración y Finanzas on the executive body of the PSOE from 1988–1993 and DIPUTADO for the CONGRESO from 1977 to 1993. GALEOTE resigned his duties in 1993 as a result of his implication in the CASO FILESA (which concerned the illegal financing of the PSOE).

GALERÍAS PRECIADOS

A chain of department stores founded in 1929. In 1979 the chain began to experience financial problems due to competion from EL CORTE INGLÉS and has been bought and sold several times since that date by a number of foreign companies, including *Mountleigh* and *Mantequerías Leonesas*. It was finally bought by EL CORTE INGLÉS in 1995.

GALICIA

GALICIA is one of Spain's autonomous regions. It has a population of 2.8 million and covers an area of 29,434 square kilometres. GALICIA is in the north-west region of Spain and borders on Portugal to the south. It has four provinces, Pontevedra, Lugo, Orense and La Coruña. Agriculture and fishing have tradionally been its most important industries with 37% of the population engaged in farming. Agriculture is characterised by very small family holdings (*minifundios*) dedicated to cattle raising, milk production and vegetable growing. The two major ports of GALICIA are Vigo and La Coruña. Vigo has a ZONA FRANCA and is the centre of the deep-sea fishing industry with important canning factories and frozen food production. La Coruña is also important for its fishing and is a centre for ship building. SANTIAGO DE COMPOSTELA, its capital, is one of the most historic cities in Spain, where pilgrimages to the tomb of St. James (SANTIAGO) have taken place since the 8th century.

GALICIA UNIDA
Small regional party launched in 1986 by Xosé Santos Lago to provide a centrist approach to local politics.

GALLEGO
Along with CASTELLANO, GALLEGO is the official language of Galicia and is similar in character to Portuguese. It is also spoken in areas of ASTURIAS and CASTILLA Y LEÓN. Approximately 2 million people speak GALLEGO, although it is difficult to make an exact calculation as speakers have varying degrees of competence in the language. It has a literary tradition dating back to the 13th century.

GARAIKOETXEA, CARLOS (1938–   )
Presidente (or LEHENDAKARI) of the Gobierno Vasco from 1979 to 1984. After fundamental disagreements, GARAIKOETXEA was expelled by his political party the PNV and in 1986 he founded his own party, EUSKO ALKARTASUNA or EA. He is a member of the European Parliament.

GARAJONAY
This park is situated on the island of Gomera in the Canary Islands and was declared a national park in 1981. It is extensively forested. Much of its flora is native to the island and has never been disturbed.

GARCI, JOSÉ LUIS (1944–   )
Film maker whose popular *Volver a empezar* (1982) won the Oscar for Best Foreign Language film in 1983. The film deals with the generation of Spaniards who fled Spain during the Civil War and recounts the story of a Spanish Nobel prize winner who returns to Spain after forty years in the United States. He has since made *Sesión continua* (1984) and *Asignatura aprobada* (1987).

GARCÍA BERLANGA, LUIS (1921–   )
Script-writer and film director, BERLANGA is the director of many feature films such as *Plácido* (1962), *La escopeta nacional* (1977) and *La vaquilla* (1985). His most famous film, a satire about rural Spain in the 1950s, is *Bienvenido Mr. Marshall* (1952).

BERLANGA runs a publishing house which specialises in erotic literature, *La sonrisa vertical*. In 1986 he was awarded the PREMIO PRINCIPE DE ASTURIAS for his contribution to the arts.

GARCÍA CALVO, AGUSTÍN (1926–   )

Essayist and linguist, GARCÍA CALVO is a professor at the COMPLUTENSE in MADRID. Among other works, he has written *Sermón de ser o no ser* and *¿Qué es el estado?* He wrote the words to the anthem of the COMUNIDAD DE MADRÍD

GARCÍA DAMBORENEA, RICARDO (1940–   )

Former socialist leader in the Basque country, GARCÍA DAMBORENEA is implicated in the GAL affaire and has in his turn, implicated other politicians, including JOSE BARRIONUEVO and FELIPE GONZÁLEZ. In 1995 he was briefly imprisoned for belonging to an outlawed organisation, and kidnapping and plotting the murder of Segundo Marey.

GARCÍA OBREGÓN, ANA

Actress and television presenter. She appears frequently in the gossip magazines.

GARRIDO, IGNACIO

Young golfer, he won the German Open in June 1997. He is the son of another famous golfer, Antonio Garrido who was a Ryder Cup player.

GARZÓN, BALTASAR (1955–   )

Member of the judiciary involved in investigating the GAL and the ROLDÁN affairs and briefly a member of FELIPE GONZÁLEZ' government when he worked on the *Plan Nacional sobre Drogas*. He resigned this post and his seat in Parliament to return to his job as examining magistrate in 1994.

GAS NATURAL, S.A.

This holding company was constituted from *Catalana de Gas*, *Gas Madrid* and REPSOL *Butano*. REPSOL holds a 45% share, *La* CAIXA 25.5% and SEPI 3.8%. It is the leading piped gas distributor in Spain as well as being involved in gas installation, construction, meter and gauges, engineering, data processing and chemical products storage.

GASODUCTO MAGREB-EUROPA
This $2.3 million natural gas pipeline was opened in 1996. It will eventually transport 10,000 million cubic metres of natural gas per year from Hassi R'mel in Algeria to Europe. Spain will take 6,000 million cubic metres and Portugal 2,500.

GASTEIZ
The Basque name for the city of Vitoria.

GEMIO, ISABEL (1961–   )
This radio and television presenter, has hosted shows such as *Hoy por ti*, *Lo que necesitas es amor* and *Esta noche, sexo*, on the private television station, ANTENA 3. In 1997, she hosted the popular TV programme *Sorpresa, sorpresa*.

GENERAL TEXTIL ESPAÑOLA
New name for the former *Intelhorce, S.A.*, a large textile company based in the south of Spain. The company had been in financial difficulties in the late 1980s and was purchased by the state and relaunched. However, its general state of finance has not improved and it is threatened with closure with the accompanying threat to many jobs in ANDALUCÍA.

GENERALITAT
The CATALÁN autonomous government, founded in 1289. Abolished under the Bourbons in the 18th century it was recreated in 1931 when the Spanish Republic was declared. It was again suppressed during the FRANCO era and its leaders went into exile, but it was revived as part of the ESTADO DE LAS AUTONOMÍAS and has regained control over CATALÁN affairs. Its most famous presidente was Josep Tarradellas who was in fact president in exile until his return to Spain after the death of General FRANCO.

GENERALITAT VALENCIANA
Parliament of the autonomous region of VALENCIA, (the COMUNIDAD VALENCIANA). It considers itself the upholder of Valencian traditions, especially with regard to CATALUÑA.

GEO See: *GRUPO ESPECIAL DE OPERACIONES*

GERNIKA

The 'sacred' town of the Basques and one of the symbols of Basque nationalism. FRANCO allowed the Nazis to use the Condor Legion to bomb the town on 26th April 1937, as the Basques had supported the Republicans in the Spanish Civil War (1936–9). GERNIKA is the subject of a famous painting by Picasso, housed in the MUSEO NACIONAL CENTRO DE ARTE REINA SOFÍA.

GES SEGUROS Y REASEGUROS

This insurance company was founded in 1928 and specialises in motor insurance which accounts for almost half its business.

GESTO POR LA PAZ

Popular movement which works to reintroduce peace to the PAÍS VASCO. This pressure group organises demonstrations in support of individuals who have been kidnapped by ETA.

GESTORAS PRO AMNISTIA

Basque association, close to ETA's militant wing, which seeks an amnesty for all Basque prisoners. Some of its members also belong to HERRI BATASUNA.

GESTORÍA ADMINISTRATIVA

An agency which undertakes to complete an administrative service for a client, such as obtaining a driving licence. The agency visits the appropriate offices and completes the paper work.

GIBRALTAR

Known as *La Roca*, this rocky outcrop on the south-west coast of Spain has been a British colony since it was taken in the War of the Spanish Succession in July 1704. Since then it has been a source of much conflict between Spain and the United Kingdom. Although the British are prepared to discuss Spain's claim to sovereignty, (its strategic importance at the western entrance to the Mediterranean is no longer important), the Gibraltarians themselves are reluctant to become Spaniards.

GIL See: *GRUPO INDEPENDIENTE LIBERAL*

GIL Y GIL, JESÚS

Politician and entrepreneur, he is presidente of the Madrid

football team ATLÉTICO DE MADRID and mayor of MARBELLA. He is a very controversial figure because of his outspoken and autocratic behaviour.

GIL-ROBLES, ALVARO (1944–   )

DEFENSOR DEL PUEBLO from 1988 to 1993. Son of José María Gil-Robles, the former leader of CEDA (*Confederación Española de Derechas Autónomas*) and former leader of the Republican Government.

GIMÉNEZ, EDUARDO (1940–   )

Tenor, born in BARCELONA. Has sung widely in Italy and at the LICEU in BARCELONA. He is well known in the Italian repertoire and also for his Mozart roles.

GIMFERRER, PERE (1945–   )

CATALÁN writer and poet. His collection of poetry, *Arde el mar*, won the *Premio Nacional de Literatura* in 1966. In 1985 he was elected to the REAL ACADEMIA ESPAÑOLA. His latest poem, *Mascarada*, was written in CATALÁN and published in 1996

GLE See: *GRAN LOGIA DE ESPAÑA*

GOBERNADOR CIVIL

The civil governor is the maximum representative of the state in each province. He is a political appointee who is responsible for implementing government policies at provincial level. He is in charge of the state police and security forces within his area and plays an important role in emergencies such as flood or fire. The post of GOBERNADOR CIVIL is scheduled to disappear in the near future.

GOBIERNO CIVIL

This institution is responsible for central government administration at provincial level.

GODO

Family which owns the GODO group of newspapers, including the highly prestigious BARCELONA newspaper, LA VANGUARDIA. The group originally owned the radio station ANTENA 3 and was a major shareholder in the television channel of the same name. It later withdrew from these activities.

GONZÁLEZ, ÁNGEL (1925–)

Poet and member of the REAL ACADEMIA ESPAÑOLA since 1996. He is a member of the 'Generación de los cincuenta'. He won the PREMIO PRÍNCIPE DE ASTURIAS in 1985 and the *premio Reina Sofía de Poesía Iberoamericana* in 1996.

GONZÁLEZ MÁRQUEZ, FELIPE (1942–)

Presidente of the Spanish government since 1982 when the socialists won 202 of the 305 seats in the CORTES. He had been SECRETARIO GENERAL of the PSOE since 1974 when he was elected during the *Suresnes* conference. As *presidente*, he was instrumental in Spain's joining the European Union (1985) and since that date, he has been prominent in international affairs, especially with relation to Latin America. Since the general strike in 1988, however, the GONZÁLEZ government was increasingly caught up in the corruption scandals which have been endemic in Spain in recent years. (See: JUAN GUERRA, FILESA, IBERCORP, ROLDÁN, GAL, CESID). In July 1995 GONZÁLEZ was called by BALTASAR GARZÓN to declare before the TRIBUNAL SUPREMO about his role in the GAL affaire. GONZÁLEZ lost his office in 1996 when JOSÉ MARÍA AZNAR won the general election. In June 1997 he resigned from his position as *secretario general* of the PSOE.

GONZÁLEZ PACHECO, ANTONIO (1943–)

Otherwise known as *Billy el niño* (Billy the kid), this policeman was well known during the transitional years after the death of FRANCO for his extreme right-wing opinions. He was convicted of using unreasonable pressure on detainees in 1974, accused by FRANCISCO LOBATÓN. (LOBATÓN is now a well-known television and radio investigative journalist). He also subjected José María Mendiluce (currently a member of the European Parliament) to harsh interrogations. He was thought to have connections with GRAPO and other extreme right-wing organisations.

EL GORDO

The monthly draw of the PRIMITIVA which offers a larger prize than normal. It is drawn on the last Sunday of the month; each ticket costs 500 pesetas.

GOROSÁBEL ELORZA, ANTONIO (1946–   )

ETA terrorist, also known as *Willy*. He has been on the run since he was convicted of terrorist activities in 1983.

GOYTISOLO, JUAN (1931–   )

Important and prolific novelist, he is the author of novels such as *Fiestas* (1958), *La isla* (1961) and a trilogy, *Conde Julián, Juan sin tierra* and *Señas de identidad* (1966). GOYTISOLO was a bitter enemy of the FRANCO régime and spent much of his life in self-imposed exile in France and Morocco. His latest book *De la ceca a la Meca* is an account of journeys through various Arab countries.

GRADUADO ESCOLAR

A student who has completed the EGB course successfully is awarded the title of GRADUADO ESCOLAR. If he or she is unsuccessful, the *Certificado de Escolaridad* is awarded instead and the student is allowed to proceed to FORMACIÓN PROFESIONAL (primer grado).

GRAN CANARIA

Island in the CANARIAS archipelago. Its tourist industry is important, as is the production of bananas, sugar cane and tobacco. Its chief town is LAS PALMAS.

GRAN LOGIA DE ESPAÑA

Body which incorporates the 163 Masonic lodges in Spain. The Masons have long been the object of mistrust in Spain but in 1996 the first step towards their acceptance by the Catholic Church was taken when the Grand Master of the Lodge, Lluís Salat Gusils, was given funeral rites in the Basilica of Santa María del Mar in BARCELONA.

GRAN TIBIDABO

Holding company run by JAVIER DE LA ROSA and MANUEL PRADO. It is currently the subject of judicial proceedings because of malpractice. It takes its name from the hill in BARCELONA which is a popular park.

LA GRAN VÍA

Important avenue which links the *Plaza de Cibeles* and the *Plaza de España* in MADRID. It is known for its shops and cinemas.

GRANDES, ALMUDENA (1960–   )

Young Spanish novelist who leapt to fame with her first, erotic novel, *Las edades de Lulú*, which later became a film. Her novel, *Malena es un nombre de tango* appeared in 1994: it also was made into a successful film. Her latest work, a collection of seven short stories, is entitled *Modelos de mujer*.

GRANDES SUPERFICIES

Generic name for super- and hyper-markets such as HIPERCOR.

GRANJA CASTELLÓ

CATALÁN dairy which produces two brands of baby milk *Nadó 1* and *Nadó 2*. In 1995 they broke the monopoly of Spanish chemists in the selling of baby milk by invoking European law.

GRAPO See: *GRUPOS REVOLUCIONARIOS ANTIFASCISTAS PRIMERO DE OCTUBRE*

GRUPO 16

Media group, comprising the weekly magazine CAMBIO 16 and the daily newspaper DIARIO 16. Highly influential in the 1980s, it has since lost many prestigious journalists and is no longer so important.

GRUPO DURO-FELGUERA, S.A.

This group is in the general engineering sector and manufactures and sells metallic constructions, boilers, smelting machinery and consumer goods. It is also involved in energy production, solid and liquid fuel, electronics and naval transport.

GRUPO ESPECIAL DE OPERACIONES

Crack police squad, formed to deal with terrorist seiges. One of its most famous operations was the storming of the *Banca Central* in BARCELONA when over 100 hostages were released.

GRUPO INDEPENDIENTE LIBERAL

Political party founded by the businessman JESÚS GIL Y GIL.

GRUPO LA SEDA
Holding company, based in BARCELONA, in the chemical and textile sector. It holds 75% of *Catalana de Polímeros*, 100% of *Viscoseda*, 95% of *Industrias Químicas Asociadas (IQA)* and 40% of *Poliseda y Cydeplsat PET*. In 1997 the company suffered a loss of 2,424 million pesetas.

GRUPO MIXTO
In the CONGRESO, a parliamentary group made up of DIPUTADOS from parties whose numbers do not justify their having their own group.

GRUPO TORRAS
Holding company whose vice-president was JAVIER DE LA ROSA. In 1992, the Kuwaiti company KIO suspended payments in the company as a result of fraud and misappropriation of funds. The group consisted of 21 separate companies and employed 30,000 people.

GRUPOS ANTITERRORISTAS DE LIBERACIÓN
An illegal right-wing organisation, responsible for a series of terrorist attacks in both France and Spain and for 27 murders of suspected Basque separatists between 1983 and 1988. It is alleged that the Spanish government financed the organisation and several members of the government, including the Prime Minister, FELIPE GONZÁLEZ, have been implicated.

GRUPOS PARLAMENTARIOS
These groups perform the major part of parliamentary work. Each group consists of the members of a particular political party. Parties too small to have a group of their own, belong to the GRUPO MIXTO.

GRUPOS REVOLUCIONARIOS ANTIFASCISTAS PRIMERO DE OCTUBRE
GRAPO is one of the small groups of extreme left-wing militants affiliated to ETA. It became especially active after 1977 and is known for its extreme violence.

GU See: *GALICIA UNIDA*

GUADALQUIVIR

River which flows through SEVILLA and is 657 km in length. It rises in the Sierra of Cazorla and enters the Atlantic at Sanlúcar de Barrameda. It is navigable as far as SEVILLA. It has reservoirs for irrigation and hydroelectric power.

GUADALUPE (NUESTRA SEÑORA DE)

Image of the Virgin found in the town of Guadalupe (Cáceres). She is the patron of all Spanish-speaking peoples and is especially revered in Mexico.

GUADARRAMA (SIERRA DE)

Mountain-range to the north of MADRID which divides the provinces of MADRID and Segovia. NAVACERRADA is an important ski-resort.

GUADIANA

River, 778 km in length, which rises in Ruidera and flows through Mérida and Badajoz to Portugal and the Atlantic.

GUARDIA CIVIL

Police force, founded in the last century to combat banditry on the highways; it has had a chequered history. It is military in character in that its members carry arms and live in barracks. It had a somewhat unsavoury reputation in the FRANCO era, which was compounded by the participation of some of its members in the military coup of 1981. It has also been accused of torture (primarily of ETA suspects) and corruption. Recently, however, its image has changed: it patrols the roads outside built up areas and is heavily involved in rescue attempts, both in the air and under water. In 1997 it received much positive publicity for its role in rescuing ORTEGA LARA, who had been captured by ETA.

GUERNICA See: *GERNIKA*

GUERRA, ALFONSO (1940–)

Vicepresidente of the Socialist Government from 1982 to 1991, GUERRA was forced to resign after a financial scandal in which his brother, JUAN GUERRA was implicated. ALFONSO GUERRA has been a member of the left since 1960, the year in which he joined

Juventudes Socialistas and in 1962 he joined PSOE. He was *vicesecretario general* of the party from 1972 and has been a member of parliament since 1976. Towards the end of the GONZÁLEZ term in office, there was a rift between the Prime Minister and GUERRA in which GUERRA lost much of his influence within the party. He resigned from the party executive, with GONZÁLEZ, in 1997.

GUERRA DEL FLETÁN

On the 9th of March 1995, three Canadian patrol vessels captured the Galician trawler *Estai*, which was fishing in international waters off the Canadian coast, about 250 miles from St. John's. Spain immediately sent a war-ship to the area; the EU was obliged to intervene in this serious diplomatic incident. The *Estai* was later released and, after negotiations, the Spanish quota for this species was reduced.

GUERRA, JUAN

Brother of the former deputy prime minister, ALFONSO GUERRA, JUAN GUERRA has been involved in a series of court cases, accused of tax evasion on property deals in ANDALUCÍA. In 1992 he underwent his first trial but was acquitted through lack of evidence. Three years later, in 1995, he was imprisoned for 18 months for illegal use of contacts.

GUERRA SUCIA

In 1995, FELIPE GONZÁLEZ was implicated in the so-called GUERRA SUCIA (dirty war) between GAL, a death squad allegedly sponsored by the state, and the Basque terrorist group ETA.

GUREAK

Association of family members of those Basque terrorists who are completing their prison sentences outside the PAIS VASCO. Along with other associations such as SENIDEAK, it works for their release or removal to prisons in or nearer the Basque Country.

GURRUCHAGA, JAVIER

Comic actor, he started his professional career with the *Orquesta Mondragón*. Among other films he has appeared in *¿Qué he hecho yo para merecer esto?*

GUTIÉRREZ ARAGÓN, MANUEL (1942–   )

Film director who became the most famous of his generation with a trilogy which appeared in the late seventies, *Camada negra* (1977), *Sonámbulos* (1977) and *El corazón del bosque* (1978). In the eighties he went on to direct *Maravillas* (1980), *Demonios en el jardín* (1982) and *La mitad del cielo* (1986). In 1991 he directed *El Quijote* for Spanish television. In 1995 he brought out *Libertarias*, which starred one of his favourite actresses, VICTORIA ABRIL.

GUTIÉRREZ, ANTONIO (1951–   )

Secretario General of COMISIONES OBRERAS since 1987. He formed part of the secretariat of the CCOO from 1978 to 1987. He has fought to make the trade union apolitical and is himself no longer a member of the Communist Party.

GUTIÉRREZ MELLADO, MANUEL (1912–1995)

Important figure in the transition from dictatorship to democracy, GUTIÉRREZ MELLADO won the respect of Spaniards for defying those members of the GUARDIA CIVIL who attempted to take over the CONGRESO DE DIPUTADOS on the 23rd of February 1981. He died in a traffic accident on the 16th of December 1995. His name is inextricably linked with the reform of the army in the transition years.

GVI GRUPO

Largest travel company in Spain. In 1995 it had a turnover of 139,949 million pesetas. It has two retail chains, *Viajes Iberia* and *Viajes Mediterráneo*. It also owns 17 hotels (*Iberostar*).

HALFFTER, CRISTÓBAL (1930–)

Possibly the best- known living Spanish composer. He has created such works as *Mural Sonante*, *Oficio de difuntos*, *Microformas* and *Misa ducal*. In 1953 he won the *Premio Nacional de Música* and in 1992 he composed the *Overtura Preludio Madrid 92* which was played at the opening ceremony of MADRID, European Capital of Culture.

HB See: *HERRI BATASUNA*

HEMICICLO

The debating chamber of the CONGRESO is often referred to as the HEMICICLO because of its semi-circular shape.

HERMIDA, JESÚS (1937–)

Television journalist, he spent ten years (1968–78) as correspondent for RTVE in New York. He began to present the news programme *Pasaporte* soon after the Spanish Constitution was approved. He now works for the independent television channel, ANTENA 3.

HERNANDO, VIOLETA (1982–)

VIOLETA HERNANDO sprung to fame in 1996 for writing a first novel at the age of 14. Her novel, entitled *Muertos o algo mejor*, was published by *Montesinos*.

HERRI BATASUNA

HERRI BATASUNA (The People's Unity Coalition) is the political wing of ETA and was founded in 1979 as a coalition of four left-wing organisations whose aim was to establish independence for the PAÍS VASCO. In the elections held in the PAÍS VASCO, HERRI BATASUNA usually polls about 17% of the vote. It is the third most important party in the regional government although its support has been steadily declining. It is especially strong in SAN SEBASTIÁN.

HIDROÉLECTRICA DEL CANTÁBRICO, S.A.

This company generates, transports and distributes electricity in ASTURIAS. Through its subsidiaries, it distributes and sells gaseous hydrocarbons.

EL HIERRO

Smallest and most westerly of the ISLAS CANARIAS. It is divided from east to west by a large mountain: the north is verdant, the south black from the volcanic lava.

HIMNO NACIONAL

The Spanish national anthem has music but no words. It is still under copyright so royalties have to be paid whenever it is played.

HIPERCOR

Chain of supermarkets belonging to EL CORTE INGLÉS. The branch in BARCELONA was the scene of a bomb blast in 1987 in which 21 persons died and 45 were injured. ETA claimed responsibility for this outrage. HIPERCOR has thirteen stores, seven thousand two hundred and fifteen employees and a turnover (data available in 1995) of 200,568 million pesetas.

HISPASAT

A number of communication satellites, sponsored by the *Instituto Nacional de Técnica Aeroespacial* (INTA) and the European Space Agency. HISPASAT 1–A was launched in 1992 from Kourou in French Guiana and serves the Spanish Peninsula, the Canary Islands and a large area of America. It provides telephone and television services as well as data communication, both for military and civil purposes. In 1993, the service was expanded with the launching of HISPASAT 1–B.

HISPAVISIÓN

Satellite television channel, belonging to the RTVE network which began to transmit from VALENCIA to South American countries in 1994. It is due to become a pay channel in 1996.

¡HOLA!

This highly popular glossy magazine founded in 1944 deals with the lives of the rich and famous in a discreet and respectful way. It sells approximately 800,000 copies a week but it is read by many more people in doctors' and dentists' waiting rooms and hairdressers throughout Spain.

HORAS EXTRAORDINARIAS

Overtime. Workers may do overtime if hours are available, but it is never compulsory. Overtime may not be done at night except in certain industries.

HORMAECHEA CAZÓN, JUAN

Former President of the autonomous region of CANTABRIA (1987–90 and from 1991–95). He has also been ALCALDE of SANTANDER (1977–78). He was found guilty in 1994 of embezzlement of public funds and perversion of the course of justice and was imprisoned. He was later given a pardon by the CONSEJO DE MINISTROS.

HORNOS IBÉRICOS ALBA, S.A.

This company's principal activity is the manufacture and distribution of cement and related products.

HORTERA

A word commonly used in Spanish for people considered to act and dress in bad taste. It was the name for male shop assistants or messengers at the turn of the century in Madrid.

HOY POR HOY

One of the most popular radio programmes in Spain, it goes out from 6 in the morning to 12.30 on CADENA SER. It is a news, interviews and features programme, hosted for the past ten years by IÑAKI GABILONDO.

HUARTE, S.A.

This company is involved in the building and civil engineering industry and in real estate.

HUELGAS

Strikes in Spain are legal if the following procedures are

respected. There must be a majority decision to strike taken at a joint meeting of workers' representatives, or a union meeting, or a joint decision of the unions involved. Five days advance warning must be given in the case of the private sector and ten calendar days for sectors providing public services. A strike committee of a maximum of 12 workers must also be formed.

HUERTA

Irrigated small-holding, especially in the VALENCIA region, producing high value fruits and vegetables. These holdings often produce more than one crop per year. Many different varieties are grown on one holding.

HULLERAS DEL NORTE, S.A.

Asturian coal mining company now in public ownership. Currently the company receives 90,000 million pesetas in subsidies, but the 11 mines will probably have to close early in the next century. Since 1991 the company has lost over 15,000 jobs and more than 9 mines have been closed.

HUNOSA See: *HULLERAS DEL NORTE, S.A.*

IARA See: *INSTITUTO ANDALUZ DE LA REFORMA AGRARIA*

IBÁRRURI, DOLORES (1895–1989)

One of the legends of the Spanish Civil War, also known as *La Pasionaria*, she was *presidente* of the PCE from 1960 to 1989. She lived in exile in Russia from March 1939 to May 1977 when she returned to Spain for the first free elections since the Republic. She was elected Member of Parliament for ASTURIAS in 1977. A symbol of feminism and of political struggle, she was the author of the famous words '*más vale morir de pie que vivir de rodillas*' – 'better to die on your feet than to live on your knees'.

IBERCORP

Financial scandal in which JAVIER DE LA ROSA and MARIANO RUBIO were both involved.

IBERDROLA, S.A.

Electricity group created in 1991 from two companies, *Iberduero, S.A.* and *Hidroeléctrica española, S.A.* It is the largest group in this sector in Spain and distributes electricity in 36 provinces. It also has interests in information technology, property and insurance.

IBERIA

The state-owned national airline has suffered many years of financial crises and in 1995 showed losses of 210,000 million pesetas. In 1995 it received 107,000 million pesetas from the European Union in a bid to place it on a sounder economic footing. As part of the deal, IBERIA had to sell one of its companies, *Aerolíneas Argentinas*, institute a programme of redundancies and impose a freeze on salaries.

IBÉRICA DE AUTOPISTAS, S.A.
This company's principal activity is the promotion, construction and maintenance of the Villalba-Adanero toll motorway and its service areas.

IBEROAMÉRICA
General term given to those countries in Central and South America which were colonised by the Spanish and Portuguese peoples.

IBIZA
This island in the ISLAS BALEARES is the most frequently visited by tourists. It was especially attractive to the hippie generation of the 1960s and still has a reputation for its wild and exotic night life.

IC See: *INICIATIVA PER CATALUNYA*

ICAC See: *INSTITUTO DE CONTABILIDAD Y AUDITORÍA*

ICE See: *INSTITUTO DE CIENCIAS DE LA EDUCACIÓN*

ICESB See: *INSTITUT CATOLIC D'ESTUDIS SOCIALS DE BARCELONA*

ICEX See: *INSTITUTO DE COMERCIO EXTERIOR*

ICONA See: *INSTITUTO NACIONAL PARA LA CONSERVACIÓN DE LA NATURALEZA*

IDÍGORAS, GUERRIKABEITIA JON (1937–   )
Basque politician and spokesman for HERRI BATASUNA, the political wing of the Basque terrorist group ETA. He has been imprisoned several times for his work with the labour movement in the Basque country and went into exile in France from 1974 to 1976. He was a founder member of the trade union LAB (LANGILE ABERTZALE BATZORDEA) and has been a member of the CONGRESO and of the autonomous Basque government since 1980. He was imprisoned again in 1996 by the judge BALTASAR GARZÓN for holding election meetings in which a subversive video was shown: in the video, hooded and armed figures spoke in support of ETA.

IESE
The most prestigious business school in Spain, based in BARCELONA and run by the OPUS DEI. It enjoys an international reputation.

IFA See: *INSTITUTO DE FOMENTO DE ANDALUCÍA*

IGAE See: *INTERVENCIÓN GENERAL DE LA ADMINISTRACIÓN DEL ESTADO*

IGLESIA DEL BUEN PASTOR
The cathedral of SAN SEBASTIÁN, which is the focus of ETA conflicts. It is here that members of SENIDEAK stage their hunger strikes and where supporters of ALDAYA held their demostrations each Tuesday and Thursday.

IGLESIAS, GERARDO (1945–   )
Secretario General of the PCE from 1982 to 1988. He succeeded SANTIAGO CARRILLO after the defeat of the Communist Party in the 1982 elections. He was instrumental in founding IZQUIERDA UNIDA but left the party in 1989 to go back to his native ASTURIAS to work as a miner.

IGLESIAS, JULIO (1945–   )
Internationally known singer and song writer, currently living in Miami. Formerly married to ISABEL PREYSLER. He first came to fame when he represented Spain in the 1970 European Song Contest and although he did not win with his song *Gwendoline*, he immediately became popular throughout Spain and Latin America. A year later he had already sold his first million records. Since then he has sold over 149 million albums and is the best known Latin singer in the world.

IKASTOLA
Schools in the PAÍS VASCO where teaching takes place exclusively through the medium of the Basque language. They were originally founded in the 1930s but have recently experienced a renaissance.

IKURRIÑA
The Basque flag, symbol of Basque nationalism. It is displayed,

along with the Spanish flag, on public buildings and at official functions in the PAÍS VASCO. It has a green and white cross on a red background. It was originally designed as a flag for the PNV by the founder of the party, Sabino de Arana Goiri.

IMAC See: *INSTITUTO DE MEDIACIÓN, ARBITRAJE Y CONCILIACIÓN*

IMADE See: *INSTITUTO MADRILEÑO DE DESARROLLO*

IMPI See: *INSTITUTO DE LA PEQUEÑA Y MEDIANA EMPRESA INDUSTRIAL*

IMPUESTO DE SOCIEDADES
Corporation tax. This has increased substantially since Spain's entry into the EU.

IMPUESTO RELIGIOSO
This is the popular name given to the 0.5% which individual taxpayers may pay to the Catholic Church if they so wish. Whatever the amount levied in this way, the Church continues to receive a block grant from the state.

IMPUESTO REVOLUCIONARIO
This 'tax' is extorted from local business men by the Basque terrorist group ETA, in order to finance their activities.

IMPUESTO SOBRE BIENES INMUEBLES
This is a tax on real estate, levied at local level by the AYUNTAMIENTO.

IMPUESTO SOBRE EL VALOR AÑADIDO
VAT, introduced in Spain when she entered the EU.

IMPUESTO SOBRE LA ACTIVIDAD ECONÓMICA
Business tax, levied at local level by the AYUNTAMIENTO.

IMPUESTO SOBRE LA RENTA DE PERSONAS FÍSICAS
Taxes levied on income and return on capital. Citizens are taxed according to their level of income: these rates apply also to tax deducted at source. The autonomous communities now have the right to administer 15% of all taxes collected by the state.

Spaniards fill out a personal tax statement in June and may be able to claim back tax.

IMPUESTO SOBRE VEHÍCULOS
Vehicle tax, levied at local level by the AYUNTAMIENTO.

INAP See: *INSTITUTO NACIONAL DE ADMINISTRACIÓN PÚBLICA*

INAS See: *INSTITUTO NACIONAL DE ASISTENCIA SOCIAL*

INCE See: *INSTITUTO NACIONAL DE CALIDAD Y EVALUACIÓN*

INCENDIOS
Spain suffers each year from a large number of fires, some of which are certainly deliberately started. Fire-raisers do so in order to clear land for building or to re-plant it with subsidised crops. Measures have been taken in certain areas to prevent summer fires, such as clearing undergrowth, installing fire-breaks and installing detection systems.

INCENTIVOS A LA CONTRATACIÓN INDEFINIDA DE JÓVENES
Employers received a subsidy of 400,000 pesetas for each young person whom they employ. Usually this person must be under 25 and have been unemployed for at least a year.

INCENTIVOS A LA CONTRATACIÓN INDEFINIDA DE MAYORES DE 45 AÑOS
Employers receive a subsidy of 500,000 pesetas for each worker over 45 years old whom they employ. These workers must have been unemployed for at least a year.

ÍNDICE DE MORTALIDAD
The death rate in Spain is 8,82 per 1,000. (1994).

ÍNDICE DE NATALIDAD
Spain's birth rate is 11,05 per 1,000. It is the lowest birth rate in Europe.

ÍNDICE DE PRECIOS AL CONSUMO
Retail price index. In 1996 this rose by 3.5%.

INDO See: *INSTITUTO DE DENOMINACIÓN DE ORIGEN*

INDURÁIN, MIGUEL (1964–)
MIGUEL INDURÁIN is one of the great cyclists of this century. In 1992 alone, he won the Giro de Italia, the Tour de France and the Vuelta de España. In 1995, he won the Tour de France for the fifth consecutive time, the first cyclist to do so. He was the first Spanish sportsman to be awarded the Order of Olympic Merit. In 1992 he won the PREMIO PRÍNCIPE DE ASTURIAS for sporting achievement. He also won a gold medal in the Atlanta Olympic Games (1995).

INDUSTRIA ESPAÑOLA DEL ALUMINIO, S.A.
Company producing and marketing aluminium, created in 1985 by the amalgamation of ENDASA (*Empresa Nacional de Aluminio*) and *Aluminio de Galicia*. It was later administered by the state holding company INI until this in turn was dissolved.

INEM See: *INSTITUTO NACIONAL DE EMPLEO*

INESPAL See: *INDUSTRIA ESPAÑOLA DEL ALUMINIO, S.A.*

INFORME ABRIL
Report published in 1991 on the reform of the health service. It recommended a joint system of private and public health care, working in *concierto* or cooperatively.

INFORME NAVAJAS
Legal dossier concerning the supposed relationship between drug dealers and the GUARDIA CIVIL at INTXAURRONDO (Guipúzcoa).

INFORME SEMANAL
Important current affairs programme, broadcast on Saturday evening at 9.30 pm on RTVE's Channel One.

INH See: *INSTITUTO NACIONAL DE HIDROCARBUROS*

INHABILITACIÓN
This term refers to the disqualification from public office of those found guilty of bribery of public officials.

INI See: *INSTITUTO NACIONAL DE INDUSTRIA*

INICIATIVA PER CATALUNYA
Left-wing Catalán party which, until 1997, maintained close links with IZQUIERDA UNIDA and belonged to the same regional and EU groupings. At the fifth congress (*V Asamblea*) of IZQUIERDA UNIDA, it was decided to withdraw support from IC.

INJUVE See: *INSTITUTO DE LA JUVENTUD*

INM See: *INSTITUTO NACIONAL DE METEOROLOGÍA*

INMOBILIARIA URBIS, S.A.
This company works in the property sector and deals in real estate; acquisition and sales, construction, promotion, management and development of real estate at all levels.

INSALUD See: *INSTITUTO NACIONAL DE LA SALUD*

INSEGURIDAD CIUDADANA
This term refers to a generalised fear of petty crime such as mugging, violence in the street, car-theft and house-breaking.

INSERSO See: *INSTITUTO NACIONAL DE SERVICIOS SOCIALES*

INSS See: *INSTITUTO NACIONAL DE SEGURIDAD SOCIAL*

INSTITUT CATOLIC D'ESTUDIS SOCIALS DE BARCELONA
ICESB was founded in 1951 to study social issues from a Christian point of view. It now has schools of social science, social work and family workers. It is involved with research in these areas and has an extensive specialist library.

INSTITUTO ANDALUZ DE LA REFORMA AGRARIA

Body empowered to expropriate land in ANDALUCÍA under the agricultural reform programme.

INSTITUTO CERVANTES

The equivalent of the Goethe Institute and the British Council, the INSTITUTO CERVANTES is designed to promote the culture and language of Spain in the outside world. It runs Spanish courses and examinations, undertakes teacher training and organises a number of cultural events in each branch. The Institute was set up in 1992 and has branches in 20 different countries, including Great Britain, the United States, the Philippines and Egypt.

INSTITUTO DE CIENCIAS DE LA EDUCACIÓN

These university colleges used to deliver the CAP or teachers' certificate. It is intended to phase out the ICES and to transfer their work to the CENTROS DE ENCUENTRO DE PROFESORES.

INSTITUTO DE COMERCIO EXTERIOR

ICEX is the agency which supports Spanish businesses trading abroad and facilitates proceedings for those who wish to do so.

INSTITUTO DE CONTABILIDAD Y AUDITORÍA

Body concerned with the regulation of accounting and audit procedures in Spanish companies.

INSTITUTO DE CRÉDITO OFICIAL

Bank which advances and administers credit for projects in the Spanish regions or in the third world.

INSTITUTO DE CRÉDITO SOCIAL PESQUERO

This body used to provide funds for the purchase, maintenance and repair of fishing vessels. This responsibility has been taken over by the BANCO DE CRÉDITO INDUSTRIAL.

INSTITUTO DE DENOMINACIÓN DE ORIGEN

This national body regulates the origin and quality of food such as cheese, olive oils and nougat (*turrón*) and of wines.

INSTITUTO DE EDUCACÍON

An INSTITUTO is a state secondary school which delivers courses to young people from 14 to 18.

INSTITUTO DE FOMENTO DE ANDALUCÍA

This body seeks to develop industry in ANDALUCÍA and has so far set up 17 companies of various sizes and activities. It is also involved in the promotion of rural tourism.

INSTITUTO DE LA EMPRESA FAMILIAR

This privately run institute supports and promotes small and medium-sized family-owned businesses.

INSTITUTO DE LA JUVENTUD

This body exists to provide activities of an academic and cultural type for young people. Among other things, it runs courses, organises competitions and sponsors exhibitions.

INSTITUTO DE LA MUJER

This body was created by the Spanish government in 1983 to promote equality between the sexes and to encourage the participation of women in political, cultural, economic and social life. The INSTITUTO was the only formal channel for womens' political demands and played a crucial role in consciousness-raising among women in Spain. It played an important part in key legal reforms and anti-discriminatory measures. It also published influential studies on the position of women in Spain (*La mujer en cifras*; *Segundo plan para la igualdad de oportunidades de las mujeres*; *La mujer en España, situación social y política*). It was abolished in 1996 by the AZNAR government.

INSTITUTO DE LA PEQUEÑA Y MEDIANA EMPRESA INDUSTRIAL

This is a state-run body whose function is to support and promote small and medium-sized industries. It comes under the aegis of the MINISTERIO DE INDUSTRIA, ENERGÍA Y TURISMO.

INSTITUTO DE MEDIACIÓN, ARBITRAJE Y CONCILIACIÓN

This mediation, arbitration and conciliation council was originally set up in 1979 within the *Ministerio de Trabajo y Seguridad Social*. Its functions were later transferred to the *Subdirección General de Mediación, Arbitraje y Conciliación*. The body exists to mediate between employers and employees and so avoid having recourse to the law in industrial disputes.

INSTITUTO DE REFORMA AGRARIA

This agency absorbed the SERVICIO DE CONCENTRACIÓN PARCELARIA and took over its role of encouraging the development of larger agricultural holdings.

INSTITUTO DE SALUD CARLOS III

This Institute is the research body directly accountable to the MINISTERIO DE SANIDAD. Its function is to carry out basic research (on the COLZA syndrome for example) and to teach, evaluate, inspect and accredit other bodies concerned with health in Spain.

INSTITUTO ESPAÑOL DE COMERCIO EXTERIOR

Government agency, formerly known as INFE and created in 1982. It is responsible for the promotion of exports.

INSTITUTO GEOGRÁFICO NACIONAL

Government agency responsible for research in astronomy, geophysics and for mapping and meteorology.

INSTITUTO MADRILEÑO DE DESARROLLO

Public development institute for the MADRID region.

INSTITUTO NACIONAL DE ADMINISTRACIÓN PÚBLICA

Government agency responsible for the selection and training of civil servants.

INSTITUTO NACIONAL DE ASISTENCIA SOCIAL

Welfare agency, originally responsible for non-contributory pensions. It was later absorbed into INSERSO.

INSTITUTO NACIONAL DE CALIDAD Y EVALUACIÓN

This body was created as a result of the 1990 Education Act or LOGSE and exists to assess results throughout the school system and to monitor the functioning of the system as a whole.

INSTITUTO NACIONAL DE EMPLEO

Employment Office, responsible for all areas related to employment such as unemployment benefits, employee protection and so on. It acts as an employment agency, especially for those workers most difficult to place – the young, the long-term unemployed and women. It also runs training courses and gives career advice. In 1994, its monopoly on placing job seekers in work was broken with the creation of the AGENCIAS DE CONTRATACIÓN.

INSTITUTO NACIONAL DE HIDROCARBUROS
Group of companies in the petrol and petrochemical sector: they were originally brought together in 1981. They currently form part of the SEPI holding company.

INSTITUTO NACIONAL DE INDUSTRIA
This state holding company was created in 1941 to reconstruct basic industry in Spain after the Civil War. It operated by creating or expanding existing companies through the injection of equity capital. Current funds were raised from dividends or profitable INI companies, through foreign equity subscriptions and through the issue of bonds. Its major fields of operation were in power generation and supply, mining, manufacturing, aerospace and electronics. INI was Spain's largest industrial group; INI companies produced 25% of the nation's electricity, refined 40% of its oil imports, mined 60% of its coal and produced 45% of its steel. IBERIA, the state airline, was owned by INI. The company was liquidated in July 1996 by the AZNAR government and a new company was set up in its place – the AGENCIA INDUSTRIAL DEL ESTADO or AIE. The function of this company is to restructure or close down loss-making enterprises within the former INI.

INSTITUTO NACIONAL DE LA SALUD
The Spanish National Health Service, established in 1978 to manage the public health system in Spain. It is responsible for outpatient clinics (*ambulatorios*), hospitals, medical and daycentres. Currently INSALUD only controls 10 out of the 17 regional health budgets as some AUTONOMÍAS have had responsibility for health devolved to them. In modern Spain, 99% of the population has the right to receive health care free of charge.

INSTITUTO NACIONAL DE METEOROLOGÍA
Organisation responsible for weather forecasting.

INSTITUTO NACIONAL DE REFORMA Y DESARROLLO AGRARIO

This state body is responsible for the technology used in agricultural production and rural development. It also implements the EU's sociostructural policy. It comes under the aegis of the MINISTERIO DE AGRICULTURA.

INSTITUTO NACIONAL DE SEGURIDAD SOCIAL

Autonomous body with its own budget and staff. Its major role is the management of funds for the social security system. It is responsible for the administration of social security benefits, such as old-age, invalidity and widows' pensions.

INSTITUTO NACIONAL DE SERVICIOS SOCIALES

This autonomous government body is responsible for social services. Like other similar bodies (INSALUD and INSS) it manages its own budget and is responsible for its own legal and financial affairs. It manages services such as residential homes and day centres, provides assistance for the disabled and handicapped, and runs holidays for the elderly.

INSTITUTO NACIONAL DE TÉCNICA AEROESPACIAL

This body was established in 1942 to promote and develop research in aeronautical and space engineering. It answers directly to the *Secretaría de Estado para la Defensa*.

INSTITUTO NACIONAL DEL CONSUMO

Body directly accountable to the MINISTERIO DE SANIDAD whose function is to work in the field of consumers' rights. Among other duties, it undertakes consumer research, education and protection.

INSTITUTO NACIONAL PARA LA CONSERVACIÓN DE LA NATURALEZA

This agency, known as ICONA, is a department of the MINISTERIO DE AGRICULTURA and existed also under the FRANCO régime. It was created in 1971. It is responsible for the environment and for the maintenance of national parks.

INSTITUTO PARA LA DIVERSIFICACIÓN Y AHORRO DE LA ENERGÍA

This body which aims to reduce energy consumption now works within the MINISTERIO DE FOMENTO.

INSTITUTO SOCIAL DE LA MARINA

This body exists to provide social security for those employed in the fishing and shipping industries. Like the INSS it is an autonomous entity which manages its own budget and financial and legal affairs.

INSTITUTOS DE FORMACIÓN PROFESIONAL

Technical schools which train youngsters from 16 upwards to occupy jobs in areas such as plumbing, the construction industry and hairdressing.

INSTRUCCIÓN

In criminal cases, the *juez de* INSTRUCCIÓN is responsible for gathering evidence, collecting statements and exhibits and so on. A report or *sumario* is then drawn up and handed to the court trying the case.

INSUMISOS

Term referring to those who refuse to do military service or the alternative community service. Many of these young people are from the PAÍS VASCO.

INTA See: *INSTITUTO NACIONAL DE TÉCNICA AEROESPACIAL*

INTERINIDAD

This term is used for those situations in which employees leave their posts temporarily: these positions are then filled by workers on short-term contracts. The average length of these contracts is three months.

INTERVENCIÓN GENERAL DE LA ADMINISTRACIÓN DEL ESTADO

This auditing department is part of the MINISTERIO DE ECONOMÍA Y HACIENDA and has over 200 inspectors whose function is to audit the accounts of public sector departments. The IGAE also prepares the accounts for the state and its attendant bodies.

INTERVENCIÓN GENERAL DE LA SEGURIDAD SOCIAL

This body exists to regulate and control the expenditure of the social security system. It prepares plans and reports, undertakes analyses of expenditure and coordinates the accounting and auditing procedure for the three major bodies in this area – INSALUD, INSS and INSERSO.

INTERVIÚ

Magazine founded by ANTONIO ASENSIO. The first edition appeared on the 5th of May 1976 and was a mixture of sex, current affairs and political analysis. It was the first of a number of such magazines.

INTXAURRONDO

The barracks of the GUARDIA CIVIL in INTXAURRONDO are under investigation for supposed irregularities in connection with the LASA and ZABALA case. There is also thought to be a connection with the supposed murder of Mikel Zabalza Gárate whose corpse was found in the Bidasoa river in 1985 after he had attempted to escape from custody.

INVALIDEZ

Invalidity pensions may be claimed by those with disabilities. The basic monthly pension is currently 35,580 pesetas but more may be claimed as a care allowance by those with more than 75% disability.

IPC See: *INDÍCE DE PRECIOS AL CONSUMO*

IRPF See: *IMPUESTO SOBRE LA RENTA DE LAS PERSONAS FÍSICAS*

IRYDA See: *INSTITUTO NACIONAL DE REFORMA Y DESARROLLO AGRARIO*

LAS ISLAS BALEARES

The ISLAS BALEARES are an archipelago off the east coast of Spain. There are eleven islands in all, the most important being

MALLORCA, MENORCA, IBIZA, Formentera and Cabrera. The islands are an integral part of Spain and form an autonomous province. The population of the islands is just over half a million and they cover an area of 5,000 kilometres. The capital is Palma de Mallorca. Although the tourist industry is of paramount importance for the islands' economies, agricultural production is also important (cereals, vegetables, capers, citrus fruits, figs and apricots). There are a number of small industries such as footwear, textiles and furniture making. The islands have their own language, Mallorquín, a close relation of CATALÁN.

ISLAS CANARIAS
The ISLAS CANARIAS are situated in the Atlantic Oceon, to the south-west of Morocco and one hundred miles from the African coast. There are seven inhabited islands and six islets, divided into two provinces. Las Palmas has its capital in Las Palmas on GRAN CANARIA island and TENERIFE at Santa Cruz on TENERIFE island. The islands consitute an AUTONOMÍA and have a population of 1.4 million people. Tourism, shipping, fishing and agriculture are the basis of the islands' economies with tourism accounting for nearly 70% of the islands' GDP. Approximately 70% of the population is engaged in the service sector. Agriculture is also important, especially the production of bananas, tomatoes and potatoes. As with other areas in Spain, the growing shortage of water is one of the major problems facing the island. The ISLAS CANARIAS do not participate in the Common Agricultural Policy of the European Union nor in the Common Customs Regime. The islands have free port status and are a low tax area.

ISLAS CHAFARINAS
A group of islands off the Moroccan coast. Their status is that of a *plaza de soberanía* and thus they come under Spanish jurisdiction.

ISM See: *INSTITUTO SOCIAL DE LA MARINA*

ITOIZ
It is proposed to construct a dam (the ITOIZ) in the valley of the Irati (NAVARRA) to which there is considerable opposition.

Construction work has been sabotaged by members of a protest group, *Solidarios con* ITOIZ, and eight people were imprisoned in 1996 for their part in the sabotage.

ITURBE ABASOLO (1943–1987)

ITURBE ABASOLO, alias TXOMIN, was head of the Basque terrorist organisation ETA for a number of years. From his base in Algeria, he negotiated with the PSOE on possible solutions to the problems in the PAÍS VASCO. He himself was the object of various assassination attempts by the BVE or *Batallón Vasco Español*. He was killed in a traffic accident in February 1987.

IVA See: *IMPUESTO SOBRE EL VALOR AÑADIDO*

IZQUIERDA UNIDA

Coalition of left-wing parties headed by JULIO ANGUITA. It is the third most important party in the Spanish parliament. It was formed in 1986 by the PARTIDO COMUNISTA DE ESPAÑA, FEDERACIÓN PROGRESISTA, *El Partido Comunista de los Pueblos de España* y *El Partido de Acción Socialista*.

JARCHA
Pop group originally founded in 1972. It became famous for its protest song, *Libertad sin ira* ('Freedom without anger'). This song was again sung in the streets after the murder of MIGUEL ÁNGEL BLANCO GARRIDO by the Basque terrorist group ETA.

JARRAI
Illegal organisation of young Basques dedicated to obtaining independence for the PAÍS VASCO through street violence. Their average age is 17–22 and they are, for the most part, students.

JÁUREGUI, RAMÓN (1949–   )
Basque politician, currently leader of the Basque section of PSOE. He is a *consejero* in the Basque parliament and *secretario general* of the PSE. He was elected to the executive of the PSOE in June 1997 and is responsible for relations with the autonomous governments.

JEREZ
Wines produced in the area around Jerez de la Frontera, el Puerto de Santa María and Sanlúcar de Barrameda (Cádiz). In Spain it is usually drunk as an apéritif in flute-shaped glasses. The alcohol content is from 18 to 25%. Among the more famous types of JEREZ are *fino*, *amontillado* and *oloroso*.

JIJONA
Town in ALICANTE, famous for the production of TURRÓN or nougat.

ELS JOGLARS
Experimental Catalán theatre company, whose director is ALBERTO BOADELLA. Among its most popular productions have been *Columbi lapsus*, a personal vision of the papacy and death

of Pope John Paul I and *Yo tengo un tío en América*, about the discovery and conquest of America.

JONDE See: *LA JOVEN ORQUESTA NACIONAL DE ESPAÑA*

JORNADA LABORAL
The length of the Spanish working week is 40 hours: employees are not allowed to work for more than 9 hours a day. Workers less than 18 years old are only permitted to work 8 hours a day.

JOTA
Traditional dance and music, most common in ARAGÓN, but heard and seen widely elsewhere.

LA JOVEN ORQUESTA NACIONAL DE ESPAÑA
Spanish Youth Orchestra. They were the first Spanish orchestra to play at the London Promenade Concerts.

JUBILACIÓN PARCIAL
Spanish workers may take part-time retirement if they are aged between 62 and 65 years old and are eligible for a pension. They usually work a half-day and earn half-pay.

JÚCAR
River, 498 kilometres in length, which flows through the province of VALENCIA and out into the Mediterranean to the north of Gandía.

JUEGO DE ROL
Role-play games in which the participants take on a fictitious identity and act out situations in accordance with it. These games acquired notoriety in 1994 when two youths killed an elderly man because their 'script' required them to do so.

JUEGOS OLÍMPICOS 1992
BARCELONA was the host city for the JUEGOS OLÍMPICOS of 1992. The games were marked by brilliant opening and closing ceremonies and by the best showing by Spanish sportsmen in any world competition.

JUEVES NEGRO

Black Thursday, 13th May 1993. This was the day on which Spain was obliged to devalue the peseta by 13% – much more than the EMU regulations allowed.

JUJEM See: *JUNTA DE JEFES DE ESTADO MAYOR*

JUNTA DE ANDALUCÍA

Name by which the autonomous government of ANDALUCÍA is known.

JUNTA DE JEFES DE ESTADO MAYOR

After the demise of FRANCO, the MINISTERIO DE DEFENSA was established and responsibility for the military given to the JUNTA, or council of joint chiefs of staff. The JUNTA was reorganised in 1984 and its head renamed the *Jefe del Estado Mayor de la Defensa*.

JUNTA DE PORTAVOCES

Each parliamentary party elects a spokesman or *portavoz* to represent it before the PRESIDENTE (or Speaker) and on other important occasions. The spokesmen come together, in the JUNTA, once a week, to agree on matters such as agendas for meetings and debates and the dates and times of parliamentary sittings.

JUNTA DIRECTIVA NACIONAL

The most important body of the PARTIDO POPULAR between the national congresses which take place every three years. The JUNTA meets every four months to ensure that the decisions and directives of the congress are implemented and to designate the party's candidate for prime minister.

JUNTA ELECTORAL

The JUNTAS ELECTORALES oversee and administer elections throughout Spain. They are organised hierarchically, from the JUNTA ELECTORAL *Central* in MADRID, through 52 provincial JUNTAS down to the hundreds of JUNTAS ELECTORALES *de Zona*. The JUNTAS are composed of members of the judiciary.

JUNTAS GENERALES

In the PAÍS VASCO, these are the equivalent of a provincial parliament or regional council. The members are directly elected.

JURADO, ROCÍO (1945–   )

Singer and actress. She married the bullfighter Ortega Cano in February 1995. She appears regularly in the REVISTAS DEL CORAZÓN.

JUVENTUDES SOCIALISTAS

Junior branch of the PSOE.

JUZGADO

Generic name for a court of law. There are several types including the JUZGADO *de lo civil* (civil court), JUZGADO *de lo penal* (criminal court), JUZGADO *de lo social* (employment court) and JUZGADO *de lo contencioso-administrativo* (administrative court).

JUZGADO DE INSTRUCCIÓN

The office of an examining judge or magistrate.

JUZGADO DE PAZ

Lowest level of court which decides minor civil and criminal offences known as *faltas*. They are presided over by the *juez de paz* (justice of the peace) who does not require legal training.

KAS See: *KOORDINADORA ABERTZALE SOZIALISTA*

KOIPE, S.A.
This company operated in the food manufacturing sector and produces olive, sunflower and other edible oils as well as margarine and mayonnaise. It is based in the north of Spain, primarily in SAN SEBASTIÁN, SANTIAGO and PAMPLONA.

KOORDINADORA ABERTZALE SOZIALISTA
Umbrella group for extreme Basque nationalist organisations, created in 1975. It is no longer allied to the trade union LAB, JARRAI or to the womens' movement *Egizan* but HERRI BATASUNA still forms part of its membership, along with a revolutionary workers' party, LAIA, and a handful of small left-wing nationalist parties.

KOPLOWITZ, ALICIA (1952–   )
One of the famous KOPLOWITZ sisters, she is the *vicepresidenta* of the holding company FOMENTO DE CONSTRUCCIONES Y CONTRATAS. Together with her sister, she holds 56.5% of the shares. She is said to be one of the richest women in the world.

KOPLOWITZ, ESTHER (1950–   )
One of the famous KOPLOWITZ sisters, she is a business-woman who is a major share-holder in and *vicepresidenta* of FOMENTO DE CONSTRUCCIONES Y CONTRATAS. According to the American magazine *Fortune*, she is one of the richest women in the world.

KRAUS, ALFREDO (1927–   )
Internationally known lyric tenor, he made his début in Cairo in 1956, in *Rigoletto* but he first came to public attention in 1958 when he starred in *La Traviata* in Lisbon with the legendary Maria Callas. Less well-known than other tenors of the day,

KRAUS is felt by many opera lovers to be the most distinguished: he is especially appreciated in the French repertoire.

KROLL
International detective agency which was used to investigate the former head of BANESTO, MARIO CONDE.

LAB See: *LANGILE ABERTZALE BATZORDEA*

LAFORET, CARMEN (1921–)
Novelist, born in BARCELONA and winner of the PREMIO NADAL in 1944 with her novel, *Nada* (1944). Since then she has written many other novels including *La isla y los demonios*, *La llamada* and *La mujer nueva*.

LANDA, ALFREDO (1933–)
Film-actor who has appeared in over 100 films during his career. In the sixties he played a series of small comic roles in films like *Ninette y un señor de Murcia* (1965) but he progressively took on longer and more serious roles, eventually winning the prize for best actor at the Cannes Film Festival for his portrayal of *Paco* in *Los santos inocentes* (1984). He also gained considerable success as *Sancho Panza* in the television series *El Quijote* (1991).

LANGILE ABERTZALE BATZORDEA
This left-wing trade union is closely allied to HERRI BATASUNA and belongs to the KAS network of radical Basque organisations.

LANZAROTE
Eastern-most island of the CANARIAS archipelago, it appears black in colour due to its landscape of lava.

LARA HERNÁNDEZ, JOSÉ MANUEL (1914–)
Managing director and founder of the *Editorial Planeta*, which awards a prestigious literary prize annually, the *premio Planeta*. Winners have included JUAN MARSÉ, CARMEN LAFORET (1942) CARMEN RIERA and Pedro Mestre.

EL LARGUERO
Very popular sports programme presented by José Ramón de la Morena on CADENA SER. It has a daily audience of 1,463,000.

LASA ARTANO, JOSÉ ANTONIO

Together with JOSÉ IGNACIO ZABALA, LASA disappeared in Bayonne (France) in 1983. They were assumed to have been kidnapped by GAL which later claimed responsibility for their 'execution' in 1984. Corpses exhumed in Busot (Alicante) were later identified as theirs. Evidence suggests that they were shot by members of the GUARDIA CIVIL.

LATIFUNDISMO

System of land ownership in ANDALUCÍA and EXTREMADURA. Much of the land is concentrated into large estates (*latifundios*) with single landowners. Land tenure for the working man is almost impossible and wealth is concentrated in the hands of very few.

LAVADO DE DINERO

Also known as *blanqueo de dinero*, this term relates to the phenomenon of money-laundering. The problem for some Spaniards is how to put illegally acquired money into general circulation without attracting the attention of the Tax Inspectorate. Money in Spain can be acquired illegally either through trafficking in drugs or via the 'black economy' – that is, working (often in the construction or footwear industry) without declaring this to the authorities.

LAVAPIÉS

Working-class district in the heart of MADRID.

LÁZARO CARRETER, FERNANDO (1923–   )

University professor and director of the REAL ACADEMIA DE LA LENGUA. He has been a member since 1972 and became director in 1991. Among other works, he has published the *Diccionario de Términos Filológicos and Estudios de Lingüística*. He has won several prizes, including the *Premio Aznar* in 1982 and the *Mariano de Cavia* in 1984.

LAZO AZUL

The blue ribbon was worn initially by non-militant Basques as a symbol of their rejection of ETA and its policy of kidnapping prominent members of the business community and holding them to ransom. Its use has now been extended to the whole of Spain.

LECTURAS

One of the so-called REVISTAS DEL CORAZÓN and the only one edited in BARCELONA. It has a readership of almost two million. It specialises in articles on European royal families and on television and film personalities.

LEGIÓN EXTRANJERA

The foreign legion, originally modelled on the French Foreign Legion. It was founded in 1920 by Milán Astray and though originally known as the *Tercio de Extranjeros*, never had more than a sprinkling of foreign members. It has recently been renamed the *Brigada Rey Alfonso XIII*, partly in an attempt to rid it of its unsavoury reputation.

LEGISLATURA

Word used to refer to the national parliament between one election and the next.

LEGUINA, JOAQUÍN (1941–)

Presidente of the AUTONOMÍA of Madrid from 1983 to 1995. He was also *concejal de Hacienda* in the AYUNTAMIENTO of MADRID when ENRIQUE TIERNO GALVÁN was mayor. He was defeated in the 1995 elections and Alberto Ruiz Gallardón of the PARTIDO POPULAR succeeded him as *presidente*. Currently, he is on the executive of the PSOE and is responsible for *Cultura*. He is a DIPUTADO for MADRID.

LEHENDAKARI

Basque name for the leader of the Basque autonomous government. Currently (1996) the LEHENDAKARI is JOSÉ ANTONIO ARDANZA.

LEMÓNIZ

Nuclear power station in the PAÍS VASCO, currently being decommissioned. Spain has nine nuclear power stations in operation and three (LEMÓNIZ, Valdecaballeros and Vandellós 1) which are no longer functioning.

LETRADO

Parliamentary clerk. He or she has received a legal training.

LEVANTE

This term (literally meaning the east) is usually employed when referring to the coastal area from Castellón to Murcia. The word *levantino* is used for persons or things from VALENCIA, which comprises the three provinces of Alicante, VALENCIA and Castellón.

LEY ANTITERRORISTA

This law, originally passed in 1977 and subsequently modified, allows the rights of detainees to be suspended if terrorist acts are suspected. Such rights include access to a lawyer.

LEY CORCUERA

The former *ministro del Interior*, JOSÉ LUIS CORCUERA, attempted to establish a law allowing the police to enter the homes of suspected criminals, without a warrant. This law (officially known as *La Ley de Protección de la Seguridad Ciudadana*) was brought to the TRIBUNAL CONSTITUCIONAL by the party in opposition at the time (the PARTIDO POPULAR). It was eventually declared anti-constitutional.

LEY DE COMERCIO

This law was passed in 1995. It deregulated the permitted opening hours of shops, a measure which proved profoundly unpopular with small shop-keepers.

LEY DE COMPETENCIA DESLEAL

Law which forbids the sale of products at less than their cost price.

LEY DE COSTAS

This Act, passed in 1988, was designed to protect Spain's coastlines from further development.

LEY DE INCOMPATIBILIDADES DE ALTOS CARGOS

This law ensures that ministers may not occupy any other post other than their ministerial office. This is to ensure that corruption, insider dealing, etc. is avoided. Ministers must also declare their assets and extra-governmental activities. These are recorded in the *Registro de Actividades de Altos Cargos* (the Register of the Activities of Senior Civil Servants).

LEY DE INTEGRACIÓN SOCIAL DE LOS MINUSVÁLIDOS

A law, passed in 1982, whose objective was to provide better care for disabled people. Among its provisions were support for carers and mobility allowances.

LEY DE ORGANIZACIÓN Y FUNCIONAMIENTO DE LA ADMINISTRACIÓN GENERAL DEL ESTADO

A law designed to simplify and streamline administrative procedures and to clarify the links between the state and the AUTONOMÍAS. It was passed in 1983 and introduced two new grades to the Spanish Civil Service, both of which are public appointees rather than career civil servants. These grades are the SECRETARIO DE ESTADO AND THE SECRETARIO GENERAL.

LEY DE PRESUPUESTOS GENERALES DEL ESTADO

This law (or budget) establishes, annually, the salary scales for civil servants, such as teachers, post office workers, local government workers, etc.

LEY DE PROTECCIÓN Y FOMENTO DE LA CINEMATOGRAFÍA

This law was passed in 1994 with a view to protecting the Spanish cinema industry. Two articles proved especially controversial: article 7, which states that distributors must obtain a licence in order to screen dubbed American films. This licence is only granted under certain conditions. Another article decrees that exhibitors may show American films on three days, if they show European films on at least one.

LEY DE RECONVERSIÓN Y REINDUSTRIALIZACIÓN

This law, passed in 1984, aimed to modernise, rationalise and restructure some of Spain's ailing industries, including shipbuilding and the iron and steel industry. Early retirement packages and *Fondos de Promoción de Empleo* (FPE) were established for the large numbers of workers laid off or made redundant.

LEY DE REFORMA UNIVERSITARIA

This law upholds the principle of university autonomy and

divides responsibility for university education between the state, the AUTONOMÍAS and the universities themselves. Decentralisation of responsibilities has meant that individual universities now have full academic and financial responsibility and are able to hire and promote their own staff.

LEY DE REPRODUCCIÓN ASISTIDA

The law regulating artificial reproduction was passed in 1988. According to the law there is a limit of five years for conserving frozen embryos and sperm, but it does not stipulate what should happen to this material once the limit has passed. The law also decreed the creation of a Commission on Human Fertilization which would advise on ethical issues surrounding in vitro fertilisation. This Commission has never met.

LEY DE TELECOMUNICACIONES POR CABLE

Passed in 1995, this law regulates the use of the cable network throughout Spain.

LEY DE TESTIGOS PROTEGIDOS

This law aims to protect witnesses in legal cases from possible reprisals. The police is able to give these people new identities, a new home and police protection. A recent example of this policy in action is the witness known as 1964/S in the *caso* LASA and ZABALA.

LEY GENERAL DE SANIDAD

This law, passed in 1986, set out the framework for the Spanish Health Service or SNS. See also: SERVICIO NACIONAL DE SALUD

LEY ORGÁNICA DE ARMONIZACIÓN DEL PROCESO AUTONÓMICO

This law, passed in 1981, concerned the regulations for establishing the autonomous regions. It proved highly controversial as it attempted to limit Basque and Catalán autonomy to the level set by the lower aspirations of the other autonomous regions. Many of its provisions were later declared unconstitutional.

LEY ORGÁNICA DE FINANCIACIÓN DE LAS COMUNIDADES AUTÓNOMAS

Law regulating the financing of the individual autonomous

regions. The autonomies received block grants from central government: they were also allowed to retain monies from sources such as certain types of tax, fines and so on.

LEY ORGÁNICA DE LIBERTAD SINDICAL

This law came into effect in 1985. It established the rights and responsibilities of trades unions (which were illegal under the FRANCO régime) and gave all Spaniards the right to found, join or work for a trade union.

LEY ORGÁNICA DE ORDENACIÓN GENERAL DEL SISTEMA EDUCATIVO

This law, passed in 1990 and known as the LOGSE, overhauls the whole Spanish educational system and will only be fully implemented in the year 2000. Among other provisions, the law sets out quality standards with respect to facilities, teaching staff and student-teacher ratios. Private schools continue to maintain their own educational or religious philosophy, but are contracted in: that is, they are subsidized by the state, are free to students and offer the same curriculum as state schools. Under the new system, pre-school is divided into two cycles. The first ends when the child is three (so far 31% of children in this age group attend school) and the second cycle extends from 3 to 6. The first cycle of primary school includes children from 6 to 12 and the second cycle from 12 to 16. From 16 to 18, young people study for the BACHILLERATO. This programme of studies has four options. All options include core subjects such as Physical Education, Philosophy, a foreign language, Spanish Language and Literature and History. At 18, students may either continue studying (at the University) do a course in vocational training (FORMACIÓN PROFESIONAL) or enter the job market.

LEY ORGÁNICA DE PARTICIPACIÓN, EVALUACIÓN, Y GOBIERNO DE LOS CENTROS DOCENTES

This law amplifies those measures set out in the LEY ORGÁNICA DEL DERECHO A LA EDUCACIÓN: it grants further autonomy to schools and colleges, regulates the governing bodies of these institutions and deals with assessment, inspection and public accountability issues. It also establishes regulations for pupils with special needs.

LEY ORGÁNICA DE RÉGIMEN ELECTORAL GENERAL
This law, passed in 1985, lays down the rules for elections and establishes, among other things, that there be 350 members of parliament and that elections be free, universal, equal and secret.

LEY ORGÁNICA DE REGULACIÓN DEL TRATAMIENTO AUTOMATIZADO DE DATOS PERSONALES
Law which regulates the use of databases and personal information recorded thereon.

LEY ORGÁNICA DE REINTEGRACIÓN Y AMEJORAMIENTO DEL RÉGIMEN FORAL DE NAVARRA
This law was passed in 1982 to affirm the historical rights of NAVARRA by virtue of its FUEROS. It is in effect the statute of autonomy of this region and confirms its already existing powers and privileges.

LEY ORGÁNICA DEL DERECHO A LA EDUCACIÓN
This law, passed in 1985 and known as the LODE, created Schools Councils whose function is to enable all interested parties to participate in school management, including teachers, parents and students. These councils (i) elect the principal of the school (ii) approve and apply internal rules and regulations (iii) establish an annual programme of activities (iv) approve and supervise the budget (v) deal with student admissions (vi) appoint teachers (in private schools). The LODE has also attempted to democratise the intake of private schools (which make up one third of educational provision in Spain) by subsidising them and making them non fee-paying. All schools which receive state subsidies must offer free education, be governed by School Councils and adhere to the same admission requirements for all students.

LEY ORGÁNICA DEL PODER JUDICIAL
Law passed in 1997 which prohibits members of the judiciary from returning immediately to this profession if they have been

candidates in an election or have had a political appointment. They must wait for 3 years with full pay before practising as judges or magistrates. The aim of the law is to ensure the separation of the judiciary and political life.

LEY PARA LA REFORMA POLÍTICA
The first reform law to be passed after the death of FRANCO in 1976, which set Spain on the path to true democracy and the overhaul of the entire political, social and economic system.

LEY REGULADORA DE LAS BASES DE RÉGIMEN LOCAL
This law which regulates local government was passed in 1985. It sets out the framework for local government and its relation to the federal and central systems.

LEY REGULADORA DE LAS HACIENDAS LOCALES
Law passed in 1988 whose function was to simplify and coordinate local taxes. At present there are only three compulsory taxes: the tax on real estate, vehicles and certain economic activities.

LEYES ORDINARIAS
An Act of Parliament. These LEYES are the most common type of law, a simple majority being required for their approval by the CORTES. See also: LEYES ORGÁNICAS

LEYES ORGÁNICAS
These constitutional laws occupy a status midway between the CONSTITUCIÓN and ordinary laws or acts of parliament (LEYES ORDINARIAS). They can only be approved, modified or repealed by an overall majority of the CONGRESO in a final vote on the entire text of the bill.

LGS See: *LEY GENERAL DE SANIDAD*

LIBERTAD SIN IRA
Protest song first composed in the early 1970s by Pablo Herrera and José Luis Armenteros and made famous by the group JARCHA. It was sung again during the demonstrations against the murder of MIGUEL ÁNGEL BLANCO GARRIDO in July 1997.

LIBRO BLANCO DE LA EDUCACIÓN

The principal tenets of the reform of Spanish education were laid down in the LIBRO BLANCO, published in 1969. Many of these tenets became law in 1971 with the *Ley General de Educación*.

LICENCIATURA

The diploma given to students who have completed the first and second *ciclos* at the university. It is equivalent to a first degree.

LICEU

Barcelona Opera House in which many famous Spanish singers made their début, including MONTSERRAT CABALLÉ and JOSÉ CARRERAS. It was partially destroyed by fire in 1994 and is currently being rebuilt by public subscription. It has always been considered a symbol of the BARCELONA bourgeoisie.

LICOR (DE FRUTAS)

In recent years, it has become increasingly popular in Spain to finish one's meal with a liqueur. Spanish liqueurs are made with a brandy base to which various fruit extracts are added (apple, mandarine, hazel-nut, etc.). They are also called *chupitos* ('little sips') because of the small size in which these liqueurs are served, though *chupito* can refer to a small measure of any spirit or liqueur.

LA LIGA

Football competition in which each division competes (Divisions 1, 2A and 2B and 3) and each team plays each other. The best team in terms of games won and goals scored is the winner: this team then goes on to play in the *Liga de Campeones*.

LÍNEAS ERÓTICAS

In 1992, it was decided to prohibit the so-called erotic phone lines prefixed by 903. This decision was reached when it was discovered that some lines were being used to promote the prostitution of young people.

LISMI See: *LEY DE INTEGRACIÓN SOCIAL DE LOS MINUSVÁLIDOS*

LITRONA

This term refers to the litre bottle (usually of beer) which groups of youths buy in supermarkets and drink in town or city squares and streets. This phenomenon is known as the *cultura de la litrona*.

LLACH, LLUIS (1948–   )

Song-writer and singer from CATALUÑA. LLACH was an important member of the *Nova Cançó* movement and therefore only sang in CATALÁN. He is especially interested in Mediterranean music and its origins and has worked extensively with North African musicians.

LOAPA See: *LEY ORGÁNICA DE ARMONIZACIÓN DEL PROCESO AUTÓNOMICO*

LOBATÓN, PACO

Popular television journalist and presenter. One of his recent successes has been his programme on TVE-1, *¿Quién sabe dónde?* one of the most popular reality shows in Spain which attempts to find people who have disappeared.

LODE See: *LEY ORGÁNICA DEL DERECHO A LA EDUCACIÓN*

LOEWE

Prestigious Spanish company which manufactures and sells luxury leather goods. It was founded in 1846 by Enrique LOEWE Roessberg in MADRID and now has 20 shops in Spain and 60 retail outlets outside. It is particularly strong in Japan. The company was bought by *Louis Vuitton Moët Hennessy* in 1996 on the 150th anniversary of its foundation.

LOFAGE See: *LEY DE ORGANIZACIÓN Y FUNCIONAMIENTO DE LA ADMINISTRACIÓN GENERAL DEL ESTADO*

LOFCA See: *LEY ORGÁNICA DE FINACIACIÓN DE LAS COMUNIDADES AUTÓNOMAS*

LOGSE See: *LEY ORGÁNICA DE ORDENACIÓN GENERAL DEL SISTEMA EDUCATIVO*

LOLS See: *LEY ORGÁNICA DE LIBERTAD SINDICAL*

LOPEG See: *LEY ORGÁNICA DE PARTICIPACIÓN, EVALUACIÓN Y GOBIERNO DE LOS CENTROS DOCENTES*

LÓPEZ ARANGUREN, JOSÉ LUIS (1909–1996)
Philosopher and essayist, ARANGUREN specialised in religion and ethics. He was a professor at the UNIVERSIDAD AUTÓNOMA DE MADRID. Among his better known works are *Ética y política* and *Moral y sociedad.*

LÓPEZ VÁZQUEZ, JOSÉ LUIS (1922–   )
Veteran film actor, LÓPEZ VÁZQUEZ has been working in the Spanish cinema for over 40 years. He is especially known for his comic roles in films such as *La escopeta nacional* (1977) and *Todos a la cárcel* (1993) but he is also a talented character actor who has worked as such with many of the leading Spanish film directors.

LOREG See: *LEY ORGÁNICA DE RÉGIMEN ELECTORAL GENERAL*

LORTAD See: *LEY ORGÁNICA DE REGULACIÓN DEL TRATAMIENTO AUTOMATIZADO DE DATOS PERSONALES*

LOS DEL RÍO
Popular musical duo from SEVILLA. The two singers (Rafael Ruiz and Antonio Romero) shot to fame in 1996 when their song *Macarena* became an international hit.

LRBRL See: *LEY REGULADORA DE LAS BASES DE RÉGIMEN LOCAL*

LRU See: *LEY DE REFORMA UNIVERSITARIA*

LUCDEME See: *LUCHA CONTRA LA DESERTIFICACIÓN EN EL MEDITERRÁNEO*

LUCHA CONTRA LA DESERTIFICACIÓN EN EL MEDITERRÁNEO
An organisation to which Spain, Italy and Greece belong and

whose objective is to combat desertification in the countries of Southern Europe.

LUDOPATÍA

Compulsive gambling is felt to be especially prevalent in Spain, with two to four of every 100 Spaniards being gambling addicts, according to clinical psychologists. Casinos and bingo halls can be required to maintain a register of hardcore addicts and deny them entrance. The majority of those listed are on the register by their own request, but in some cases, relatives seek court injunctions to prevent their relatives from frequenting gaming halls.

EL LUTE (ELEUTERIO SÁNCHEZ) (1942–   )

EL LUTE became famous in the 1970s as the most wanted man in Spain and as a celebrated escapologist. Although he never committed any serious crime, a legend grew up around him and he became known as a heartless robber and bandit. While in prison, he studied law; he was released in 1981. A series of films was made about his life.

MACBA See: *MUSEO DE ARTE CONTEMPORÁNEO DE BARCELONA*

LOS MADEROS

Slang term for the police, whose uniform changed from grey to brown in 1978. *Madera* is the general word for wood. Prior to this date, the police were known as *los grises*.

MADRE DE ALQUILER

Surrogate mother. Surrogacy in prohibited in Spain under the 1988 LEY DE TÉCNICAS DE REPRODUCCIÓN ASISTIDA.

MADRID

MADRID is one of the AUTONOMÍAS; the city of MADRID is its regional capital, as well as being the national capital. It has a population of almost five million inhabitants and covers an area of 7,995 kilometres. It is situated in the very centre of the Spanish peninsula. The city of MADRID is the major administrative, banking and transportation centre of Spain and is the Spanish headquarters of most national and international companies. Industries include light engineering, electronic components, construction and food and drink processing. The industrial base of the city is currently being developed, especially new, high-tech industries. MADRID is also important in the service sector.

MAESTRANZA

The bull ring in SEVILLA, also known as the *Plaza de Toros de la Real*. It comes into its own during the *Fiesta de Abril*. It can seat up to 12,538 spectators.

MAESTRE, PEDRO (1967–)

Young novelist, born in Alcoi (Alicante). He won the PREMIO

NADAL in 1996 for his first novel, *Matando dinosaurios con tirachinas*.

MAESTRO

Primary school teacher who has obtained a university degree over 3 years. One must be a MAESTRO/A to be allowed to work in an *escuela primaria* or primary school. One may specialise in different areas such as foreign language teaching, physical education or music. The same qualification is required for nursery education.

MAGISTRADOS

Judges who work collectively in courts at higher levels of the judicial system.

MAHOU

Second largest brewery in Spain. Spain itself is the third largest producer of beers in Europe, preceded only by Germany and the United Kingdom. In 1996 the company was forced to close its MADRID factory due to the falling consumption of beer in Spain and high taxes.

MAKETO

Basque name for other Spaniards coming into the Basque country to live or work.

MALLORCA

The biggest of the ISLAS BALEARES. It has exceptionally attractive beaches which have led to the promotion of tourism on the coast: the interior is entirely given over to agriculture and small scale industry. Its capital, Palma de Mallorca, is also the capital of the autonomous community of the BALEARES.

MAÑAS, JOSÉ ÁNGEL (1971–   )

Novelist, the author of two books, *Las historias del Kronen* and *Mensaka* (1995). *Las historias del Kronen*, which recounts the story of young hooligans in MADRID sold over 60,000 copies. It has recently been made into a film.

MANCHEGO (QUESO)

The best-known of Spanish cheeses, made in LA MANCHA. There

are a number of types ranging from mild to strong, depending on how long the cheese has been left to mature.

MANCOMUNIDAD

Because many MUNICIPALIDADES are very small, some have come together to provide joint services to the inhabitants of a larger area or MANCOMUNIDAD.

MANDO SUPREMO DE LAS FUERZAS ARMADAS

Commander-in-Chief of the Armed Forces; this is the monarch.

MANGLANO, LUIS (1954–)

Examining magistrate in VALENCIA, Manglano investigated the *caso Naseiro* in 1990, in which ROSENDO NASEIRO, Ángel Sanchis, Salvador Palop and José Balaguer were accused of illegally financing the PARTIDO POPULAR.

MANZANARES

The river which runs through MADRID. Unlike other European capitals, MADRID does not have a developed river side with quays or promenades.

MANZANARES, JOSÉ LUIS (1930–)

Lawyer, currently *vicepresidente* of the CONSEJO GENERAL DEL PODER JUDICIAL. He has been *juez*, *magistrado* and LETRADO in the MINISTERIO DE JUSTICIA, among other professional posts.

MANZANILLA

Infusion made from camomile flowers and recommended for stomach complaints. It is also the name of a type of JEREZ.

MAPFRE

Group of Spanish insurance companies. The company began life in 1933 as the *Mutua de Propietarios de Fincas Rústicas de España* (a mutual fund founded by a group of landowners) but it gradually grew in importance until it created a network of specialist companies, dealing in travel, accident and life insurance. The *Fundación* MAPFRE, an offshoot of MAPFRE, is an educational foundation concerned with research and training in human safety, and accident prevention.

MAR EGEO

The MAR EGEO is the Greek oil tanker which foundered just off La Coruña in 1993 and caused serious pollution on the Galician coast. The seafood industry in this area has been badly affected.

MARAGALL, PASQUAL (1941–   )

Catalán politician and Mayor of BARCELONA since 1982 when he succeeded NARCÍS SERRA in this post. He was instrumental in obtaining, financing and organising the 1992 Olympic Games in BARCELONA. He is a very popular figure.

MARCA

Daily newspaper, devoted to sport, founded in SAN SEBASTIÁN in 1938. It has been published in MADRID since 1940. It has a circulation of about 113,000.

MARCOS COMUNITARIOS DE APOYO

This is the Spanish term for the (European) Community Support Framework agreements. Local regions can now bypass central government and bid directly for EU funds.

MARE NOSTRUM, S.A.

Founded in 1942, this insurance company specialises in vehicle and life insurance.

MARÍA GUERRERO

One of the most important theatres in Madrid.

MARÍAS, JAVIER (1951–   )

Author of a number of very successful novels, including *Mañana en la batalla piensa en mí*, *Corazón tan blanco* and *Todas las almas*. His latest work, a collection of short stories entitled *Cuando fui mortal*, was published in 1996. Also in 1996, a film version of *Todas las almas* was directed by GRACIA QUEREJETA. This proved a rather controversial adaptation and was not approved by MARÍAS himself. MARÍAS has won many prizes including the *Premio Herralde de Novela*, the *Premio Ciudad de* BARCELONA and the *Premio de la Crítica*.

MARICHALAR, JAIME DE (1963–   )

A Spanish aristocrat who married the eldest daughter of King

JUAN CARLOS in 1995. He was born in Pamplona in 1963. After specialising in business studies and marketing he began his career in international banking and currently works in the private banking sector.

MARISCAL DE GANTE, MARGARITA (1954–)

Ministro de Justicia, appointed by JOSÉ MARÍA AZNAR in 1996. Formerly a member of the CONSEJO GENERAL DEL PODER JUDICIAL, this former judge is the first woman minister for Justice in Spain.

MARISCAL, JAVIER (1950–)

Designer and graphic artist, born in VALENCIA. He became internationally famous for inventing COBI, the mascot of the 1992 Olympic Games in BARCELONA. His cartoons frequently appear in EL PAÍS *Semanal* the weekly supplement to EL PAÍS.

MARISMAS

The marsh-lands in the GUADALQUIVIR basin in ANDALUCÍA. This is where the world famous COTO DOÑANA is located; it is also the largest rice-growing area in Spain.

MARISOL (1948–)

MARISOL (Josefa Flores González) was discovered at the age of eleven, by the film producer Manuel J. Goyanes and appeared in a number of musical comedies in the 1960s including *Cabriola* (1965) by Mel Ferrer and *La nueva cenicienta* (1964) by George Sherman. In the 1970s she began to work in more erotic films such as *La chica del Molino Rojo* (1976). Later she changed her name to Pepa Flores and appeared in *Bodas de Sangre* (1981) and *Carmen* (1983), both directed by CARLOS SAURA. She has since retired from show business.

MARIVENT

The summer palace of the Royal Family in Mallorca. It is a former museum which overlooks a bay just outside Palma.

MARSANS

Second largest travel organisation in Spain with a turnover of 130,000 million pesetas in 1995. Its two retail chains are *Viajes* MARSANS and *Viajes VIE*. It has a 51% share in an airline (SPANAIR) and owns 9 hotels (*Hotetur*).

MARSÉ, JUAN (1933–   )

CATALÁN writer; in 1995 he won the *Premio Europa* (awarded by the EU) for his latest novel, *El embrujo de Shanghai*. Among his others novels are: *La muchacha de las bragas de oro* (later made into a film which won the *Premio Planeta* in 1978) and *Últimas tardes con Teresa* (which received the *Premio Biblioteca Breve*).

MARSILLACH SORIANO, ADOLFO (1928–   )

Theatre director, he runs the *Compañia Nacional de Teatro Clásico*. He is well-known for his staging of world classics.

MARTES Y TRECE

Popular comedy duo. They take their name from Tuesday the 13th, an unlucky day in Spain. They appear frequently on Spanish television and host one of the most important programmes of the year on New Year's Eve. They have also made several comedies for the cinema. In 1997 the pair split up and each began separate television careers.

MARTÍN GAITE, CARMEN (1925–   )

Novelist, translator and writer, CARMEN MARTÍN GAITE has won numerous literary prizes, including the *Premio Café de Gijón* in 1954 for El Balneario, the PREMIO NADAL in 1958 for *Entre visillos* and the *Premio Nacional de la Literatura* in 1978 for *El Cuarto de atrás*. Her latest novel, *Lo raro es vivir*, was published in 1996.

MARTÍNEZ BORDIÚ, CRISTÓBAL (1922–   )

General FRANCO's son-in-law. He was trained as a surgeon and as a doctor, and was in attendance at FRANCO's death bed. Latterly he has devoted himself to the FRANCO family's financial affairs.

MARTÍNEZ, CONCHITA

Tennis player. She won Wimbledon in 1994 and the Italian Open in 1995.

MARTÍNEZ-BORDIÚ, CARMEN (1951–   )

General FRANCO's grand-daughter, originally married to Alfonso de Borbón Dampierre, the grandson of Alfonso XIII. She separated in 1979 and married a Frenchman, Jean-Pierre Rossi. As Carmen Rossi, she frequently appeared in the popular press as a member of the jet set. She divorced Rossi in 1995.

MARTÍNEZ-BORDIÚ, MARÍA DEL CARMEN (1956–   )

MARÍA DEL CARMEN ('Merry') is one of General FRANCO's grand-daughters. Originally married to the journalist, Jimmy Jiménez Arnau from whom she is divorced. She is now resident in the United States.

MASÍA

Large farm with its attendant farm-house in CATALUÑA. In this area, land was usually left to the eldest son and thus fragmentation of property was avoided. See also: MINIFUNDIO

MASIFICACIÓN

Term used to denote chronic over-crowding, usually in the university system.

MATERNIDAD

Persons of either sex can take paid maternity leave if they have made a minimum of 180 days social security payments in the previous five years. Paid leave can last up to 16 weeks (18 for a multiple birth), 4 of which can be taken by the father if the mother so chooses. Shorter periods of paid leave are available for those adopting.

MATRIMONIO CIVIL

Since the coming of democracy it is quite usual for couples to have a civil rather than a religious wedding: that is, they marry in court, before a judge. One may also be married by the mayor (ALCALDE) in some town halls.

MATUTES, ABEL (1941–   )

Politician from the ISLAS BALEARES, MATUTES has been a DIPUTADO (from 1979 to 1986), SENADOR (from 1977 to 1979), and a European Commissioner (from 1986 to 1994). He has represented the PARTIDO POPULAR in the European Parliament and was appointed *ministro de Asuntos Exteriores* in the 1996 government of JOSÉ MARÍA AZNAR. He is one of the principal landowners in the ISLAS BALEARES and a very successful businessman.

MAURA, CARMEN (1945–   )

Distinguished film actress who first rose to prominence in the films of PEDRO ALMODÓVAR. She has appeared in *¿Qué he hecho* *yo para merecer esto?*, *La ley del deseo* and *Mujeres al borde de un ataque de nervios*. In 1989 she quarrelled with ALMODÓVAR and since then has not appeared in any of his productions, preferring to work instead with other directors such as CARLOS SAURA and MARIO CAMUS. One of her most famous roles was that of the variety artiste Carmela in *¡Ay Carmela!* (SAURA, 1989). In 1993 she played a more dramatic role, that of *Ana*, an ex-Basque terrorist, in *Sombras en una batalla* (CAMUS, 1993). She has since appeared in *Pareja de tres* (1995), *El palomo cojo* (1995), and *Hay amores que matan* (1996). She was recently honoured by the French government (1996).

MAYOR OREJA, JAIME (1951–   )

Basque politician, OREJA started his political career in 1977 with the UCD. He joined the PARTIDO POPULAR in 1989 and has been presidente of the PP in the PAÍS VASCO since 1990. In 1996 he became *ministro del Interior* in the AZNAR government.

MCA See: *MARCOS COMUNITARIOS DE APOYO*

MCC See: *MONDRAGÓN CORPORACIÓN COOPERATIVA*

MDT See: *MOVIMIENTO DE DEFENSA DE LA TERRA*

MEC See: *MINISTERIO DE EDUCACIÓN Y CULTURA*

MECANO

A very popular '80s pop group from MADRID with three members; Ana Torroja (born 1959) and two brothers, José María Cano (1959) and Nacho Cano (1963). They received a number of awards including a prize from the World Music Awards for the group with the highest sales in Spain. They appear twice in the *Guinness Book of Records*, for having sold more than 5 million discs in Spain and for having remained in the charts for 83 consecutive weeks. The group split up in the early '90s after their international hit *Una rosa es una rosa*.

MEDEM, JULIO (1958–   )

Young Basque film director. To date, Medem has directed three films, *Vacas*, *Ardilla Roja* and *Tierra*. He has won a number of national and international prizes for his blend of surrealism, violence, humour, hate and pride in being Basque.

MEDICUS MUNDI ESPANA
Spanish branch of a charitable organisation founded in Germany in 1962. It works in third world countries primarily in the field of health care and on nutrition, education and construction projects.

MEDINA FERNÁNDEZ DE CÓRDOBA, RAFAEL
RAFAEL MEDINA is the *duque de Feria* and has been tried on two occasions for corruption of minors. He is presently in jail in Sevilla. His former wife is NATI ABASCAL, a member of the jet-set.

MELILLA
A Spanish enclave on the North African coast. It is administered as an integral part of Spain. MELILLA has a population of 58,449 and an area of 14 square kilometres. Its existence, along with that of CEUTA, is deeply resented by Morocco and by its Muslim inhabitants, but since they predate Morocco as nations, there is no easy solution.

MÉNDEZ, CÁNDIDO (1952–   )
Chemical engineer and trade-union leader, he was re-elected *secretario-general* of the UGT in April 1995. He was elected a member of Parliament for PSOE at the age of 28 and was also a member of the Andalusian Parliament.

MENDILUCE, JOSÉ MARÍA (1951–   )
MENDILUCE has worked with the United Nations since 1980 and has sat in the European Parliament as an independent since 1994. During the Yugoslavian conflict, he worked as an envoy for the European Union.

MENDOZA, EDUARDO (1943–   )
Writer, born in BARCELONA, whose first novel, *La verdad sobre el caso Savolta* (1975) was an immediate success and which was later made into a film. It won the *Premio de la Crítica*. He has since written *El misterio de la cripta embrujada* (1979), *La ciudad de los prodigios* (1988), *La isla inaudita* (1992) and *Una comedia ligera* (1996).

MENORCA
Island in the ISLAS BALEARES archipelago. Its population is concentrated in the two largest towns, Ciudadela and Mahón. Ciudadela was occupied by the English throughout the 18th century and conserves many vestiges of this occupation. MENORCA is also interesting for its numerous megalithic monuments.

MERCADO RUIZ, ROSENDO (1954–   )
Rock musician, especially famous as a guitarist. His most important album has probably been *Loco por incordiar*. Among his better known songs are *Cucarachas*, *El Tren* and *Maneras de Vivir*.

MERCADOS CENTRALES DE ABASTECIMIENTO
Central market for the wholesale of meat, fish, fruit and vegetables.

MERCAMADRID
Biggest wholesale fruit, vegetable and meat market in MADRID.

MERCASA See: *MERCADOS CENTRALES DE ABASTECIMIENTO*

MERCHERO
Slang name for a peddlar or hawker.

MERINO, JOSÉ MARÍA (1941–   )
Novelist who explores the relation between life and fiction, dream and reality. His best known novel is *La orilla oscura*.

MESA DEL CONGRESO
The MESA DEL CONGRESO comprises the *Presidente*, two *vicepresidentes* and two *secretarios*. Its function is to organise parliamentary business, to draw up the order of business, to prepare a draft budget and supervise its implementation, and to evaluate all parliamentary papers and documents.

METROBUS
A ticket which is valid both for bus and underground travel.

METROPOLITANO DE MADRID
The full name of the underground train network in MADRID,

known popularly as the *metro*. Work was begun in 1917; today it has 11 lines and 126 stations.

MIGUEL, ARMANDO DE (1937–   )

Professor of sociology since 1970, he is the author of many books analysing Spanish society. Recently (1994–5) he represented the PARTIDO POPULAR at RTVE and acts as an official spokesman for the party on social affairs.

MILÁ, MERCEDES (1951–   )

Television journalist, she came first to public attention in 1978 with a programme of interviews which she made with Isabel Tenaille. In 1982 she presented a series called *Buenas Noches* and since that time she has worked on documentaries, news and current affairs programmes. In 1995 she made and presented a series which described Spain's movement towards democracy, entitled *La transición española*. In 1996 she published a book with the same title.

MILANS DEL BOSCH, JAIME (1915–   )

A high ranking soldier in the Spanish army, he was chief of the military region of VALENCIA in 1981. He took part in the failed coup against the democratic state on 23rd of February 1981and was sentenced to thirty years in prison. He was freed in 1990 when he reached his seventy-fifth birthday.

MILITANTES

These are card-carrying members of political parties.

MILLÁS, JUAN JOSÉ (1946–   )

Novelist and journalist. His best known novel is *El desorden de tu nombre* which has no fewer than 22 editions. His latest novel, *Tonto, muerto, bastardo e invisible*, was published in 1995. He won the PREMIO NADAL in 1990 for *La soledad era esto*.

MINER   See: *MINISTERIO DE INDUSTRÍA Y ENERGÍA*

MINGOTE, ANTONIO

Born in Sitges in 1919, MINGOTE began his career as a cartoonist in 1946 with the satirical magazine *La codorniz*. He has published a daily cartoon in ABC since 1953. He has also written two novels, *Las palmeras de cartón* (*Planeta*, 1948) and *Adelita en su desván* (*Planeta*, 1991). He was awarded the *Premio Nacional de Periodismo* in 1980, and was elected a member of the REAL ACADEMIA in 1987.

MINIFUNDIO
Small-holding, particularly in GALICIA. Property became more and more sub-divided with each generation, due to inheritance laws which ensured that all children had a right to an equal share in the property. Nowadays, many of these *minifundios* are sublet to people from nearby towns or to emigrants who have returned to GALICIA.

MINISTERIO DE ADMINISTRACIONES PÚBLICAS
This ministry is responsible for state bureaucracy at all levels – it heads the entire Civil Service, liaises with the autonomous governments and all local authorities, and transfers staff and resources from central to regional government.

MINISTERIO DE AGRICULTURA, PESCA Y ALIMENTACIÓN
The Ministry of Agriculture, Fishing and Food. At present, the minister is Loyola de Palacio del Valle-Lersundi. This ministry negotiates very actively with the EU on questions such as the transport of live animals, the olive industry, milk and fishing quotas etc.

MINISTERIO DE ASUNTOS EXTERIORES
The Foreign Office. The minister is currently (1997) ABEL MATUTES.

MINISTERIO DE DEFENSA
The Ministry of Defence which is responsible for the armed forces, and internal and external security. At present (1997) the minister is Eduardo Serra Rexach. INTA, the INSTITUTO NACIONAL DE TÉCNICA AEROESPACIAL, is part of this Ministry.

MINISTERIO DE ECONOMÍA Y HACIENDA
Ministry of Economy and Finance. This Ministry deals with state finance, economic planning and expenditure: with small and medium-sized companies: with tourism and the PARADOR net-

work. The INSTITUTO NACIONAL DE ESTADÍSTICA also falls within its ambit.

MINISTERIO DE EDUCACIÓN Y CULTURA
This Ministry is located in MADRID and is responsible for the education in all those AUTONOMÍAS to which responsibility for education has not been transferred. For many years it was known as the *Ministerio de Educación y Ciencia*: *Cultura* was a separate Ministry.

MINISTERIO DE FOMENTO
New name for what was originally known as MOPTMA, the MINISTERIO DE OBRAS PÚBLICAS, TRANSPORTES Y MEDIO AMBIENTE. This ministry is responsible for traffic and transport, for the CENTRO DE ESTUDIOS DE EXPERIMENTACIÓN DE OBRAS PÚBLICAS (CEDEX) and for AENA (AEROPUERTOS ESPAÑOLES Y NAVEGACIÓN AÉREA).

MINISTERIO DE INDUSTRIA Y ENERGÍA
The Ministry of Industry and Energy. Among other things, this ministry is responsible for distributing and administering government grants in technological fields.

MINISTERIO DE JUSTICIA
Ministry responsible for the Spanish legal system. At present the minister is MARGARITA MARISCAL DE GANTE Y MIRÓN.

MINISTERIO DE LA PRESIDENCIA
The minister of this government department is responsible for protocol and the prime minister's personal safety. He or she also controls appointments, combining the role of spokesperson for the prime minister with that of goverment secretary. The CIS and BOE are organisations which answer directly to this minister.

MINISTERIO DE OBRAS PÚBLICAS, TRANSPORTE Y MEDIO AMBIENTE
Large ministry, originally responsible for roads, public transport and the environment. In AZNAR's government, some of these responsibilities were transferred to the MINISTERIO DE FOMENTO and to the *Ministerio del Medio Ambiente*.

MINISTERIO DE SANIDAD Y CONSUMO
The Ministry for Health and as such responsible for the National Health Service.

MINISTERIO DE TRABAJO Y ASUNTOS SOCIALES
Ministry for Employment and Social Affairs.

MINISTERIO DEL INTERIOR
Ministry of Home Affairs. This department is responsible, among other things, for the police, the GUARDIA CIVIL, PROTECCIÓN CIVIL, security and traffic. It was briefly combined with the MINISTERIO DE JUSTICIA, with BELLOCH as Minister under the Socialist Government of FELIPE GONZÁLEZ.

MINISTERIO FISCAL
Government attorney service. This department is responsible for acting as public prosecutor in civil cases.

MIÑO
River, 310 kilometres in length, which flows through a large part of GALICIA. Its largest tributary is the Sil.

MIRALLES, ENRIC (1955–   )
Catalán architect and teacher. He designed the Avenida Icaria in the Olympic Village in BARCELONA.

MIRÓ, JOAN (1893–1983)
Artist, born in Montroig (CATALUÑA). He studied in Paris and BARCELONA and exhibited in the 1920s with the surrealists. He spent the majority of his working life in France. His works are predominantly abstract and painted in vivid colours. He also designed stage sets and produced sculptures, murals and tapestries. He died in Palma, MALLORCA.

MIRÓ, PILAR (1940–1997)
Controversial film and television director and one-time head of RTVE. Her most famous film is *El crimen de Cuenca*, (1979) banned by the UCD government because of its depiction of torture inflicted by the GUARDIA CIVIL at the beginning of the century. MIRÓ is famous for the so-called *Ley Miró* which guaranteed grants for Spanish film makers. Other films she has made are

Gary Cooper, que estás en los cielos (1980) and *Beltenebros* (1991) adapted from the novel of the same name by ANTONIO MUÑOZ MOLINA. In 1996, she directed *El perro del hortelano* which was a huge success at the box office and was awarded 7 GOYA prizes in 1997. Her last work was to film the wedding of the Princess CRISTINA DE BORBÓN in October 1997. She died later that month.

MOCEDADES
Well-known pop group, popular in the 1970s. It has now disbanded.

MOCIÓN DE CENSURA
A motion of no-confidence in the government of the day. Besides being critical in character, it must also propose an alternative prime minister. Only two such motions have been presented, neither of which was successful.

MOCIÓN DE REPROBACIÓN
This is a censure motion which condemns the actions of an individual member of parliament.

MODELO
Large prison in BARCELONA

MOIX, TERENCI (1943–   )
Popular CATALÁN novelist, MOIX first rose to fame with *No digas que fue un sueño*, which won the *Premio Planeta* in 1986. Prior to this novel, however, MOIX had already won the PREMIO JOSEP PLÁ for *Olas sobre una roca desierta*. The first part of his autobiography, *El peso de la paja*, was published in 1990 and was an immediate best seller. Moix is also a translator and journalist. In 1995 he published *Mujercísimas*, a novel which deals with the lives of women who belong to the Spanish jet set. In 1996 he was awarded the PREMIO DE NOVELA FERNANDO LARA for his novel *El amargo don de la belleza*.

MOLINA, ANGELA (1955–   )
Born into a family of actors and singers, ANGELA MOLINA began her film career in the early seventies and it was with BUÑUEL's *Ese oscuro objeto del deseo* (1977) that she became internationally

famous. During the 1980s and 1990s she appeared in many excellent films directed by both Spanish and European directors, including *El corazón del bosque* (GUTIÉRREZ ARAGÓN, 1987), *Las cosas del querer* (CHÁVARRI, 1989), *El hombre que perdió su sombra* (Tanner, 1991) and *El ladrón de niños* (de Challonge, 1991). In 1995 she appeared in *Las cosas del querer 2*, set in Argentina, and in 1997 she starred in *Carne trémula* (ALMODÓVAR).

MOLINS, JOAQUIM (1945–)

Industrial engineer and politician. He has been a member of parliament since 1979 when he was elected for *Centristes de Catalunya* (the CATALÁN branch of UCD). He is currently spokesman for CiU in the CONGRESO.

MONARQUÍA

Spain has a constitutional monarch according to the 1978 CONSTITUCIÓN. The function of the monarch is to represent the state. According to article 62 of the CONSTITUCIÓN, the monarch also sanctions and promulgates laws, summons and dissolves LAS CORTES, calls elections, proposes candidates for the presidency and is head of the armed forces.

LA MONCLOA

Official residence of the Spanish Prime Minister.

MONDRAGÓN CORPORACIÓN COOPERATIVA

Group of small and medium-sized firms based in Mondragón (PAÍS VASCO), which are cooperative in character. This collective is internationally famous for its early experiments in worker participation in industry.

MONEO, RAFAEL (1937–)

Internationally recognised architect, he has designed such prestigious buildings as the Thyssen-Borja museum in Madrid.

MONTE

Generic name for scrubland which is particularly prone to forest fires. See also: INCENDIOS

MONTEJURRA

A hill near PAMPLONA where the Carlists traditionally make an annual pilgrimage. The Carlists traditionally supported Don Carlos against Isabel II and fought for the nationalists in the Civil War.

MONTERO, ROSA (1951–   )

Feminist writer and journalist. ROSA MONTERO has a regular column in EL PAÍS. She has written short stories and novels such as *Crónica del desamor*, *Bella y oscura* and *Te trataré como a una reina*. She has won the *Premio Mundo* for her interviews and in 1980 she was awarded the *Premio Nacional de Periodismo*.

MONTIEL, SARA (1928–   )

Veteran film actress, SARA MONTIEL started her career in the forties but it was a series of films made in Mexico in the early fifties which catapulted her into fame. She also appeared in three excellent American films, *Veracruz* (Aldrich, 1954) *Dos pasiones y un amor* (Mann, 1955) and *Yuma* (Fuller, 1957). In the sixties she returned to Spain and starred in a number of very popular musical comedies, but this formula eventually ran dry and in the seventies she turned to television and theatre variety performances.

MONTJUÏC

Mountain which overlooks BARCELONA. It was the home of the *Exposición Internacional* in 1929 and later many of the 1992 Olympic installations were built there also. It is a recreational area for the people of BARCELONA, in that it has sports and cultural facilities, parks and gardens. From the funfair, one gets an excellent view of the city and port.

MONTSERRAT

Catalán monastery, upholder of Catalán nationalism throughout the centuries. The monastery is famous for its shrine to the Black Virgin, its boys' choir and its music school. It published material in CATALÁN when this was forbidden under the FRANCO régime.

MOPTMA See: *MINISTERIO DE OBRAS PÚBLICAS, TRANSPORTES Y MEDIO AMBIENTE*

MORÁN FERNANDO (1926–   )

Ministro de Asuntos Exteriores with FELIPE GONZÁLEZ from 1982 to 1985. He was Spanish Embassador to the United Nations from 1985 to 1986 and has been a member of the European Parliament since 1987. It was he who took Spain into the European Union in 1985.

LOS MORANCOS
Comedy duo from ANDALUCÍA. They appeared in a popular television show called *Llévatelo calentito* in which they presented sketches about Spanish working-class life and people from show-business.

MORDILLO (1932–   )
Cartoonist. He first started out as an illustrator for childrens' books and later moved into television cartoons. He now publishes a weekly cartoon in EL PAÍS *Semanal*.

MOREIRAS, MIGUEL
Judge working at the AUDIENCIA NACIONAL. In 1996 he was fined 300,000 pesetas for revealing classified information concerning the Caso Argentina Trust in which MARIO CONDE was involved. He has the reputation of being capricious and loquacious and has made controversial decisions which he has later revoked.

MORENTE, ENRIQUE (1943–   )
One of the best-known *cantaores* (flamenco artistes) outside Spain, MORENTE has sung in venues all over the world, has made many records and in 1995 won the *Premio Nacional de Música*. MORANTE is famous for his unorthodox approach to flamenco and the pureness of his *cante jondo*. He has put the poetry of Federico García Lorca Miguel Hernández and Antonio Machado to music with flamenco rhythms.

MORGAN, LINA
Popular comic actress. Among her recent successes has been her role as *Reme* in the TV sitcom *Hostal Royal Manzanares*.

MOSSOS D'ESQUADRA
The autonomous police force of CATALUÑA. It has partially replaced the CUERPO NACIONAL DE POLICÍA in this AUTONOMÍA.

LA MOVIDA MADRILEÑA

During the late 1970s and 1980s MADRID became an exciting and experimental cultural centre with a vibrant night life. Figures such as the film director PEDRO ALMODÓVAR, actors and singers like MIGUEL BOSÉ, and photographers such as Ouka Lele suddenly became fashionable. New restaurants and bars sprung up with extravagant décors, and youth culture and street style became paramount. Magazines such as *La luna de Madrid*, and *Madrid me mata*, were founded and art galleries created. Much of this cultural activity was promoted and funded by the PSOE. The most important supporter of the movement was the ALCALDE of MADRID, ENRIQUE TIERNO GALVÁN.

MOVIMIENTO DE DEFENSA DE LA TERRA

Catalán separatist group, active in the 1980s.

MOVIMIENTO VASCO DE LIBERACIÓN NACIONAL

Broad independence movement in the PAÍS VASCO, composed of trades unions, youth organisations and pro-amnesty groups.

EL MUNDO

An independent daily newspaper founded in 1989 with a circulation figure of 150,000 during the week and 220,000 on Sundays. It has the third largest circulation in Spain, though this has been falling recently. It has international connections with other European newspapers such as The Guardian in the United Kingdom. It began as a rival of EL PAÍS but in recent years has become more sensationalist and investigative in style.

MÚGICA GARMENDIA, FRANCISCO (1953–   )

Also called *Pakito*, MÚGICA GARMENDIA has been leader of the Basque terrorist group ETA since the death of TXOMIN ITURBE in 1987. He went to France as a refugee in 1975 and joined the military wing of ETA in 1977. He was arrested in Bidart (France) in 1992.

MULTINACIONAL ASEGURADORA, S.A.

This insurance company specialises in vehicle insurance which has accounted for 95% of its activity in recent years.

MUNICIPIO
The fundamental unit of local administration, administered by the Town Hall or AYUNTAMIENTO. The PROVINCIA is composed of a number of MUNICIPIOS.

MUÑOZ MOLINA, ANTONIO (1956–)
Born in 1956 in ANDALUCÍA, MUÑOZ MOLINA is a novelist and journalist. Among his works are *Beatus ille*, *Beltenebros*, *El jinete polaco* and *El invierno en Lisboa*. *El jinete polaco* won the *Premio Planeta* in 1991 and in 1987 he won both the *Premio de la Crítica* and the *Premio Nacional de Literatura*. In 1995 he was elected a member of the REAL ACADEMIA ESPAÑOLA and, at 39, became its youngest member.

MUNT, SILVIA (1956–)
Distinguished film and theatre actress, SILVIA MUNT has appeared in films such as *Sal gorda* (TRUEBA, 1983) and *Alas de mariposa* (ULLOA, 1991).

MUSEO DE ARTE CONTEMPORÁNEO DE BARCELONA
This museum of modern art was opened in 1995 by the King and Queen of Spain. It is situated in the very heart of the city, near the RAMBLAS and was designed by the American architect Richard Meyer.

MUSEO DEL PRADO
The most important art gallery in Spain, the PRADO houses a unique collection of paintings from the 12th to the 19th centuries.

MUSEO NACIONAL CENTRO DE ARTE REINA SOFÍA
Museum of contemporary art, inaugurated in 1986 and housed in the former general hospital of the city of MADRID. A number of important modern art collections were moved into these premises, including that from the PRADO museum. Picasso's *Gernika* is now also exhibited in the museum.

MUSEO THYSSEN-BORNEMISZA
This museum was endowed in 1992 by the Baron Hans Heinrich Thyssen-Bornemisza and his Spanish wife Tita (CARMEN CERVERA) and is housed in the *Palacio de Villahermosa* in MADRID. The

Palace was refurbished by RAFAEL MONEO as a backdrop for a magnificent collection of paintings, sculptures and furniture ranging from the 14th to the 20th centuries.

MUTUAL GENERAL DE SEGUROS
This insurance company was founded in 1907. Its principal source of income is vehicle insurance, followed by fire, personal accident and life.

MUY INTERESANTE
A popular science magazine, covering astronomy, geology, chemistry, genetics and the environment. Founded in 1981, it has a circulation of about 300,000. It appears monthly.

MVLN See: *MOVIMIENTO VASCO DE LIBERACIÓN NACIONAL*

NACIONAL DE REASEGUROS, S.A.
Insurance company, founded in 1939 and specialising in fire insurance.

NACIONAL HISPÁNICA, S.A. DE SEGUROS Y REASEGUROS
Insurance company, founded in 1945 and principally involved in marine and industrial business. It is owned by the *Banco Vitalicio de España*.

NASEIRO, ROSENDO (1937–)
The principal defendant in the political scandal known as the *Caso* NASEIRO, NASEIRO was treasurer of the PP and was arrested in April 1990 on charges of bribery and misuse of public funds and the illegal financing of the party. NASEIRO and his co-defendant, Salvador Palop, were released, as evidence from taped telephone conversations was deemed inadmissable.

NAVACERRADA
Ski resort 60 kilometres to the north of MADRID. One of the earliest holiday resorts, it has been a popular destination for the people of MADRID in summer as well as winter.

NAVARRA
NAVARRA is an AUTONOMÍA situated between the PAÍS VASCO and the French border. It is felt by Basque nationalists to belong historically to the PAÍS VASCO, along with the Basque provinces in France. However, the majority view in NAVARRA is against union with the PAÍS VASCO. It has a population of half a million and covers an area of 10,421 square kilometres. It is an important region for agriculture and produces fresh, dried and canned vegetables, as well as other food products and table wines. It has a number of car assembly plants, including SEAT. Its capital is PAMPLONA.

NAVARRA has retained more of its ancient rights or FUEROS than other AUTONOMÍAS, chiefly because it supported the nationalists in the Civil War. Its official name is the *Comunidad Foral de Navarra* and the name of its regional government is the *Diputación Foral.*

NIF See: *NÚMERO DE IDENTIFICACIÓN FISCAL*

NISSAN MOTOR IBÉRICA, S.A.
This company manufactures, assembles and sells commercial and private vehicles, deisel engines, aerospace equipment, textile machinery and marine products. Its major shareholder is Nissan (Japan).

NORMATIVAS, CLÁUSULAS
Clauses in workers' contracts which ensured that salaries, work schedules and working conditions were strictly regulated and that the provisions of an expired contract continued to apply until a new contract was agreed upon. Gradually these clauses are being eroded to allow for more flexibility in labour negotiations.

NOTARIO
Lawyer who has passed the appropriate OPOSICIÓN or competitive examination. *Notarios* are therefore civil servants: they are authorised to process contracts, wills and legal certificates and are especially involved in property purchase and sales. The number of *notarios* per city is strictly limited.

EL NOTICIERO UNIVERSAL
Evening newspaper, published in BARCELONA.

NOU CAMP
120,000 capacity stadium, home to BARÇA, the BARCELONA football team, which is as much a symbol of national unity as the CATALÁN language or flag.

NUESTRA SEÑORA DEL PILAR
This élite school in MADRID is run by the Marianist fathers and has produced a large number of Spaniards who have been

important in public life. JOSÉ MARÍA AZNAR and JAVIER SOLANA are both old boys of the school.

NUEVA ORGANIZACIÓN DEL EJÉRCITO DE TIERRA
This plan was approved in 1994: its object was to slim down, restructure and modernize the army.

NUEVAS GENERACIONES
The youth wing of the PARTIDO POPULAR.

LOS NUEVOS DIRECTORES DE CINE
In recent years, the Spanish film industry has taken on a new lease of life, with a host of new directors emerging on the international scene. Comedies have become even more ebullient since the arrival of PEDRO ALMODÓVAR, with young directors such as Manuel Gómez Pereira (*Todos los hombres sois iguales* – You men are all the same, 1994; *Salsa rosa* – Hot sauce, 1991; *¿Por qué lo llaman amor cuando quieren decir sexo?* – Why do they call it love when they really mean sex?, 1993) and Rosa Vergés (*Boom Boom*, 1990; *Souvenir*, 1994). BIGAS LUNA follows a similar though overtly bawdier line, with his trilogy: *Jamón, jamón* (Ham, ham), *Huevos de oro* (Golden Balls), 1993 and *La teta y la luna* (The tit and the moon), 1993. A more sombre note is struck by JUANMA BAJO ULLOA in *Alas de mariposa* (Butterfly Wings), 1991 in which a young girl takes revenge on her family and her baby brother. His second feature, *La madre muerta* (The dead mother), 1993, is similarly disturbing in atmosphere and subject matter.

EL NÚMERO COMPLEMENTARIO
An additional number used in the PRIMITIVA and the BONOLOTO. This number is added to 5 or 6 winning numbers for an even larger pay-out.

NÚMERO DE IDENTIFICACIÓN FISCAL
Tax number which is the same as that of one's DNI and passport. It is hoped that in the future, the Spanish driving licence will carry the same number.

EL NÚMERO DE REINTEGRO

The last two numbers on a national lottery ticket. The owner of the lottery ticket receives a refund if these numbers come up.

NUMERUS CLAUSUS

A number of universities and faculties within universities now operate a system of NUMERUS CLAUSUS for the admission of students: that is, they operate a quota system in which only a certain number of places are awarded. In the past, all students with the BACHILLERATO were assured of a university place.

O CORREO GALEGO
The first daily paper to be published entirely in GALLEGO, it was founded in 1994 in SANTIAGO DE COMPOSTELA and has a circulation of 10,000. It is sponsored by the regional parliament, the XUNTA DE GALICIA.

O'SHEA, PALOMA
Patron of the arts, she founded the *Concurso de Piano de Santander*. In 1996 she received the *Premio Montblanc de Cultura*: she is married to the *presidente* of the BANCO DE SANTANDER, EMILIO BOTÍN.

OBIOLS GERMÁ, RAIMON (1941–   )
Catalán politician, he is a DIPUTADO in the CATALÁN parliament, *presidente* of the PSC and on the PSOE executive, responsible for International Relations.

OBJETOR DE CONCIENCIA
Conscientious objector or person who refuses to complete his military service. Recently, numbers have grown to such an extent that the PP government of 1996 intends to abolish military service entirely.

OBRA BENÉFICO-SOCIAL
The CAJAS DE AHORRO may give up to 50% of their profits to charities, enterprises or initiatives in the area in which they operate. The amount given is usually about 18% per annum.

OBS See: *OBRA BENÉFICO-SOCIAL*

OCASO, S.A. SEGUROS Y REASEGUROS
Insurance company founded in 1920 and specialising principally in insurance for burial expenses.

OCHOA DE ALBORNOZ, SEVERO (1905–1993)
Biochemist, OCHOA DE ALBORNOZ has lived and worked almost entirely in the United States. He won the Nobel Prize for Medicine in 1959.

OFICINA DE EMPLEO
Local employment office, run by INEM. These offices register the unemployed, undertake to help them find work, give career advice and run training courses.

OFICINA DE MARCAS
The Patent Office.

OFICINA DE OBJETOS PERDIDOS
Lost property office located in some police stations.

OFICINA RECAUDADORA
Local tax office.

OLANO, ABRAHAM
1995 World Champion in cycling. In 1997, he joined the BANESTO team, in the place of INDURÁIN, who retired, and was placed 4th in the Tour de France in that year.

OLAZÁBAL, JOSÉ MARÍA (1966–   )
Born in Fuenterrabia (Guipúzcoa) in 1966, OLAZÁBAL won his first golfing trophy at the age of 9 and became a professional player in 1986. He was declared best new player of that year. In 1990 he became the only golfer to have won tournaments in three continents: in Europe, Japan and the United States.

OLEA, PEDRO (1938–   )
Film director and critic, his most important work is a trilogy about MADRID which he made in the seventies. His most successful film to date is *Un hombre llamado 'Flor de Otoño'* (1978). In 1992 he made *El maestro de esgrima*, based on the novel by ARTURO PÉREZ REVERTE.

OLMO, LUIS DEL (1937–   )
Important radio journalist, he first worked with RADIO NACIONAL DE ESPAÑA. He then presented the popular programme

Protagonistas on the COPE radio station from 1983 to 1991. In 1991 he signed a multimillion contract with ONDA CERO.

ONCE See: *ORGANIZACIÓN NACIONAL DE CIEGOS ESPAÑOLES*

ONDA CERO RADIO
Radio station, based in MADRID and owned by the ONCE group. Its director is Santiago Galván. It is the third most listened to radio network in Spain after CADENA SER and COPE. Two of its most popular programmes are *Protagonistas* (with LUIS DEL OLMO) and *Las tardes de Julia* (with Julia Otero).

ONETO, JOSÉ (1942–   )
Journalist and broadcaster, ONETO has been editor of the weekly magazine *Tiempo* from 1987. Prior to this he was editor of CAMBIO 16 from 1976 to 1985.

ONG See: *ORGANIZACIÓN NO GUBERNAMENTAL*

ONZE DE SETEMBRE
Feast day in CATALUÑA which commemorates the defeat of the Spaniards in 1714.

OPERACIÓN GALAXIA
Name given to a plot to kidnap the King and Prime Minister, so called from the café where the plot was hatched by members of the Armed Forces, including TEJERO.

OPERACIÓN NÉCORA
One of the first large-scale drug raids mounted in Spain in which a number of important drug dealers in GALICIA were captured, tried and sentenced. The principal defendants were Laureano Oubiña, his wife Ester Lago and Manuel Charlín. Many Spaniards considered that the sentences awarded were too light.

OPOSICIONES
Competitive examinations for posts in the civil service. The examinations are oral as well as written and take place before a jury or *tribunal*. Candidates who are successful are assured of a job for life. Candidates for posts in the POLICÍA NACIONAL, the

GUARDIA CIVIL, in the prison and education systems are all required to take these examinations.

OPTECAL

Cable company with rights to provide cable facilities in CASTILLA Y LEÓN. ENDESA is an important share-holder in this company, along with *Retecal* (11 local cable companies).

OPUS DEI

The OPUS DEI (also known as *La Obra*) is a religious order for both lay people and the ordained. It was founded by Josemaría Escrivá de Balaguer in 1928 in order to implant religious values in the world. To this end, the OPUS recruits members who are, or will be, influential on a national and international scale. Its members belong to the world of education (the *Universidad de* NAVARRA is run by the OPUS), politics (its members hold important positions in most of the Spanish political parties) and banking. It believes in maximum discretion and thus it it is not clear who, or who does not, belong to the order. It is currently very influential in the Vatican.

ORA

Area of restricted car parking.

ORDENANZAS LABORALES

Rules and regulations concerning job demarcation. Until recently, these enabled workers to quit with full severance pay and access to unemployent benefit, rather than accept a geographical transfer or change of job. Many of these rules have now been eliminated and the AZNAR government hopes to renegotiate those regulations which still remain outstanding.

ORDESA Y MONTE PERDIDO

National park in Huesca and the second to be declared in Spain after COVADONGA. It is famous for its wild life and spectacular views of the Pyrenees. UNESCO is currently considering an application for it to be declared a *Patrimonio de la Humanidad*.

ORDÓÑEZ, GREGORIO (1958–1995)

Former leader of the Basque section of the PARTIDO POPULAR and candidate for mayor of SAN SEBASTIÁN. He was murdered by ETA in January 1995 while in a restaurant.

ORGANIZACIÓN NACIONAL DE CIEGOS ESPAÑOLES
This organisation was founded in 1938 to help improve the lot of blind people in Spain. Its chief source of funds is a daily lottery whose proceeds pay the blind men and women who sell the tickets. The ONCE is one of the largest companies in Spain and among its investments is a 25% stake in a commercial TV channel, TELE 5.

ORGANIZACIÓN NO GUBERNAMENTAL
Non-government organisation, which often takes the form of pressure groups active in the field of social affairs and the environment. There are about 120 in Spain including *Manos Unidas*, *Intermón* and MEDICUS MUNDI ESPAÑA.

ORQUESTA MONDRAGÓN
Dance band, founded in MADRID in 1979 under the leadership of Javier Gurruchaga. Among their hits have been *Bon Voyage*, *Bésame tonta*, and *Esto es la guerra*. In recent years, the band has taken second place to its conductor.

ORQUESTA SINFÓNICA DE RADIO TELEVISIÓN ESPAÑOLA
The official orchestra for Spanish television and radio, founded in MADRID in 1965. Its principal conductor is Sergiu Comissiona.

ORTEGA LARA, JOSÉ ANTONIO (1958–   )
Prison officer, he was kidnapped by the Basque terrorist organisation ETA in January 1996. This was the first time that ETA had two people in custody at the same time. Since there was no ransom demand, it was assumed that ETA wished to force the Government to reverse its policy of placing ETA prisoners in jails outside the PAÍS VASCO. ORTEGA LARA was released after 532 days' imprisonment, on the 1st of July, 1997.

ORUJO
Spirit made from the lees of wine and typical of GALICIA. Usually drunk with coffee after a meal or as the base for a *queimada* (a type of punch).

OSBORNE, BERTÍN
Singer and actor, originally specialising in Latin-American soap-

operas. He is currently a presenter with TELE 5. He belongs to the famous OSBORNE family from Jerez de la Frontera which has important interests in the wine trade. He appears frequently in the gossip magazines.

OTAN

Organización del Tratado del Atlántico Norte (NATO). Despite initial opposition to Spain's joining the North Atlantic Treaty Organisation, the government of FELIPE GONZÁLEZ backtracked on this issue and urged the Spanish people to vote in favour of joining the organisation. A referendum took place in 1986 which approved Spain's membership. In 1996 Parliament voted to become a full member. Its current secretary-general is a Spaniard, JAVIER SOLANA.

PA See: *PARTIDO ANDALUCISTA*

PABLO, LUIS DE (1930–)
Composer from the PAÍS VASCO, he is the author of two well-known operas, KIU (1982) and *El viajero indiscreto* (1988).

PACHARÁN
A sticky red liqueur, made by marinating sloe berries in anisette; it is a product of the NAVARRA region of Northern Spain. It became especially popular in the 1980s as a digestive and as a result, the regional government is currently supporting a planting programme for a domesticated sloe-tree with more fruit and fewer thorns.

PACTO DE AJURIA ENEA
Agreement signed in January 1988 by all Basque political parties (except HERRI BATASUNA) to work together in the fight against terrorism. It is currently (1996) in abeyance, due to the lack of accord between these political parties as to how terrorism and violence should be tackled. AJURIA ENEA is the name of the official residence of the Basque Prime Minister.

PACTO DE TOLEDO
An agreement which sets out the laws for the Spanish pension system, based on social security contributions, rather than on private pension plans.

PACTOS DE LA MONCLOA
A series of fiscal, economic, social and political reforms, agreed upon in 1977 after discussion and negotitation between all political parties. Some of these ideas later became articles of the new CONSTITUCIÓN.

PADE See: *PARTIDO DE ACCIÓN DEMÓCRATA ESPAÑOLA*

PADRES DE LA CONSTITUCIÓN
The founding fathers of the 1978 CONSTITUCIÓN. These include statesmen such as MANUEL FRAGA and ADOLFO SUÁREZ.

PAGA EXTRAORDINARIA
All wage-earners receive two extra pay-checks, one at Christmas and another at a time agreed upon by the employer and the union.

PAGARÉS DEL TESORO
Treasury bonds: they usually give about 5% interest.

EL PAÍS
Spain's leading and most prestigious daily newspaper. It published its first issue on 1st May 1976. Under Juan Luis Cebrián as its editor-in-chief, it soon became a symbol of the transition from dictatorship to democracy. It publishes a weekly international edition and its daily circulation figures approach 400,000 during the week and over one million copies on Sunday. Its Sunday edition appears with numerous supplements, including a colour supplement called EL PAÍS *Semanal* and another for children, *El Pequeño País*.

PAÍS VASCO
The PAÍS VASCO is situated in the north of Spain between the French border and CANTABRIA to the west. It is one of the three historical AUTONOMÍAS, along with CATALUÑA and GALICIA. It comprises three provinces, Vizcaya, Guipúzcoa and Álava in Spain and three in France, Labourd, Soule and Basse Navarre. It is one of the three major industrial regions of Spain, along with MADRID and BARCELONA. BILBAO is Spain's largest port and has major container-handling facilities. It has two power stations, an oil refinery and large shipbuilding yards. The province of Vizcaya is the most heavily industrialised region in the area and is the home of ship building, heavy engineering, oil refining and the chemical industry. SAN SEBASTIÁN, on the coast, is the capital of Guipúzcoa and an important tourist centre with a famous Film Festival each summer. It is also a centre for machine-tool making and the electronics industry. Vitoria is the capital of this autonomous region and the administrative centre. It also has a Mercedes-Benz van

assemby and Michelin tyre production plants. There is much support for Basque separatism in the region and the area is the home of ETA, the terrorist organisation which struggles nationally and internationally for Basque independence. This has led to disinvestment in local industry and a climate of fear among the Basque people.

PAJARES, ANDRÉS (1940–   )

Very popular comic actor in the 1980s, in films such as *La Lola nos lleva al huerto* (1983). In the 1990s he began to be taken more seriously and was awarded the prize for best actor at the Montreal Film Festival for his role in *¡Ay Carmela!* (1990). Since then he has appeared in two films by Carlos Suárez, *Makinavaja, el último choriso* (1990) and *Makinavaja 2* (1993). He has also appeared in the popular television series, *¡Ay, señor, señor!* and in IMANOL URIBE's *Bwana* (1996).

PALACIO DE ORIENTE

Another name for the PALACIO REAL, the home of the Spanish monarchs.

PALACIO DE SANT JORDI

Olympic stadium, built for the BARCELONA Olympic Games in 1992. It has a capacity of 17,000 spectators and can accommodate track and field events, ice skating and hockey. It has an unusual roof which is 45 metres high.

PALACIO DE SANTA CRUZ

Another name for the MINISTERIO DE ASUNTOS EXTERIORES. It is the name of the official residence of the Minister for Foreign Affairs.

PALACIO REAL

The 18th century PALACIO REAL or PALACIO DE ORIENTE is the traditional home of the Spanish monarchs and it is there that official royal business is conducted. In practice, the royal family lives in the ZARZUELA, a much smaller mansion outside MADRID.

LA PALMA

Island in the CANARIAS, sometimes known as the *isla verde* (the 'green island'). Because of its high humidity, it tends to stay green throughout the year.

PALMA, ROSSY DE

An actress who first rose to fame through the films of PEDRO ALMODÓVAR. Famous for her aquiline, almost 'cubist' looks, she starred in films such as *La ley del deseo* and *Mujeres al borde de un ataque de nervios*. She also works in advertising and as a model.

PAMIES, SERGI (1960–   )

Young CATALÁN novelist with a marked predilection for the absurd and astonishing. Influenced in his writing by the cinema and advertising, his novel *Sentimental*, originally written in CATALÁN, was published in Spanish by *Anagrama* in 1996.

PAMPLONA

Originally capital of the kingdom of NAVARRA and now capital of the province. It has a university and ancient cathedral. It is here that the bullrunning takes place which Hemingway describes in *For Whom the Bell Tolls*.

PANTOJA, ISABEL (1956–   )

Singer and actress. Her real name is María Isabel Martín. She was born in the gypsy quarter of SEVILLA and made her debut there at the age of 7. In 1983 she married the bullfighter, PAQUIRRI who died in a bull fight in CÓRDOBA in 1984. Her most important records are *Marinero de luces*, *Desde Andalucía*, and *Cambiar de ti*.

LA PAPELERA ESPAÑOLA, S.A.

This company operates in the packaging, paper and printing sector and manufactures pulp, newsprint, writing and printing paper, tissue etc. It is based in the PAÍS VASCO.

PAR See: *PARTIDO ARAGONÉS REGIONALISTA*

PARADOR

The PARADOR is a luxurious state-owned hotel, often situated in a building of historic importance or in an exceptional geographical location. These hotels are run by an enterprise called the *Paradores de Turismo de España, S.A.*

EL PARDO
Former country estate on the edge of MADRID which now belongs to the city itself. General FRANCO used it as his private home; today it is used for offical visitors to the city.

PARLAMENTARIOS
This term refers to both DIPUTADOS (members of the CONGRESO or Lower House) and SENADORES (members of the SENADO, or Upper House).

PARLAMENTO VASCO
The Basque autonomous parliament is composed of 75 members. It has legislative powers, approves budgets, controls the *Gobierno Vasco* (which is the executive and administrative body) and nominates the president. Its official name is *Eusko Jauralitza*.

PARTIDO DE ACCIÓN DEMÓCRATA ESPAÑOLA
Political party founded in 1997 to represent voters further to the right than members of the PP. It celebrated its first party conference in January 1998, at which its national executive was elected. Juan Ramón Calera was elected president. Previously he had held the post of spokesperson for the PP in the Spanish parliament.

PARTIDO ANDALUCISTA
This party has changed radically since its inception as the PSA in 1984. It has known mixed fortunes since its heyday in 1989 when it won two congressional seats. The party improved its declining position in the regional elections of 1995: in 1996 it became influential in the regional parliament, since the Socialists were dependent on its support in order to maintain a stable administration.

PARTIDO ARAGONÉS REGIONALISTA
Right-wing party founded in 1977. Over the years it has fought for the widest possible autonomy for ARAGÓN. It is currently third in the regional parliament, but holds the balance of power. It has 11,000 members.

PARTIDO COMUNISTA DE ESPAÑA
Members of the PSOE left the party in 1921 to form the PCE. The movement was especially important in the 1930s during the Spanish Republic and also in the 1960s in anti-FRANCO campaigns.

In 1982 the PCE suffered a major setback after the expulsion of some of its more progressive members. A further split let to the founding of the PTE or *Partido de los Trabajadores de España*, headed by SANTIAGO CARRILLO. This splinter group was later dissolved. At the present time, the PCE is the dominant partner in the IU (IZQUIERDA UNIDA) coalition. The leader of IU is JULIO ANGUITA.

PARTIDO DEMOCRÁTICO DE LA NUEVA IZQUIERDA

Party, led by CRISTINA ALMEIDA and Diego López Garrido, which broke away from IZQUIERDA UNIDA. It is considered by some to be ideologically closer to the PSOE than to IU.

PARTIDO JUDICIAL

District courts '*de la primera instancia*' – that is, courts which first deal with the vast majority of cases. They are presided over by a *juez* or judge with legal training and usually act as the JUZGADO *de* INSTRUCCIÓN or examining court.

PARTIDO LIBERAL

Formed in 1977, the PL absorbed the smaller *Unión Liberal* in 1985. The party joined the PP in 1989 although it retained its independance as a legal entity.

PARTIDO NACIONAL VASCO

The PNV, together with the PSOE, currently governs the PAÍS VASCO and is also represented in the CORTES, where it holds 5 seats. It is a nationalist party, founded by Sabino Arana y Goiri, the founder of Basque nationalism. During the FRANCO years, it formed a government-in-exile but in 1977 it was invited to negotiate the new Constitution along with other nationalist groups and representative bodies. In the 1996 government the party supports the ruling PARTIDO POPULAR.

PARTIDO POPULAR

The PARTIDO POPULAR is the party of the Spanish right, founded in 1977 by MANUEL FRAGA IRIBARNE, and originally known as ALIANZA POPULAR (AP). In 1982 it won over 100 seats in the elections and established itself as the main opposition party. The present party leader is JOSE MARÍA AZNAR, under whose leadership it won the 1996 elections with a slim majority. It depends on the support of the Catalán and Basque nationalist parties.

PARTIDO REGIONALISTA CÁNTABRO

The PRC is a moderate conservative party which won 6 out of 39 seats in the 1995 regional assembly elections in CANTABRIA.

PARTIDO RIOJANO

A centre-left formation in Spain's principal wine-growing region, the PR won 1 seat in the 1993 general elections and 2 in the 1995 regional elections.

PARTIDO SOCIALISTA DE EUSKADI

Regional organisation of the PSOE in the PAÍS VASCO. In 1984 it formed a coalition with PNV which revived the latter's fortunes and enabled it to control much of the local government in the region.

PARTIDO SOCIALISTA DE GALICIA-ESQUERDA UNIDA

This nationalist party won 2 seats in the regional elections of 1989 but none in 1993.

PARTIDO SOCIALISTA OBRERO ESPAÑOL

The PSOE is the oldest political party in Spain and was founded in 1879 by Pablo Iglesias. The renovation of the party has largely been due to its leader, FELIPE GONZÁLEZ, who has occupied the position of *secretario general* of the party almost continuously since 1979. During its years in opposition, the party modified the ideological content of its principles, abandoning its Marxist roots and is now very much a Western European social-democratic party. Since 1979, the PSOE has governed in most of the large cities in Spain and from the 1982 general elections, has also governed federally. The party finally lost power in the 1996 elections, after 14 years in government.

PARTIDO VERDE ESPAÑOL

A group of pacifists, feminists and ecologists, the PVE (known as *los verdes* or the greens) became established as a formal party in 1984 and convened their first congress in 1985.

PARTIT DELS SOCIALISTES DE CATALUNYA

This party is a branch of the PSOE in CATALUÑA and was formed in 1978 from several small socialist groups. It does well in general elections in CATALUÑA but loses out to CIU in the regional elections.

PASCUA MILITAR

This military ceremony is conducted annually on January 6th by the King in his role as MANDO SUPREMO DE LAS FUERZAS ARMADAS or Commander-in-Chief of the Armed Forces. The speech which he gives to officers of all three armed forces, to the Prime Minister and to the Minister of Defence comments on the state of the armed forces. The ceremony takes place in the *salón del Trono* in the PALACIO REAL.

PASCUAL HERMANOS, S.A.

Food manufacturing company engaged in the production, packaging and distribution of fresh fruit and vegetables.

PASEO DE LA CASTELLANA

The principal artery of MADRID, lined with modern buildings, many of which are the headquarters of international companies, banks or ministries.

PASQUAL, LLUIS (1951–   )

Important Catalán theatre director. Together with Fabiá Puigserver, he founded the *Teatre Lliure* in 1976. He is currently director of the Odéon in Paris.

PASTOR, ROSANA

Actress and singer from the Canary Islands. She appeared as *Blanca* in Ken Loach's *Tierra y Libertad*.

PATA NEGRA

The Iberian pig which is indigenous to Spain roams freely in areas of southern Spain, feeding on acorns, grass and grubs. The ham which is produced from the pig is justly famous. Traditional DENOMINACIÓN DE ORIGEN areas producing this ham include Guijelo in Salamanca, La Dehesa in EXTREMADURA and Jamón de Huelva, in ANDALUCÍA.

PATERA

Small boats in which illegal emigrants travel from Morocco to the southern coast of Spain. See also: BALSEROS

PATI 2 See: *PLAN DE ACCIÓN DE TECNOLOGÍA INDUSTRIAL*

PATRIMONIO DEL ESTADO
State holding company, created in 1964 to administer public companies such as TABACALERA, BANCO EXTERIOR and TELEFÓNICA.

PCE See: *PARTIDO COMUNISTA DE ESPAÑA*

PDNI See: *PARTIDO DEMOCRÁTICO DE LA NUEVA IZQUIERDA*

PEAN
Plan Económico Andorra: this programme seeks to develop certains regions of Teruel, including Andorra itself, Ariño and Alcorisa with grants and loans from both private and public sources. These monies are made available to small and medium sized companies and those seeking to establish their own businesses.

PECES-BARBA, GREGORIO (1938–   )
Rector of the UNIVERSIDAD CARLOS III and *ex-presidente* of the CONGRESO during the first legislature (1982–86). He was the representative for PSOE in the team which drew up the new CONSTITUCIÓN in 1978.

PELLÓN, JACINTO (1935–   )
Comisario general for the 1992 World Trade Fair in SEVILLA.

PELOTA
Ball-game which is very popular in the PAÍS VASCO. It can be played with hand, glove, racket or bat. In the Basque country it is often played with a wicker basket attached to the forearm in which the ball is caught and flung. It is one of the fastest games in the world. Outside Spain it is also known as *jai-alai*.

PEN See: *PLAN ENERGÉTICO NACIONAL*

PENA DE MUERTE
The death penalty in Spain was abolished under the 1978 constitution.

PENEDÉS
Area in the north-east of Spain, famous for its wine and especially for the sparkling wine known as CAVA.

PEÑON DE ALHUCEMAS
Island off the Moroccan coast. It is a so-called *plaza de soberanía* and as such comes under Spanish jurisdiction.

PEÑON DE VÉLEZ DE LA GOMERA
Island off the Moroccan coast. It is a so-called *plaza de soberanía* and as such comes under under Spanish jurisdiction.

PEQUEÑAS Y MEDIANAS EMPRESAS
The promotion and growth of small and medium-sized industries is one of the goals of current Spanish industrial policy. Measures have been drawn up to promote international cooperation in this sector, to provide credit facilities and to offer information and advice to businessmen working in this area.

PER See: *PLAN DE EMPLEO RURAL*

PER
Well known partnership of architects, specialising in minimalist and conceptual work.

PÉREZ REVERTE, ARTURO (1951–   )
Novelist, journalist and war correspondent. Two of his novels, *El maestro de esgrima* (1988) and *La tabla de Flandes* (1990) have been made into films. His novel, *La piel del tambor* (1995) has sold over 150,000 copies. In 1997 he published a novel in conjunction with his daughter Carlota, entitled *El capitán Alatriste*. The sequel to *El capitán* was published later that year, entitled *Limpieza de sangre*.

EL PERIÓDICO
Newspaper which belong to the ZETA newspaper chain and is more popular in appeal than EL PAÍS or LA VANGUARDIA. It is based in CATALUÑA. In 1997 it became the first newspaper in Spain to publish the same edition in two languages, CASTELLANO and CATALÁN. It is the fourth most widely read newspaper in Spain with a daily circulation of 210,000 copies.

PERIÓDICO DE CATALUNYA
Independent morning newspaper, edited in BARCELONA and owned by *Ediciones Primera Plana, S.A.*. It invested in the most advanced technology of the time and is justly renowned for its visual presentation. It has a circulation approaching 200,000 during the week and almost 400,000 on Sundays.

PERMISO DE CONDUCIR
Spaniards can obtain driving licences at the age of 16 for 125cc motor bikes, at 18 for cars and at 21 for buses, cars with trailers and heavy goods vehicles.

PERMISO DE TRABAJO
All non-members of the EU wishing to work in Spain must obtain a work permit. There are several categories of work permit: *A*, for workers engaged in seasonal or cyclical work: *B*, for those wishing to work in a specific geographical area: *C*, for those employed in any activity and in any geographical area.

PEROTE PELLÓN, JUAN ALBERTO
Ex-head of the *Agrupación Operativa* of CESID, he was imprisoned in 1995 for removal of classified documents of importance for national security. Some material (transcripts of bugged telephone calls) were published by the Spanish daily EL MUNDO. It has been alleged that PEROTE passed classified information to the Libyan government.

PETRÓLEOS DEL MEDITERRÁNEO
Petrochemical company, acquired in the 1980s by *British Petroleum*. It is now known as *BP Oil España, S.A.*

PETROMED See: *PETRÓLEOS DEL MEDITERRÁNEO*

PFC See: *PROGRESO Y FUTURO DE CEUTA*

PICOS DE EUROPA
Mountain chain in the north of Spain in the provinces of ASTURIAS, LEÓN and CANTABRIA. The area now forms the largest national park in Europe with over 65,000 hectares.

PIÑAR, BLAS (1918–   )
Leader of the extreme right party FUERZA NUEVA, he was especially active during the transition to democracy in the late 1970s.

PINEDA, EMPAR
A leading feminist, PINEDA was an important figure in the MC (*Movimiento Comunista*) in CATALUÑA during the transition. She later became leader of the *Colectivo de Feministas Lesbianas de Madrid*.

PIRULÍ
Slang term given to a tower such as the Torrespaña in MADRID or the Residencia Almirante in Vigo.

PL See: *PARTIDO LIBERAL*

PLÁ, ALBERTO (1966–   )
Comic actor and singer.

PLAN DE ACCIÓN DE TECNOLOGÍA INDUSTRIAL
This new plan of action, designed to cover the period from 1994 to 1996, gave priority to the communication and information industries and aimed to strengthen small and medium-sized industries (PYMES) by improving infrastructure and resources and by providing them with low interest loans.

PLAN DE CONVERGENCIA
This plan, drawn up in 1992 as a result of the Edinburgh Summit, was designed to further restrict government spending and to adopt a harsh monetary policy with a view to joining the EMU.

PLAN DE EMPLEO RURAL
This programme provides work and/or unemployment benefits for agricultural workers in the south, on state-financed infrastructure projects. Eligibility requirements for unemployment benefits are low: as few as 40 days work a year entitles the recipient to 120 days worth of benefits. Since 1991, many beneficiaries have been women.

PLAN DE ESTABILIDAD 1997–2000
Plan drawn up by the MINISTERIO DE ECONOMÍA Y HACIENDA, with a view to meeting the requirements for the common European

currency. It predicates an economic growth of 3.2% over the period 1997–2000 and a decrease of 1.6% in public spending. Interest rates should also fall and the rate of job creation increase.

PLAN DE FORMACIÓN DE EMPRESAS
Companies with more than 200 workers may apply for grants to initiate in-service training programmes.

PLAN DE LIBERTAD Y SEGURIDAD
This plan, introduced in 1994 by JUAN ALBERTO BELLOCH, is intended to improve public safety through a series of measures which are less confrontational that those proposed in the LEY CORCUERA.

PLAN DE TRANSPORTE FERROVIARIO
The object of this plan is to modernise the Spanish railway system. Over two billion pesetas are to be invested in its infrastructure in the immediate future. The international gauge of 1,435 mm will be introduced for the new high-speed trains, with priority given to the MADRID-SEVILLA and MADRID-BARCELONA lines.

PLAN ENERGÉTICO NACIONAL
This plan was ratified in 1991 and has the following objectives: to cut energy costs, to diversify the production of power and energy, to increase domestic resources and to work towards conservation of the environment. Spain is still very dependent on oil, which accounts for 65% of her energy consumption.

PLAN HIDROLÓGICO NACIONAL
A national policy for the storing and use of water, which envisages the connecting of reservoirs (such as those on the EBRO and DUERO) with those in the south (on the GUADALQUIVIR, GUADIANA and SEGURA) so that water can be evenly distributed throughout the entire country. Since water is a scarce resource, the plan has not yet been implemented due to objections from those AUTONOMÍAS affected.

PLAN INTEGRAL DE JUVENTUD
This policy document, approved in 1991, concerns young people in Spain. It has provided over a billion and a half pesetas to fulfill

34 objectives in 5 major areas. These areas are: education, training and employment; housing, health care and the promotion of a healthy life style; equal opportunities, including actions directed towards lower income and disadvantaged young people; societies and associations directed at young people; and international projects with other European and Latin-American countries.

PLAN NACIONAL DE REFORESTACIÓN
National plan which attempts to combat deforestation in Spain by offering grants to farmers to plant indigenous species of trees.

PLAN RECTOR
Each national park has a PLAN RECTOR or strategic plan, which sets out aims, objectives and policies for the management of the area.

PLANCHUELO, MIGUEL
Jefe of the *Brigada de Información de Bilbao* from 1981 to 1984 and police chief in BILBAO from 1984 to 1988 during the time in which GAL was operative. He was tried in 1995 by GARZÓN, accused of belonging to a terrorist organisation, illegal arrest and participation in 8 murder attempts.

PLENO DEL AYUNTAMIENTO
This term – usually abbreviated to *el pleno* – refers to the city or town council and is the elected body of the municipal government.

PLENOS
PLENOS are plenary sittings of Parliament which tend to take place on Tuesday and Wednesday afternoons and all day Thursday.

PLURIEMPLEO
Practice of holding several jobs at one time: this was made illegal under the GONZÁLEZ government. It ensures that employees such as doctors may not work concurrently in the private and public sector.

PLUS ULTRA COMPAÑIA DE SEGUROS Y REASEGUROS

This insurance company was founded in 1887 and specialises principally in life insurance.

PNB See: *PRODUCTO NACIONAL BRUTO*

PNN See: *PROFESOR NO NUMERARIO*

PNR See: *PLAN NACIONAL DE REFORESTACIÓN*

PNV See: *PARTIDO NACIONAL VASCO*

PODERES FÁCTICOS

This expression is often used with reference to the Catholic Church and to the army – that is, to the de facto powers as opposed to the de jure powers (the monarchy, government, the judiciary and the civil service).

POLEO-MENTA

Type of infusion, very popular in the COMUNIDAD VALENCIANA, and drunk after a meal to help the digestion.

POLICÍA LOCAL/MUNICIPAL

Police force working within urban areas. Their duties include traffic control, protection of population and property, patrolling parks and open places, and crowd control.

POLICÍA NACIONAL

The name of the national police force until its amalgamation in 1986 with the *Cuerpo General*. It is now known as the CNP or CUERPO NACIONAL DE POLICÍA. Three regions have their own force (CATALUÑA, EL PAÍS VASCO and NAVARRA) and three have assumed responsibility for the national force (ANDALUCÍA, GALICIA and VALENCIA).

POMBO, ÁLVARO (1939–   )

Author of novels such as *Relatos sobre la falta de sustancia* (1977) and *Los delitos insignificantes*. He is concerned with themes such as appearance and reality and the nature of personality and human identity. He received the *Premio Herralde de Novela* for *El héroe de las mansardas de Mansard*.

PONENCIAS

These are working parties nominated by the various parliamentary committees to prepare specialised materials and documents for meetings. They reflect the relative importance of each political party.

PORT AVENTURA

Largest theme park in Spain, it was opened in 1995 and is situated in Salou (Tarragona). Its five themes are: the Mediterranean, the Far West, Polynesia, China and Mexico. It is jointly owned by LA CAIXA, FECSA, the Pearson Group and the American company *Anheuser Busch*, which conceived and designed the park.

PORTAVOZ DEL GOBIERNO

The spokesman/woman for the Government was responsible for managing the media with relations to political affairs. This ministerial portfolio acquired a separate ministry in 1988. In 1992, this portfolio was subsumed into the MINISTRERIO DE LA PRESIDENCIA or Prime Minister's Office.

PORTLAND VALDERRIVAS, S.A.

This company is active in the construction industry, in both the public and private sectors. It also produces cement, concrete and clinker, and has interests in real estate.

POSADAS, CARMEN (1953–   )

Writer and member of the jet set, she was married to the business man MARIANO RUBIO in the 1980s. She has written for the cinema and television. Her latest novel is entitled *Cinco moscas azules*, a detective story set amid the rich and aristocratic society of MADRID. She also published a collection of 14 short stories in 1997.

POTOTO

Alias of Julián Atxurra Egurola, third in command of the Basque terrorist group ETA. He was arrested by the French police in Pau in July 1996.

PP See: *PARTIDO POPULAR*

PR See: *PARTIDO RIOJANO*

PRACTICANTES
Practising members of the Church. Although Spain is a Catholic country, only 30–40% of adults are regular church goers.

PRÁCTICAS
Short-term work experience of a duration of not less than six months and not more than two years. The salary earned must be not less than 60% in the first year and 75% in the second year of that earned by the employee who normally occupies that position.

PRADO Y COLÓN DE CARVAJAL, MANUEL (1931–   )
International financier, he was *Presidente* of IBERIA in 1975 and was also a SENADOR. He has also been *presidente* of the *Instituto de Cooperación Iberoamericana* and ambassador *en misión extraordinaria*. In the mid-eighties he began to work with JAVIER DE LA ROSA, first as vice-presidente of the CNL (*Consorcio Nacional del Leasing*, later GRAN TIBIDABO). As a result of mismanagement and malpractice in the latter company, he is currently (1995) on trial in the Spanish courts.

EL PRAT
Airport located in BARCELONA.

PRAT, JOAQUÍN (1929–1995)
Game-show host, he compered the massively successful show *Un, dos tres* for a number of years. As a result of this show he became a household name in Spain.

PRC See: *PARTIDO REGIONALISTA CÁNTABRO*

PREJUBILACIÓN
Some workers may elect to go on to a period of short-time working prior to retirement, or they may be required to do so. These workers earn a pro-rata salary.

PREMIO CERVANTES
The most important literary prize awarded to any writer writing

in the Spanish language. Among those who have won the prize are Octavio Paz (1981), Ernesto Sábato (1984) and Francisco Ayala (1991).

PREMIO DE NOVELA FERNANDO LARA
Annual literary prize awarded by the *Editorial Planeta* and worth 20 million pesetas. It is the second largest literary prize awarded in Spain.

PREMIO JOSEP PLÁ
Annual literary prize awarded to novels written in CATALÁN and worth 1 million pesetas.

PREMIO NACIONAL DE POESÍA
Annual prize previously awarded by the *Ministerio de Cultura* (now the MINISTERIO DE EDUCACIÓN Y CULTURA) and worth 2.5 million pesetas. In 1996 it was awarded to Felipe Benítez Reyes.

PREMIO NADAL
Annual literary prize awarded by the publishers *Ediciones Destino* for the best novel of the year and worth three million pesetas. The first PREMIO NADAL was awarded in 1942 to CARMEN LAFORET, for her novel *Nada*. It is always awarded on the 6th of January and is considered to be one of the most important literary prizes in Spain.

PREMIO PRÍNCIPE DE ASTURIAS
Prizes awarded annually by the PRÍNCIPE DE ASTURIAS, (FELIPE DE BORBÓN) in such areas as sports, culture, literature and the sciences. Among the winners have been MIGUEL INDURÁIN, LUIS BERLANGA and MARIO VARGAS LLOSA.

PREMIOS GOYA
Equivalent to the Oscars in the United States, these prizes are awarded annually, in January, by the *Academia del Cine*. Prizes are awarded for the best film, best script, best actor and so on.

PRENSA ESPAÑOLA, S.A.
Media group which owns ABC. Its current chairman (1977) is Guillermo Luca de Tena.

PRESIDENCIA DEL PARTIDO POPULAR
The presidency or inner cabinet of the PP consists of the founder president (MANUEL FRAGA), the president (currently JOSÉ MARÍA AZNAR) and the general secretary. The founder president's position is purely honorary. It is the president who wields most power in this triumvirate.

PRESIDENTE DE AUTONOMÍA
The *presidente* is the head of an autonomous region and also of the regional executive. He has three functions: he represents the community in its relations with the monarchy, central government and in foreign affairs; he is responsible for making political decisions which affect the community; and he nominates and discharges the members of the regional executive also.

PRESIDENTE DEL CONGRESO
The PRESIDENTE (or Speaker) of the CONGRESO DE LOS DIPUTADOS has many functions in common with the *presidente* of the SENADO. Their main task is to supervise the everyday organisation of the CORTES, to draw up the legislative agenda and to exercise parliamentary discipline.

PRESIDENTE DEL GOBIERNO
The prime minister. According to article 99 of the 1978 Constitution, the King proposes a candidate to be prime minister. This candidate then presents his programme to the CORTES and, if it gains approval, he is duly appointed by the King.

PRESOS POLÍTICOS
ETA and other terrrorist organisations in Spain consider any of their members who are imprisoned to be political prisoners and therefore entitled to special treatment and privileges.

PRESTACIÓN FAMILIAR POR HIJO
Family allowances are payable to those with children under 18. The amount received is 36,000 pesetas (double in the case of a handicapped child).

PRESTACIÓN SOCIAL SUSTITUTORIA
Those young men who are conscientious objectors and who do not wish to do military service may opt to do social work of dif-

ferent types (in schools, prisons and hospitals). This lasts one year.

PRESTACIONES CONTRIBUTIVAS
These are contributory state benefits: that is, they are payable only to those who have made sufficient contributions to the state insurance system.

PRESTACIONES ECÓNOMICAS
These are state benefits which are financial only. See also: PRESTACIONES TÉCNICAS.

PRESTACIONES TÉCNICAS
These are state benefits in kind, such as free health care.

PREYSLER, ISABEL (1951–   )
Originally from the Philippines, ISABEL PREYSLER has had three rich and famous Spanish husbands JULIO IGLESIAS, the Marqués de Griñon and MIGUEL BOYER (Formerly *Ministro de la Economía* in the GONZÁLEZ government). ISABEL PREYSLER is known throughout Spain as a member of the jet set. She regularly appears in publications such as ¡HOLA!. She is especially known for her television appearances advertising for the ceramics company, *Porcelanosa*.

PRIMA INMOBILIARIA, S.A.
This company is a holding company for a group whose main activities lie in the real estate sector. It develops urban and tourist projects, buys, sells, leases and develops leisure and sports facilities.

PRIMER CICLO
First stage of university education, lasting three years. Students may continue on to the SEGUNDO CICLO. These courses are taught not only in the universities, but also in the COLEGIO UNIVERSITARIO which offers no facilities beyond this level but which enables students to go straight into the SEGUNDO CICLO at the university to which the COLEGIO is affiliated.

PRIMER PLAN PARA LA IGUALDAD DE OPORTUNIDADES DE LA MUJER
A government policy document with 120 measures designed to

promote specific policies concerning womens' rights. These measures have resulted in educational programmes for women, an increase in the resources and services directed at women (such as shelters for battered wives), and subsidies for non-governmental agencies working with and on behalf of women.

PRÍNCIPE DE ASTURIAS
Title used by the eldest son of the monarch and heir to the throne.

PRISA See: *PROMOTORA DE INFORMACIONES, S.A.*

PRISIÓN PREVENTIVA
Remand prisons where offenders reside prior to trial. Offenders serving minor sentences of less than a year also serve their time in these prisons.

PRODUCTO NACIONAL BRUTO
GNP. In 1996, Spain's GNP was 2.4%, a similar figure to that of other European countries.

PROFESOR ADJUNTO
University teacher, equivalent to assistant professor grade. They must hold a doctorate plus have at least one year's experience as an AYUDANTE or in scientific research.

PROFESOR AGREGADO
University teacher equivalent to associate professor grade. They hold a doctorate and a qualification in education.

PROFESOR AYUDANTE
Assistant lecturers must have a first degree (LICENCIATURA) or equivalent. They are appointed for one year with the possibility of renewal for a maximum of four successive years.

PROFESOR NO NUMERARIO
Untenured university teachers of whom large numbers were recruited in the 1980s to deal with the enormous expansion in university education.

PROFESOR TITULAR
Permanent or tenured lecturer at a university.

PROGRAMA DE DESARROLLO GITANO
State programme which attempts to integrate the gypsy into mainstream Spanish life, but also to preserve gypsy culture and traditions.

PROGRAMA DE INCENTIVOS REGIONALES
Regional incentives programme. This scheme, administered by the MINISTERIO DE ECONOMÍA Y HACIENDA, funds special projects in the regions, thus creating employment and developing regional infrastructures.

PROGRAMA DE INTEGRACIÓN ESCOLAR
Programme whose object is to integrate the vast majority of disabled children within mainstream education.

PROGRAMA DE PRIVATIZACIÓN DEL SECTOR PÚBLICO
The government of JOSÉ MARÍA AZNAR has approved a four phase plan to privatise public sector companies such as TELEFÓNICA and REPSOL.

PROGRESO Y FUTURO DE CEUTA
Regional party, which won 6 of the 25 CEUTA seats in the legislative assembly in 1995 and which provided the president of the assembly, Basilio Fernández López.

PROMOTORA DE INFORMACIONES, S.A.
This media group, usually known as PRISA, controls EL PAIS, CADENA SER and CANAL PLUS. It was established in 1976 to provide an independent source of information and thus help Spain's move towards democracy and modernity.

PROMOTORA SOCIAL DE VIVIENDAS
A cooperative, founded to create reasonably priced living accommodation. It belongs to the UNIÓN GENERAL DE TRABAJADORES. In the 1990s it was at the centre of a financial scandal, accused of misappropriation of funds. It is largely financed by the ARGENTARIA and CAJAMADRID (two of the largest Spanish savings banks) and has a membership of about 12,000.

PROPINA

Tipping is not required in Spain but many people do tip waiters and taxi-drivers. If the service has beens satisfactory, a tip of between 5% and 10% of the bill is adequate.

PROPOSICIONES DE LEY

These are parliamentary bills which are not proposed directly by the government. They can issue from parliamentary groups or individual members of parliament (with the backing of 15 other DIPUTADOS).

PROSEGUR, S.A.

Founded in 1976, this is now the largest company in the security sector with a turnover of 56,000 million pesetas. It trains personnel in the use of firearms, driving security vehicles and in the legislation relevant to the security industry. It provides transport and handling, as well as electronic security systems (camera systems, alarms, perimeter systems etc.). It has an annual growth rate of over 25%.

PROTECCIÓN – PRESTACIÓN POR DESEMPLEO

State benefit payable to workers who have become unemployed. In order to claim this benefit, workers must have paid national insurance contributions for a minimum of one year in the six years preceding the period of unemployment. The longer one has contributed to the national insurance scheme, the longer one is eligible for this benefit. Once it has run out, the unemployed person may apply for the SUBSIDIO POR DESEMPLEO.

PROTECCIÓN A LA FAMILIA

Child support benefit. It is a contributory benefit, only payable to those who have made sufficient contributions into the national insurance system.

PROTECCIÓN CIVIL

National organisation composed of full-time and voluntary workers whose responsibility is to take charge in national, regional and local emergencies, such as winter blizzards, forest fires and floods.

PROVINCIA
Administrative, electoral and legal unit, made up of a number of MUNICIPIOS. The maximum representative of the state in the PROVINCIA is the GOBERNADOR CIVIL. Each province (of which there are 50) is governed by the DIPUTACIÓN, elected by the different AYUNTAMIENTOS. The province is the unit from which DIPUTADOS and SENADORES are elected to the lower and upper chambers.

PROYECTO DE LEY
Bills or draft laws, proposed by the government or a regional parliament.

PRYCA
Most important supermarket chain in Spain, owned by the French company *Carrefour*. In 1995 it had 51 stores, 14,200 employees and a turnover of 543,374 million pesetas.

PSC See: *PARTIT DELS SOCIALISTES DE CATALUNYA*

PSE See: *PARTIDO SOCIALISTA DE EUSKADI*

PSG-EG See: *PARTIDO SOCIALISTA DE GALICIA ESQUERDA GALEGA*

PSOE See: *PARTIDO SOCIALISTA OBRERO ESPAÑOL*

PSV See: *PROMOTORA SOCIAL DE VIVIENDAS*

PUENTE
If a public holiday takes place on a Thursday or Tuesday it is customary for Spaniards to '*hacer puente*' ('make the bridge'): that is, to have a long weekend by making Monday or Friday a holiday too.

PUENTING
Sport consisting of tying oneself to the top of a cliff or bridge and jumping into the void.

PUERTO BANÚS
This holiday resort near Marbella is one of the few which have been entirely artificially created. Its extensive marinas attract wealthy tourists from all over the world, especially from the Arab countries.

PUERTO OLÍMPICO
Marina created for the BARCELONA Olympic Games in 1992 and situated in the Poble Nou on the Paseo Marítimo, near the Olympic Village.

PUÉRTOLAS, SOLEDAD (1947–   )
Novelist. Her favourite themes are the passage of time, love and its reversals and the fragility of life. She has published six novels including *El bandido doblemente armado* (1980), *Queda la noche* (1989) and *La corriente del golfo* (1993). *Queda la noche* won the *Premio Planeta*.

PUJOL, JORDI (1930–   )
President of the CATALÁN GENERALITAT since 1980 and leader of the CiU (CONVERGENCIA i UNIÓ). PUJOL has been president since his party won the first autonomous elections in 1980. He was imprisoned from 1960 to 1963 for organising a cultural event in which the Catalán national anthem was sung in CATALÁN. He is a fervent Catholic and nationalist and deeply respected in CATALUÑA. He was a key figure in the negotiations which led to the formation of the government of the PARTIDO POPULAR after the parliamentary elections of 1996.

PULEVA-UNIÓN INDUSTRIAL AGRO-GANADERA, S.A.
This company operates in the food manufacturing sector and produces dairy foods, pasteurised and long-life milk, milk shakes, butter, cream and cheese. It also manufactures baby milk and powdered food. Products are marketed throughout Spain under the *Puleva* trade-mark.

PVE See: *PARTIDO VERDE ESPAÑOL*

PYME See: *PEQUEÑAS Y MEDIANAS EMPRESAS*

QUADRA-SALCEDO, TOMÁS DE LA (1946–   )
Ministro de Administración Territorial (1982–85) and *ministro de Justicia* (1991–93) in the government of FELIPE GONZÁLEZ. In 1981 he formed part of the commision on the AUTONOMIAS.

QUEREJETA, ELÍAS (1935–1997)
International film producer. He has produced thirteen of CARLOS SAURA's films including *La caza* (1965), *La prima Angélica* (1973) and *Deprisa, deprisa* (1980) and has produced many of the most important films to come out of Spain. All (apart from *La familia de Pascual Duarte*) are based on original scripts and many have won prizes at the major European festivals. He died in Cuba in 1997.

QUEREJETA, GRACIA (1962–   )
Member of the younger generation of film directors, she has made two films – *El último viaje de Robert Rylands* and *Una estación de paso*. *El último viaje* was based on a novel by JAVIER MARÍAS and proved rather controversial.

QUINIELA
Spanish version of the football pools. It began in 1946 with the name *Apuesta Mutua Deportiva Benéfica*. All profits go to charity.

QUINIELÓN
An easier version of the traditional QUINIELA or football pools in which 15 correct results are the maximum correct forecast.

QUINTERO, JESÚS (1946–   )
Journalist and radio presenter, known as *El loco de la colina*. He has hosted a programme of the same name for several years, first with RNE (RADIO NACIONAL DE ESPAÑA) and later with CADENA SER.

QUO
Popular monthly magazine dealing with social and scientific issues, it was founded in 1995 and is a competitor of magazines such as MUY INTERESANTE.

RABAL, FRANCISCO (1926–)

Veteran film actor who has worked not only with Spanish directors but with many important European film makers also. It was probably his work with LUIS BUÑUEL in *Viridiana* (1961) and *Nazarín* (1958) which brought him his early fame, but throughout the 1980s he played in a number of important films including *Los santos inocentes* (CAMUS 1984) for which he won the prize for best actor at the Cannes Film Festival.

RACE See: *REAL AUTOMÓVIL CLUB DE ESPAÑA*

RADIO ESPAÑA DE MADRID

This radio group is also known as *Cultural Radio Española*. Based in MADRID, it is part of *Cadena Ibérica*. It was founded in 1924 and is currently directed by Eugenio Fontán Pérez.

RADIO LIBERTY

RADIO LIBERTY, sited on the beach at Pals (Girona) was a radio station originally owned by the CIA and used to broadcast anti-communist material to the USSR. It ceased broadcasting in November 1995.

RADIO NACIONAL DE ESPAÑA

State-owned radio network, under the aegis of RTVE. Faced with the competition from the commercial stations, RNE is losing audience share.

RADIO OCHENTA SERIE ORO

Chain of sixteen radio stations, owned by ANTENA 2 and specialising in 'golden oldies'.

RADIO POPULAR

More popularly known as COPE, this radio broadcasting network has 45 medium wave and 121 FM stations. Its chairman is Silvio González Moreno.

RADIO TELEVISIÓN ESPAÑOLA
The state-owned radio and television network with two channels, TVE-1 and TVE-2. The first is aimed at the general public and offers uninterrupted programming from early in the morning to late evening: it has the largest audience (almost 25% of viewers in 1997). TVE-2 specialises in sports broadcasts and live broadcasts of important cultural events. It has an audience of about 7 million viewers (8.6% in 1997). Both channels are financed by publicity and this income is also used to subsidize the radio system (known as RNE, RADIO NACIONAL DE ESPAÑA).

RAHOLA, PILAR (1958–   )
Member of Parliament for ERC (*Esquerra Republicana de Catalunya*) she is a leading member of the movement for Catalán independence without violence or armed struggle.

RAIMÓN (1940–   )
This song-writer and singer from VALENCIA was involved in the *Nova Cançó* movement. See also: MARÍA DEL MAR BONET, JOAN MANUEL SERRAT, LLUIS LLACH

RAJOY BREY, MARIANO (1955–   )
Lawyer and politician in GALICIA and member of the XUNTA de Galicia. Originally DIPUTADO for Pontevedra in the CONGRESO and later *vicesecretario general* of the PP. In 1996 he became *ministro de Administraciones Públicas*.

LAS RAMBLAS
Avenue in BARCELONA which links the city centre with the sea. It is famous for its cafés, flower stalls, street artistes and bird-sellers.

RASTRO
Flea market in MADRID. Open on Sunday mornings only, it is to be found in the area around Ribera de Curtidores, off the Plaza Mayor.

RATO FIGAREDO, RODRIGO (1949–   )

Former spokesman for the PP in the CONGRESO. Earlier he was a DIPUTADO for AP between 1982 and 1989 and *secretario general adjunto* of the parliamentary party under Miguel Herrero de Miñon. He was appointed *vicepresidente segundo* and *ministro de Economía y Hacienda* in the 1996 government of JOSÉ MARÍA AZNAR.

REAL ACADEMIA DE LA LENGUA/REAL ACADEMIA ESPAÑOLA

The Royal Academy of the (Spanish) Language was founded in 1713 by Felipe V. It establishes norms for the correct use of the Spanish languge. It also produces a dictionary, the DRAE or DICCIONARIO DE LA REAL ACADEMIA DE LA LENGUA ESPAÑOLA. The headquarters of the REAL ACADEMIA are in MADRID but there are other *Academias de la Lengua* throughout the Spanish-speaking world which, in turn, establish norms for the correct use of Spanish in their own countries. There are 36 members of the Spanish ACADEMIA: in 1978 the first woman member was admitted, the poet CARMEN CONDE. Each seat has a letter of the alphabet: it is only when the holder of a particular seat dies or resigns that another member is elected to take his or her place.

REAL AUTOMÓVIL CLUB DE ESPAÑA

Association which assists its members when they have accidents or breakdowns on the road.

REAL MADRID

One of the two first division football teams in MADRID and one of BARCELONA's great rivals. The team has won the European Cup six times. In 1996, Lorenzo Sanz was appointed *presidente*. They are known as the *merengues* ('meringues') because of their white strip.

REALES DECRETOS

These decrees are of the highest importance and must be signed by both the king and a minister. They were used frequently in the 1980s and 1990s to transfer powers and responsibilities from central government to the autonomous regions.

RECTOR DE UNIVERSIDAD
The vice-chancellor of a university. He or she is the top official of the university and as such is responsible for its management and administration. He or she is elected from the entire body of CATEDRÁTICOS or full professors.

RED ELÉCTRICA ESPAÑOLA
Public company which provides high tension electricity throughout Spain. Its latest project is to lay 25 kilometres of cable on the sea bed from Spain to Morocco, via Tarifa.

RED NACIONAL DE FERROCARRILES ESPAÑOLES
The Spanish railway system, 12,570 kilometres in length. It operates all the wide-gauge lines (the network is 233 mm wider than the European standard gauge). It radiates from MADRID with two lines going to the French border, another to ANDALUCÍA and VALENCIA and the high speed tracks to SEVILLA, Cadiz and Huelva. See also: FEVE.

REDONDO, NICOLÁS (1927–   )
Secretario general of the UGT from 1976 to 1994. He became a member of the union at 18 when he was an apprentice at the naval dockyards in Sestao. He has been in prison more than a dozen times for his opposition to the government, the first time being in 1951 and the last in 1974. He was a DIPUTADO in the CONGRESO from 1977 to 1987 when he resigned. In 1994 he was succeeded as leader of the UGT by CÁNDIDO MÉNDEZ. He was held for questioning in 1994 on his role in the collapse of PSV. See also: PSV.

REE See: *RED ELÉCTRICA ESPAÑOLA*

REFERÉNDUM
Under article 92 of the CONSTITUCIÓN, the King may call a REFERÉNDUM, at the request of the PRESIDENTE DEL GOBIERNO on matters of supreme importance to the Spanish State. Referenda have been called to approve the transition to democracy (1976) and in 1978 to approve the CONSTITUCIÓN. They can only be called by the state and not by individual AUTONOMÍAS or MUNICIPIOS.

REFRENDO
Expression used to signify the endorsement by the prime minis-

ter (or another minister) of any official document signed by the King. This is a means of limiting the power of the King but also of absolving him of responsibility for political decisions.

REGÀS, ROSA (1934–   )
Catalán novelist who won the PREMIO NADAL in the fiftieth anniversary of its inception with a novel entitled *Azul*. She had only published one earlier novel, *Memoria de Almator*, published in 1991.

REGIÓN DE MURCIA
Official name of the autonomous region based in MURCIA, to the south of the COMUNIDAD VALENCIANA. Its regional parliament is known as the GOBIERNO.

REGISTRO CIVIL
Register of births, marriages and deaths. The phrase can also refer to a Registry Office. This department is accountable to the MINISTERIO DE JUSTICIA.

REGISTRO DE LA PROPIEDAD MOBILIARIA E INMOBILIARIA
Land register or land registry office. This department is directly accountable to the MINISTERIO DE JUSTICIA.

REINSERCIÓN
Policy of reintegrating into normal society those members of terrorist organisations such as ETA and GRAPO. The policy has been criticized by those who do not approve of convicted prisoners being released early. Also, the organisations themselves view REINSERTADOS as traitors and some have been murdered after their release by former comrades. See also: YOYES

REINSERTADO(S)
This name is applied to former ETA terrorists who leave the organisation to live a normal life.

RENFE See: *RED NACIONAL DE FERROCARRILES ESPAÑOLES*

REPSOL
Until 1995, a state-owned oil company. By March 1996 only 10%

of its assets were in state hands. It has considerable interests outside Spain, including a 20% stake in *Atlantic LNG*, a company which manufactures natural gas in the Caribbean, as well as interests in Egypt where it is the third largest foreign oil company and in South American, especially Argentina, Ecuador, Perú and Bolivia.

RESIDENCIA DE TERCERA EDAD
State-run old people's home. The majority of these are new and have good facilities but only cover 40% of demand. The shortfall is met by privately-run homes.

RETEVISIÓN
Recently privatised telecommunications company which beams television signals to both public and private networks. It is second only to TELEFÓNICA in this sector.

EL RETIRO
Madrid's largest park, originally the grounds of a palace built by Philip IV in the 17th century. In the heart of the city, it has a lake (the *estanque*) and a series of avenues flanked by statues. It is popular with *madrileños* (inhabitants of MADRID) throughout the year but especially in fine weather when it is crowded with families, tourists, street artistes and vendors.

REVISTA DEL CORAZÓN
Type of gossip/society magazines which are very popular in Spain. They range from publications such as DIEZ MINUTOS to the best-selling ¡HOLA!.

REVISTA
Show or revue, which comprises music, dialogues and dance, originally confined to the theatre but popular now on television also.

REY, FERNANDO (1917–1995)
Veteran film actor who leapt to international fame with his appearance in *Viridiana* (BUÑUEL, 1961). As a result of this he went on to play important roles in non-Spanish films such as *Chimes at Midnight* (Orson Welles, 1965) and *Quintet* (Altman, 1979). He also played the lead in other BUÑUEL films such as *El*

discreto encanto de la burguesía (1972) and *Ese oscuro objeto del deseo* (1977). In 1976 he was awarded the prize for best actor at the Cannes Film Festival for his role in CARLOS SAURA's *Elisa, vida mía*. He has appeared in over 200 films including Don Quijote himself, in the television series of that name (GUTIÉRREZ ARAGÓN, 1991).

LOS REYES

The three Kings or Magi who traditionally leave presents for Spanish children on the night of the 5th of January. The Kings often parade through Spanish towns, scattering sweets and chocolates. They sometimes arrive spectacularly by boat or helicopter.

RIBEIRO

Wine-growing region in the province of Orense (GALICIA). The wine produced here is drunk in small china bowls often accompanied by *pulpo a la gallega* (Galician-style octopus).

RIDRUEJO, MÓNICA (1963–)

Until recently director of RTVE: she was appointed in 1996. Trained as an economist in the United States, she has worked for corporations such as *Citibank*, the *First National Bank of Chicago* and the *Chase Manhattan*. In recent years, she has worked as a financial consultant and later with CANAL+, the *BBC* and *NBC*.

RIERA, CARMEN (1948–)

CATALÁN novelist, winner of the *Premio Nacional de Literatura*. Her latest novel, *En el último azul*, appeared in 1996.

RÍO CABRIEL

River which divides the two provinces of Cuenca and VALENCIA. Its gorges were declared a national park (*Las Hoces del* CABRIEL) in 1995. This has led to much debate as to whether the motorway from MADRID to VALENCIA should be diverted away from this area.

RIOJA, (VINOS)

One of the best-known Spanish wines, especially famous for the oaky character of its reds. These wines are kept in oak barrels for several years which gives the wine this particular flavour.

LA RIOJA

LA RIOJA is one of the AUTONOMÍAS. It has a population of 253,259 and covers an area of 5,032 kilometres. Its capital is Logroño. It is home of the famous red and white wines, but it also has a significant industrial base, including the production of printing machinery, packaging materials and car parts. It is the home of Spain's principal manufacturer of knitting wools and threads as well as having an important footwear industry. The official name of its regional parliament is the *Gobierno*.

RÍOS, MIGUEL (1944–)

Known originally as the *rey del twist* ('king of twist'), MIGUEL RÍOS first rose to fame in the early sixties with the advent of rock and roll, under the name of Mike RÍOS. In the 1970s, he assumed his own name once again and adopted a more personal and socially committed style. His summer tours around Spain are still enormously popular, especially with the 1960s generation which first heard his songs.

RIVERA, FRANCISCO (PAQUIRRI) (1948–1984)

Bull fighter, married to the singer ISABEL PANTOJA. He was gored to death in Pozoblanco, CÓRDOBA, in 1984.

RNE See: *RADIO NACIONAL DE ESPAÑA*

ROCA JUNYENT, MIQUEL (1940–)

Catalán politician, lawyer and university professor, formerly leader of CONVERGENCIA DEMÓCRATICA DE CATALUNYA. As a member of the coalition party of CiU, he represented the party in MADRID and was one of the committee which drew up the 1978 CONSTITUCIÓN. He retired from politics in 1995.

ROCA, MARIA MERCE (1958–)

Novelist and script writer. She is the author of the popular Catalán soap opera, *Secrets de familia*.

EL ROCÍO

Festival held in ANDALUCÍA at Whitsuntide, in which the faithful go on pilgrimage to the shrine of *Nuestra Señora del ROCÍO* in Ayamonte (Huelva). The pilgrimage takes several days and leaves from SEVILLA: pilgrims wear traditional Andalusian costume and ride on horseback, drawing highly decorated carriages.

RODRÍGUEZ GALINDO, ENRIQUE (1939–   )

Head of *Comandancia 513* of the GUARDIA CIVIL in Guipúzcoa from 1981 to 1995. He led the fight against ETA during the time in which more than 100 commando groups were broken up. The most important operations which he carried out were the discovery of the so called '*papeles de Sokoa*' in which valuable information about ETA operations was seized and the capture of the ETA leadership in Bidart (France) in 1992. After the 1996 elections, the case of the deaths of LASA and ZABALA were reopened and GALINDO was accused of having been implicated. As a result of his involvement in the *guerra sucia* or dirty war, he was imprisoned in June 1996.

RODRIGUEZ PORTO, BLANCA

Wife of LUIS ROLDÁN. She was arrested in June 1994 on charges of tax evasion and concealment (*encubrimiento*), having previously sought refuge in the Chilean Embassy. (She holds both Spanish and Chilean nationality). See also: LUIS ROLDÁN.

ROIG, MONTSERRAT (1946–1991)

Catalán novelist and journalist, she is the author of *Los refugiados en los campos nazis*, *Tiempo de cerezas* and *La hora violeta*. She won the *Víctor Catalá* prize in 1971 and the *Sant Jordi* in 1976.

ROJAS-MARCOS, ALEJANDRO (1940–   )

Member of parliament from 1979 to1982 and mayor of SEVILLA from 1991 to 1995 for the PA (PARTIDO ANDALUCISTA). ROJAS-MARCOS occupies a left of centre position within the nationalist party but he was supported by the PP in his position as ALCALDE during the 1992 World Fair in that city.

ROLDÁN, LUIS

Head of the GUARDIA CIVIL from 1986 to 1993, he was indicted on a number of charges, including the charging of illegal commision, tax fraud, embezzlement, bribery and misappropriation of funds. He escaped to Laos in 1994 and was recaptured 10 months later.

In 1995, he was put on trial together with his wife and has been in preventive detention ever since.

ROMAY BECCARIA, JOSÉ MANUEL (1934–   )

Lawyer and politician from GALICIA. Originally worked with MANUEL FRAGA and in the MINISTERIO DE SANIDAD during the FRANCO régime. During the transitional years, he joined the AP and became vicepresidente of the XUNTA DE GALICIA. He is currently *ministro de Sanidad* (1996).

ROMERÍA

The ROMERÍA is a festival or holiday, held at a local shrine (usually in the countryside) and with a marked religious character. See also: EL ROCÍO

ROMERO, CARMEN (1946–   )

Member of Parliament for PSOE for Cádiz since 1989. Despite being the wife of FELIPE GONZÁLEZ, CARMEN ROMERO has always tried to keep herself and her children away from the limelight, and has kept a low profile although for many years she was second lady in the country. Before entering politics in her own right, she was a teacher.

ROMERO, EMILIO (1917–   )

Journalist and writer. He was editor-in-chief of the daily paper *El Pueblo* from 1952 to 1975. He was fired from his post at EL PAÍS by JUAN LUIS CEBRIÁN for supposedly being too generous in his opinions of those implicated in the attempted coup of the 23rd of February 1981. He won the *Premio Planeta* for his novel *La paz empieza nunca*.

RONCAL (QUESO DE)

Cheese made in the *Valle del* RONCAL in the Pyrenees. It is hard in texture and strong in flavour.

RONDA

City in the south of Spain (Málaga). It is famous for its *plaza de toros* which is the oldest in Spain, constructed in 1785.

ROTA

Ex-US army base in the province of Cádiz.

RTVE See: *RADIO TELEVISIÓN ESPAÑOLA*

RUBIA, LA

Colloquial name for the peseta. It acquired its name from the golden colour of the metal from which it is made and because one side has the face of a young woman with flowing hair.

RUBIO JÍMENEZ, MARIANO (1931–)

Business man and financier. *Ex-gobernador* of the BANCO DE ESPAÑA, RUBIO was dismissed from this post for his implication in the IBERCORP scandal. He and a colleague, Manuel de la Concha are accused of tax evasion and falsification of documents. RUBIO is alleged to have had a bank account with 115 million pesetas which had not been declared to the tax office. He was imprisoned briefly in 1994 but later released on bail.

RUDI, LUISA FERNANDA (1951–)

One of a small number of women mayors in Spain, LUISA RUDI is the ALCALDESA of ZARAGOZA. Originally an accountant, she is a member of the PP and was a member of parliament for 10 years, before moving to her post in local government.

RUEDA, GERARDO (1926–1996)

Painter and sculptor, RUEDA was one of the co-founders of the *Museo de Arte Abstracto de Cuenca* together with Fernando Zóbel and Gustavo Torner. He was a member of the *Academia de Bellas Artes de San Fernando* and one of the best-known Spanish abstract artists.

RUIZ DE LA PRADA, ÁGATA (1960–)

Designer. She works in many fields, including women's and children's fashion. She has recently moved into the creation of accessories such as luggage, scarves and cosmetics. She has also designed suites in the Hotel Alcalá in MADRID and created designs for EL CORTE INGLÉS, Swatch and Absolut. She is married to the director of EL MUNDO, Pedro Ramírez.

RUIZ SOLER, ANTONIO (ANTONIO) (1921–1996)

The most famous Spanish dancer of his day, ANTONIO and his partner, Rosario, travelled extensively abroad, taking Spanish dance (primarily flamenco) to America and Europe. ANTONIO was famed for his astonishing technique, especially in the *zapateado* (rhythmic stamping) which was always the climax of his shows.

RUIZ-GALLARDÓN, ALBERTO (1958–)

Presidente of the *Comunidad Autónoma de* MADRID from 1995 (the youngest *presidente* in Spain), he has been a SENADOR for PP since 1989. He was *secretario general* of AP from 1986 to 1988. A law graduate, he is crown prosecutor (FISCAL) with the AUDIENCIA of Málaga.

RUIZ-GIMÉNEZ, JOAQUIÍN (1912–)

Lawyer and politician. He co-founded the magazine *Cuadernos para el diálogo* in 1963 and was the *presidente* of the *Partido Demócrata-Cristiano*; this party was unsuccessful in the 1977 elections and was subsequently dissolved. In 1982 he became DEFENSOR DEL PUEBLO, in which post he remained until 1987.

RUIZ-MATEOS, JOSÉ MARÍA (1931–)

Head of the RUMASA group of companies, which was expropriated in 1983 by the government of FELIPE GONZÁLEZ. Since that time he has been at the centre of many scandals: he fled to England, was imprisoned in Germany and later in MADRID, he insulted MIGUEL BOYER (responsible for the expropriation) in public, dressed up and paraded around as Superman and so forth. RUIZ-MATEOS is still under investigation for tax evasion, misappropriation of funds, fraud and insulting Don Juan Carlos. He attempted to enter politics by founding his own political party and is now the owner of a football club, Rayo Vallecano.

RUMASA

Large holding company founded by JOSE MARIÁ RUIZ-MATEOS which controlled banks, insurance companies and numerous agricultural and manufacturing companies. It collapsed spectacularly in 1983 and was expropriated by the government of FELIPE GONZÁLEZ.

RUPÉREZ, JAVIER

Former leader of UCD, he was kidnapped in November 1979 by ETA and remained in their custody for 31 days before being released.

SÁENZ DE SANTA MARÍA, JOSÉ ANTONIO
Former leader of the POLICÍA NACIONAL and instrumental in suppressing the attempted coup of 1981. He was also responsible for setting up the GRUPO ESPECIAL DE OPERACIONES.

SAINZ, CARLOS (1962–)
SAINZ began his career as a rally driver when he won the *Copa Nacional Renault* at the age of 18. With Luis Moya as his co-pilot, he won the San Remo Rally in 1990 and became the youngest world champion ever. He has a reputation of being a cold and calculating driver.

SAL See: *SOCIEDAD ANÓNIMA LABORAL*

SALAMANCA
Important historic city on the River Tormes in the *Comunidad de CASTILLA Y LEÓN*. It has almost 400,000 inhabitants. The university of SALAMANCA is the oldest in Spain and dates from the thirteenth century. One out of every four inhabitants of the city is a student. Today SALAMANCA is an important centre for Spanish language teaching to foreigners.

SALANUEVA, CARMEN (1948–)
Directora general of the BOE from 1984 to 1991. She was arrested in 1993 for embezzlement of public funds and fraud, having bought paper for the BOE at prices in excess of the normal rate. She was also sentenced to four years imprisonment in 1995, for buying paintings at below market prices by passing herself off as a friend of the Queen and of CARMEN ROMERO.

SALARIO MÍNIMO INTERPROFESIONAL
Minimum wage agreed by the state and by the trade unions. In 1996, the minimum wage for workers older than 18 was 2,164

pesetas a day or 64,920 per month. For workers younger than 18, the established wage is 1,674 pesetas a day or 50,220 pesetas per month. These sums may be increased to cover transport costs, bonuses, PAGAS EXTRAORDINARIAS etc.

SALARIO SOCIAL

Type of income support, provided by some of the regions for those no longer in receipt of unemployment benefit.

SALAS, MARGARITA

A distinguished biologist, SALAS is a research worker at the *Centro de Biología Molecular Severo Ochoa*. She is currently head of the *Insituto de España*, a body which coordinates the work of the eight *Reales Academias*.

EL SALER

Premier golf course, situated in Cullera (VALENCIA) and designed by Javier Arana in 1968. It is one of the few public courses in Spain and has hosted many national and international competitions.

SAMARANCH, JUAN ANTONIO (1920–)

Sportsman, politician and business man. He was ambassador to the Soviet Union from 1977 to 1980. He was *presidente* of the *Comité Olímpico Español* until 1980, when he was elected *presidente* of the COI (*Comité Olímpico Internacional*). He was re-elected to the post in 1989. In 1988 he was awarded the PREMIO PRÍNCIPE DE ASTURIAS for his services to sport. As a CATALÁN, he was especially gratified to preside over the 1992 Olympic Games in BARCELONA.

SAMPEDRO, JOSÉ LUIS (1917–)

Writer and economist. SAMPEDRO has been a SENADOR and chaired the *Comisión de Medio Ambiente* in the Upper House. Among his most important works are *El río que nos lleva*, *Octubre octubre* and *La sonrisa etrusca*. In 1990 he was elected to the REAL ACADEMIA ESPAÑOLA.

SAN MIGUEL

The fourth largest manufacturer of beer in Spain, SAN MIGUEL is well known outside the peninsula also. The French company *Danone* is the principal share-holder.

SAN SEBASTIÁN

Along with BILBAO and Vitoria, SAN SEBASTIÁN is one of the three capital cities of the PAÍS VASCO. Its Basque name is Donostia. It is one of the loveliest cities in Spain because of its geographical situation on the northern coast. It has 180,000 habitants and hosts an important film festival in September.

SÁNCHEZ CASAS, JOSÉ MARÍA (1945–97)

Co-founder of the extreme left-wing terrorist organisation GRAPO. He was recently released from prison after serving a sentence of 18 years for the attack on the *California* café in MADRID and for the murders of General Muñoz Vázquez and the magistrate Cruz Cuenca.

SÁNCHEZ FERLOSIO, RAFAEL (1927–   )

SÁNCHEZ FERLOSIO is the author of numerous novels, essays and articles. His most well-known novels are *Industrias y andanzas de Alfanhuí* (a sort of modern day picaresque novel) and *El Jarama* (1956). *El Jarama* is an important example of the Spanish neo-realist novel and was awarded the PREMIO NADAL in 1955 and the *Premio de la Crítica* in 1956.

SÁNCHEZ- GIJÓN, AITANA (1969–   )

A television and film actress, she has appeared in films such as *El mar y el tiempo* (FERNÁN-GÓMEZ) and *Bajarse al moro* (COLOMO, 1988). Recently she has been working in Hollywood with Anthony Quinn and Keanu Reeves, and in 1997 appeared in *La camarera del Titanic* (BIGAS LUNA).

SÁNCHEZ VICARIO, ARANTXA (1971–   )

Tennis player, currently number 3 in the world. She won the French Open Championship (the Roland Garros) twice and the US Open in 1994. She has been in the top four women players since 1989.

SÁNCHEZ, CRISTINA (1972–   )

Woman bull fighter. Although there have been others, including *La Pajuerela* and *La Fragosa*, SÁNCHEZ is the only one to have reached the rank of '*matador de toros*'. She took the *alternativa* (that is, she became a fully-fledged bullfighter) in 1996, in Nîmes.

SÁNCHEZ, ENCARNA (1940–96)

A well-known radio personality, ENCARNA SÁNCHEZ presented the programme *Directamente Encarna* for many years on the COPE radio station. Her career began in the 1960s with *Radio Almería* and she became a national celebrity in 1978 with a programme entitled *Encarna de noche*, a late night phone-in. This programme became one of the most popular on the air waves. She died in 1996 from cancer.

SANCRISTOBAL, JULIÁN (1952–   )

GOBERNADOR CIVIL of Vizcaya (1982–84) and *director general de Seguridad de Estado* (1984–86), JULIÁN SANCRISTOBAL was arrested and imprisoned in 1994, accused of the following: belonging to a terrorist organisation, illegal arrest, involvement in a plot to murder and embezzlement of public funds with relation to the kidnapping of Segundo Marey. In 1995 he was allowed bail of 125 million pesetas.

SANFERMINES

Bull-running festival in PAMPLONA, which Ernest Hemingway made famous. It takes place from the 7th to the 14th of July to celebrate the feast-day of *San Fermín*. Young men dressed in white shirt and trousers with a red scarf and cummerbund, run in front of the bulls as they move through the streets towards the bull-rings.

SANGRÍA

Type of alcoholic fruit punch, very popular with visitors to Spain.

SANLÚCAR, MANOLO

Flamenco guitarist, who fused the sounds of the flamenco guitar with those of the classical orchestra. Among his most famous compositions are *Fantasía para guitarra y orquesta*, *Trebujena* and the music for a modern ballet by a Spanish choreographer (Grabero), *Medea*.

SANTANA, MANUEL (1938–   )

Tennis-player. He won the tournaments at Roland Garros in 1961 and 1964, Forest Hills in 1965 and Wimbledon in 1966. He retired in 1973.

SANTANDER
Capital of the autonomous community of CANTABRIA, SANTANDER
is both an industrial and tourist centre. It is justly famous for its
beach EL SARDINERO and its university, *La Universidad
Internacional de Menéndez Pelayo* which runs an impressive
series of conferences, lectures and summer schools and attracts
speakers from all over the world. SANTANDER has 200,000 inhabitants.

SANTIAGO BERNABEU
The REAL MADRID football stadium, built in the CHAMARTÍN area of
MADRID in 1947. It is named after one of the chairmen of the team
and can seat almost 100,000 spectators. It is one of the venues for
the Spanish cup final.

SANTIAGO DE COMPOSTELA
The cultural and administrative capital of GALICIA, SANTIAGO has
been a place of pilgrimage since the 9th century. Tradition has it
that the body of Saint James (Santiago) was brought to SANTIAGO
from the Holy Land and a cult grew up around his shrine.
Millions of pilgrims from Europe flocked to the city throughout
the Middle Ages. The 25th of July is the feast day of Saint James
and an important day for the city. SANTIAGO has 110,000 inhabitants and a very ancient university.

LOS SANTOS INOCENTES
Feast day of the Holy Innocents, celebrated on the 28th of
December. This is the day for practical jokes between the family
and friends and in the newspapers and on television.

SARDÁ, ROSA MARÍA (1941–   )
Catalán actress and director. She specialises in television comedies. Her most recent appearance was in the film ACTRICES.

SARDANA
Catalán national dance, danced in towns and villages throughout
CATALUÑA. It is a circle dance in which dancers hold hands and
perform to the music of the *cobla*, or traditional orchestra. It has
seen a revival in recent years, as part of an assertion of CATALÁN
national values.

EL SARDINERO
Famous beach in Santander. It was especially fashionable at the turn of the century, like LA CONCHA in SAN SEBASTIÁN.

SARRIO, S.A.
This company manufactures packaging and paper. It also processes and distributes cardboard.

SARTORIUS, NICOLÁS (1938–)
Member of parliament from 1981 to 1993 for PCE and IU, SARTORIUS is a union leader, and co-founder of COMISIONES OBRERAS. He was one of those imprisoned in the *Proceso 1001* affair in 1973.

SAURA, ANTONIO (1930–)
Internationally-known painter, born in Huesca, but who now divides his time between Paris and Cuenca.

SAURA, CARLOS (1935–)
A film-maker who rose to prominence in the sixties and seventies with films such as *La caza* (1965) *Ana y los lobos*, *Peppermint frappé* and *La prima Angélica* (1973). Although SAURA was critical of the FRANCO régime in these and other films, he escaped censorship by dealing with his subjects through metaphor. In later years he delighted Spanish as well as international audiences with his flamenco version of *Carmen* (1983) and *Bodas de Sangre* (1981). Currently (1997) he is making a film entitled *Tango*, with the Argentinian dancer Julio Bocca.

SAVATER, FERNANDO (1947–)
Basque writer and philosopher, he is the author of *La filosofía tachada* and *Panfleto contra el Todo*. He has also written several novels including *Caronte aguarda* and *El dialecto de la vida*.

SCHOMMER, ALBERTO (1928–)
Photographer. He specialises in portraits of the Spanish Royal Family.

SEAT See: *SOCIEDAD ESPAÑOLA DE AUTOMÓVILES DE TURISMO, S.A.*

SEAT
Originally a Spanish-owned automobile manufacturing com-

pany, SEAT continues to manufacture, distribute and sell automobiles, parts, accessories and related services. It is now wholly owned by *Volkswagen*.

SECOT
Body comprising experienced managing directors, many of whom are already retired, whose goal is to advise small and medium-sized companies and to encourage industrial development in the less-favoured regions.

SECRETARÍA
The term for a section within a government department.

SECRETARÍA GENERAL
Each of the parliamentary chambers has a secretariat whose function is to provide committees with legal, technical and administrative assistance. This is known as the SECRETARÍA GENERAL.

SECRETARIO DE ESTADO
Secretary of state – that is, a junior cabinet minister who is not a full member of cabinet although he may attend meetings to provide information only.

SECRETARIO GENERAL
General secretary – that is, a senior administrator in certain ministeries. This is a political appointment.

LA SEDA DE BARCELONA, S.A.
This company is in the textile sector and manufactures and distributes artificial silk and other synthetic fabrics and yarns. It also manufactures machinery.

SEGOVIA, ANDRÉS (1894–1987)
Internationally known guitarist. SEGOVIA was the first person to make the guitar acceptable within the classical repertoire. Many modern composers composed works for him.

SEGUNDO CICLO
To enter the SEGUNDO CICLO of higher education, students must either have completed the PRIMER CICLO at a university or COLEGIO UNIVERSITARIO, or have completed a bridging course after

graduation from an ESCUELA UNIVERSITARIA. The SEGUNDO CICLO offers two years of specialization, after which one is awarded the LICENCIATURA, *título de ingeniero* or *título de arquitecto*. To obtain this *título*, engineers and architects must have completed an end of term project (*proyecto de fin de carrera*).

SEGUNDO PLAN PARA LA IGUALDAD DE OPORTUNIDADES DE LA MUJER

This government programme took up where the PRIMER PLAN left off. The most important objective was to promote a change in attitude towards women in order to encourage their participation in the worlds of culture, politics and work. Goals included: to encourage a fairer distribution of household chores; to promote the appointment of women to posts of responsibility in public life and in the world of work; to improve women's health; to ensure that women such as prostitutes, drug addicts, single mothers and immigrants have full access to their social rights.

SEGURA

River, 325 kilometres in length. It flows through VALENCIA and out into the Mediterranean, to the south of ALICANTE.

SEGURA, ANABEL (1971–1993)

ANABEL SEGURA was kidnapped on the 12th of April 1993 while she was out jogging in La Moraleja (MADRID). Her body was found in September 1995.

SEGURIDAD SOCIAL

Most Spaniards think in terms of the Health Service when they speak of the SEGURIDAD SOCIAL, but this term also refers to the state pension system and unemployment benefit. In 1995, pensions accounted for 10% of GNP, health for 5% and unemployment benefits for 20%. All workers must pay a contribution (*la cotización*) as soon as they obtain salaried employment. The employer pays 28,3% of the basis of contribution (*la base de cotización*) and the worker pays 4,7% (1996 rates). Currently, all Spanish citizens have the right to pensions for invalidity or retirement, whether they have contributed to the system or not.

SEGURO DE CONDUCIR

Car insurance is obligatory in Spain and a currently valid insurance certificate must always be carried in the vehicle. Insurance premiums vary according to whether they are third-party (*a terceros*), all risk (*a todo riesgo*), against theft (*por robo*) and so on.

SEIS DE DICIEMBRE

The 6th of December is the *Día de la* CONSTITUCIÓN; it is an official holiday in Spain to mark the signing of the new constitution in 1976.

SELECTIVIDAD

An examination which students wishing to enter higher education must pass. Over 80% of candidates do so. They may sit the examination in either June or September. Each university sets its own examinations and students must enter the university whose exams they have passed.

SEMANA

One of the so-called REVISTAS DEL CORAZÓN, it is second only to ¡HOLA! in sales. It was founded in 1944. It specialises in television and film personalities.

SEMPRÚN, JORGE (1923–)

Novelist and essayist. *Ministro de Cultura* in FELIPE GONZÁLEZ's government from 1988 to 1991. SEMPRÚN was a member of the PCE until he was expelled in 1965 for 'revisionism and opportunism'. He has lived in France for many years and much of his work has been written in French. He received the *Premio Planeta* for the *Autobiografía de Federico Sánchez*. In 1996 he was the first foreign writer to be elected a member of the *Académie Goncourt*.

SENADO

The SENADO or Upper House has around 250 members elected, for the most part, from the 50 provinces, according to a first past the post system. Each province elects 4 senators, a system which does not allow for the huge difference in population between some provinces and others. Other senators represent, and are elected from, members of the regional Parliaments.

SENIDEAK
Association of families one of whose members has been imprisoned because of an allegiance to the Basque terrorist group ETA. The association holds demonstrations, gives press conferences and organises events such as hunger strikes, but is not legally recognised by the state.

SENYERA
The Catalán flag which is displayed, along with the Spanish flag, on public buildings and at official state functions. It is yellow and red.

SEPI See: *LA SOCIEDAD ESTATAL DE PARTICIPACIONES INDUSTRIALES*

SEPLA See: *SINDICATO ESPAÑOL DE LÍNEAS AÉREAS*

SEPP See: *SOCIEDAD DE PRIVATIZACIÓN DEL PATRIMONIO*

SER See: *CADENA SER*

SERNA, ASSUMPTA (1957–   )
Film actress, she has appeared in films such as *Dulces Horas* (SAURA, 1981) and *Matador* (ALMODÓVAR, 1986). She has also had a number of film parts with foreign directors including María Luisa Bemberg (*Yo, la peor de todas*, 1990). She has lived for several years in the United States where she starred in the television soap opera *Falcon Crest*.

SERRA Y SERRA, NARCÍS (1943–   )
Former *ministro de Defensa* (1982–91) and *vicepresidente* of the government (1991–95). He has also been mayor of BARCELONA (1979–82). He was obliged to resign from his government post in 1995, having been implicated in the CESID affair concerning illegal telephone tapping. He was cleared in 1996.

SERRAT, JOAN MANUEL (1943–   )
A song-writer and singer from BARCELONA, SERRAT was heavily involved in the *Nova Cançon* movement. He is famous for setting to music the poems of writers such as Antonio Machado, Rafael Alberti and Miguel Hernández. He sings both in CATALÁN

and Spanish. Among his most famous albums are *Mediterráneo*, *Para piel de manzana* and *Fa vint anys que tinc vint anys*.

SERVICIO DE CONCENTRACIÓN PARCELARIA

State scheme which aimed to create larger agricultural holdings by encouraging owners to exchange or sell smaller plots. It was later absorbed by the INSTITUTO DE REFORMA AGRARIA.

SERVICIO INTERCONFEDERAL DE MEDIACIÓN Y ARBITRAJE

Joint union-employer mediation and arbitration service. It was established in 1986 as part of the legislation for out-of-court settlements of industrial disputes.

SERVICIO MILITAR

Currently, military service is compulsory in Spain and lasts nine months. Young men from the age of 17 are liable for service but can be excused on medical grounds, if they have family commitments or if they are conscientious objectors. Conscientious objectors must perform the PRESTACIÓN SOCIAL SUSTITUTORIA or social service. Students may postpone their service until they have completed their studies. In practice, the *mili*, as it is popularly known in Spain has become so unpopular that the PARTIDO POPULAR is planning to abolish military service and introduce an entirely professional army.

SERVICIO NACIONAL DE SALUD

Spanish Health Service, modelled on the British National Health Service. Health care is free at the point of delivery. 99% of Spaniards are entitled to this free health care, although 40% of the cost of prescriptions has to be paid unless the patient is exempt.

SETIÉN, JOSÉ MARÍA (1928–   )

Bishop of SAN SEBASTIÁN since 1972. A controversial figure, he is politically active in the fight against ETA.

SEVILLA

Spain's third city, located on the river GUADALQUIVIR, with almost one and a half million inhabitants. It is the capital of the COMUNIDAD AUTÓNOMA DE ANDALUCÍA. It is an important port and

tourist centre. In 1992, it hosted an international fair, the EXPOSI-
CIÓN UNIVERSAL.

SEVILLANO, TRINIDAD (1969–   )
Prima ballerina at the age of 15 with the *Ballet Nacional*, she
retired in 1996 after a glittering international career, including
seasons with the London Festival Ballet and the Boston Ballet.

SIDA
Síndrome de Inmunodeficiencia Adquirida, the Spanish term for
AIDS. Spain has more AIDS cases than any other European country
with 180 patients per million inhabitants. Since 1981 there have
been 41,598 cases of which more than half have died. Drug users
have been the most at risk. In 1996 there was a slight decrease in
the number of cases, giving cause for optimism.

SIDRA
Cider, produced and drunk mainly in the north-west of Spain in
ASTURIAS and GALICIA. It is poured into the glass from a height in
order to aerate it.

SIERRA DE GUADARRAMA
Mountain range about 50 kilometres to the north of Madrid. It is
used by the inhabitants of MADRID (*madrileños*) as a ski resort in
winter and a place for rambling and climbing in summer.

SIESTA
Although Spain is famed for the *siesta* or afternoon nap, not
many modern day urban Spaniards continue to take one.

SILOS
Monastery in the province of Soria, which shot to fame in 1994
when a record of Gregorian chant sung by monks at the
monastery sold 3 million copies in 32 countries.

SIMA See: *SERVICIO INTERCONFEDERAL DE
MEDIACIÓN Y ARBITRAJE*

SINDIC DE GREUGES
The name for the Ombudsman in CATALUÑA.

SINDICATO DE OBREROS DEL CAMPO

This is a radical trade union, based in ANDALUCÍA and founded in 1976 in Antequera. Members have frequently staged protests (such as occupying the land) in defense of the unemployed and day labourers.

SINDICATO ESPAÑOL DE PILOTOS DE LÍNEAS AÉREAS

Union of Spanish airline pilots.

SINDICATURA DE CUENTAS

This is the Catalán equivalent to the state TRIBUNAL DE CUENTAS – that is, it is responsible for examining and controlling all public sector accounts in CATALUÑA.

SMI See: *SALARIO MÍNIMO INTERPROFESIONAL*

SNIACE, S.A.

This company manages areas of forestry, and produces and sells chemical pastes, paper, bleach, artificial and synthetic fibres and sodium sulphite.

SNS See: *SERVICIO NACIONAL DE SALUD*

SOBRESALIENTE

This is the highest qualification awarded in examinations, either public or at school. It is followed by *notable*, *bien*, *suficiente* and *insuficiente* (or fail).

SOC See: *SINDICATO DE OBREROS DEL CAMPO*

SOCIEDAD ANÓNIMA

Public limited company. Its acronym *S.A.* appears after the name of the company.

SOCIEDAD ANÓNIMA LABORAL

Type of company in which the workers are share-owners. It is similar in kind to the American or British ESOP (Employee Share Ownership Plan). 85% of permanent employees must be shareholders and own at least half the shares in the company. As in a normal company, each share carries a vote.

SOCIEDAD COLECTIVA
A firm in which the partners are personally liable in case of bankruptcy. These firms are identified by the suffix *y Compañía* (*y Cía*) after their name.

SOCIEDAD COMANDITA
A company in which the partners are personally liable in the event of bankruptcy, but whose liability is limited according to the amount of capital they initially invested. The name of the company has the suffix *SC* attached.

SOCIEDAD DE PRIVATIZACIÓN DEL PATRIMONIO
Organism created by the AZNAR goverment to oversee the sale of companies such as TABACALERA, TELEFÓNICA and ARGENTARIA, whose shares are held by the DIRECCIÓN GENERAL DEL PATRIMONIO.

SOCIEDAD DE RESPONSABILIDAD LIMITADA
This is an alternative to the SOCIEDAD ANÓNIMA and was designed to cater for smaller companies whose minimum share capital is less than 10 million pesetas. There are over 500,000 companies in Spain which fall into this category.

SOCIEDAD ESPAÑOLA DE CARBUROS METÁLICOS, S.A.
Company producing different types of gases, industrial, compressed, liquid and domestic. Some of these are destined for medical use.

SOCIEDAD ESPAÑOLA DE RADIODIFUSÍON
More popularly known as CADENA SER, this radio network was founded in 1924 and has 45 medium wave and 121 FM stations.

SOCIEDAD ESPAÑOLA DEL ACUMULADOR TUDOR, S.A.
The company and its subsidiaries are principally engaged in the manufacture and marketing of batteries.

SOCIEDAD ESTATAL DE PARTICIPACIONES INDUSTRIALES
More commonly known as SEPI, this body was created by the GONZÁLEZ government to hold the shares of the economically

healthy firms which were previously held by TENEO as part of INI.

SOCIEDAD GENERAL AZUCARERA DE ESPAÑA, S.A.
This food-manufacturing company owns factories which produce sugar, sweeteners, alcohol and yeast. Factories are situated in Vitoria, Jerez de la Frontera and Málaga.

SOCIEDAD GENERAL DE AGUAS DE BARCELONA
This company supplies drinking water to 20% of the population of Spain. It also purifies household and industrial waste water and sells bottled mineral water, and runs a water sports leisure centre.

SOCIEDAD PARA EL DESARROLLO INDUSTRIAL DE ANDALUCÍA
Body set up to promote industrial growth in ANDALUCÍA. It belongs to the TENEO group.

SOCIEDAD PARA EL DESARROLLO INDUSTRIAL DE CANARIAS
Body set up to promote industrial growth in the Canary Islands. It belongs to the TENEO group.

SOCIEDAD PARA EL DESARROLLO INDUSTRIAL DE EXTREMADURA
Body set up to promote industrial development in EXTREMADURA. It belongs to the TENEO group.

SOCIEDAD PARA EL DESARROLLO INDUSTRIAL DE GALICIA
Body originally belonging to the TENEO group which was founded to promote industrial development in GALICIA. It has recently been privatised.

SOCIEDAD PARA LA PROMOCIÓN Y RECONVERSIÓN ECONÓMICA DE ANDALUCÍA
This company promotes economic activities throughout ANDALUCÍA and itself has majority and minority holdings in numerous smaller enterprises.

SOCIEDAD REGULAR COLECTIVA
This is a business partnership with unlimited liability. This type of company is not particularly common in Spain.

SOCIEDADES BENÉFICAS
Charitable organisations. There are fewer of these in Spain than in other western European countries, as formerly most social needs were provided by the Church or the family.

SOCIEDADES DE DESARROLLO INDUSTRIAL
These companies were created in the poorer regions of Spain (EXTREMADURA, ARAGÓN, CASTILLA-LEÓN and CANARIAS) in order to promote industrial development. They belong to the holding group TENEO. They are known by the acronym SODI which is placed before the first letters of the region's name. See also: SODIEX, SOCIEDAD PARA EL DESARROLLO INDUSTRIAL DE GALICIA, DE ANDALUCÍA etc.

SODI See: *SOCIEDADES DE DESARROLLO INDUSTRIAL*

SODIAN See: *SOCIEDAD PARA EL DESARROLLO INDUSTRIAL DE ANDALUCÍA*

SODIEX See: *SOCIEDAD PARA EL DESARROLLO INDUSTRIAL DE EXTREMADURA*

SODIGA See: *SOCIEDAD PARA EL DESARROLLO INDUSTRIAL DE GALICIA*

SOFÍA DE GRECIA (1938–   )
Born in Greece, and eldest daughter of King Paul and Queen Federica of Greece, SOFÍA married JUAN CARLOS I in 1962. Together with her husband, she ascended the throne in 1975.

SOGECABLE
The most important satellite television company in Spain, it controls CANAL+ and *Canal Satélite Digital*. It has recently signed an agreement with Warner Brothers to be the sole distributor of their films and television programmes in Spain. The agreement also includes the rights to CNN programmes and the Hanna Barbera cartoons.

SOL, LAURA DEL (1961–   )

Trained as a flamenco dancer, LAURA DEL SOL was discovered by Emiliano Piedra, the producer of SAURA's *Carmen* (1983). Having achieved a great success as the heroine in that film, she went on to play in other SAURA movies including *Los zancos* (1984) and *El amor brujo* (1985). She has also appeared in *El rey pasmado* (1991) directed by IMANOL URIBE.

SOL MELIÁ

Important chain of hotels with establishments in 22 countries. Hotels with the names *Meliá Hoteles*, *Sol Hoteles*, *Sol Inn Hoteles* and *Paradisus* all belong to this chain. The company belongs to the Escarrer family from Mallorca and has 19,000 employees. It is the third largest European company in this sector.

SOLANA, JAVIER (1942–   )

Politician, SOLANA has been *ministro de Cultura* (1982), *de Educación y Ciencia* (1988) and *ministro de Exteriores* (1992). In 1995 he was appointed head of NATO in spite of having campaigned earlier against Spain's entry into the North Atlantic Treaty Organisation.

SOLANA, LUIS (1935–   )

Lawyer. Socialist member of parliament for Segovia from 1977 to 1982, *presidente* of TELÉFONICA from 1982 to 1989 and director of RTVE from 1989 to 1990.

SOLBES MIRA, PEDRO (1942–   )

Politician, he has worked closely with colleagues in the European Union and indeed was a participant in the negotiations on Spain's entry into the the EU. SOLBES was appointed *ministro de Agricultura* in the 1991 government shuffle and worked closely on the Common Agricultural Policy of the EU. In 1993 he was appointed *ministro de Economía y Hacienda*.

SOLCHAGA, CARLOS (1944–   )

Politician. Appointed *ministro de Industría y Energía* in 1982 and *ministro de Economía y Hacienda* from 1985 to 1993.

SOPREA See: *SOCIEDAD PARA LA PROMOCIÓN Y RECONVERSIÓN ECONÓMICA*

SOTOGRANDE

Luxurious housing development in Cádiz, frecuented by million-aires and members of European royal families. It is internation-ally known for its private health clinics. The development is entirely private and it is difficult for outsiders to penetrate the complex.

SPAIN-MOROCCO TUNNEL

It was agreed in 1996 to construct a tunnel joining Spain and Morocco. The terminal in Spain is to be built near the city of Tarifa and in Morocco, near Tangiers. It will be similar to the Channel tunnel in construction, with two tunnels for trains and a third for services. A budget of 64,000 million pesetas has been set aside for the project.

SPANAIR

Originally a charter airline, it now runs scheduled flights. Its headquarters is in Palma de Mallorca. 51% of its shares are owned by *Viajes* MARSANS and 49% by *SAS*.

SPANISH GUN LAWS

The GUARDIA CIVIL administers the granting of fire-arms licences, of which 1 million are held by people who hunt. Security and military personnel (including those who have retired) are also allowed to own arms. There are three million guns held legally in Spain.

SRC See: *SOCIEDAD REGULAR COLECTIVA*

SRL See: *SOCIEDAD DE RESPONSABILIDAD LIMITADA*

SUÁREZ, ADOLFO (1932–)

ADOLFO SUÁREZ held several important posts in the FRANCO régime, including GOBERNADOR CIVIL of Segovia and *director general* of RTVE. As leader of the UCD, he won the first democratic elections in Spain after the death of General FRANCO and was appointed *primer ministro* in 1976, which post he held until 1981. Earlier, he had been chosen by JUAN CARLOS to oversee the transi-tion between FRANCO's dictatorship and the new democratic state. In 1982 he founded another party, the CDS (CENTRO DEMOCÁTICO Y

SOCIAL), which did relatively well in the 1986 elections, winning 19 parliamentary seats. He resigned the party leadership after its disastrous showing in the local and regional elections of 1991.

SUÁREZ, EMMA (1964–   )

She was chosen at the age of 15 to play the lead role in *Memorias de Leticia Valle* (Miguel Angel Rivas, 1979) and since then has played important parts on radio, television and in the cinema. The most recent films in which SUÁREZ has appeared are *Vacas*, *La ardilla roja* and *Tierra* by JULIO MEDEM. In 1996 she appeared in PILAR MIRÓ's *El perro del hortelano*, and worked with Imanol Arias in the TV series *Querido maestro* in 1997.

SUÁREZ, GONZALO (1934–   )

Originally a journalist and novelist, SUÁREZ turned his attention to the cinema in the sixties. After a series of adaptations of novels for the cinema he found his personal style in films such as *Reina Zanahoria* (1978), *Epílogo* (1984) and *Remando al viento* (1988).

SUBIRATS, MARINA (1943–   )

Directora of the INSTITUTO DE LA MUJER since 1993, SUBIRATS has a doctorate in Philosophy and Letters and is Professor of Sociology at the UAB (*Universidad Autonómica de Barcelona*). Her special interest is sexism in school. She was appointed to the post at the INSTITUTO DE LA MUJER by CRISTINA ALBERDI, despite not being a member of the PSOE.

SUBIRÓS, JOSEP (1947–   )

CATALÁN novelist, SUBIRÓS won the PREMIO JOSEP PLÁ in 1996 for his novel *Cita a Tombuctú*. His two previous books were *Full de dames* (1992) and *La rosa del desert* (1993).

SUBSECRETARIO DE ESTADO

In a ministry without a secretary of state, the under-secretary or *subsecretario* is the most important figure, after the minister. He answers directly to the minister and liaises between the different departments of the ministry and with external bodies.

SUBSIDIO POR DESEMPLEO

State benefit payable to those people who are unemployed and are no longer in receipt of unemployment benefit. Those with dependents may claim it, workers over 45, emigrants who have returned to work in Spain and those recently released from prison. With certain exceptions, it is payable for up to a maximum of 18 months. It also covers payments to the SEGURIDAD SOCIAL. The benefit is 75% of the minimum wage. See also: PROTECCIÓN POR DESEMPLEO

SUMMERS, MANUEL (1935–   )
Film director and script-writer. He started his career as a television technician and cartoonist, but he turned towards the cinema in the sixties and has directed over thirty films, most of which are based on his own scripts. Many of them are comedies or films about the problems of adolescence.

SUPERDOTADOS
Gifted children. A recent ruling (1996) allows gifted children to start primary school a year early, and to leave school 2 years early, at 14.

SUQUÍA, ANGEL
Bishop who succeeeded TARANCÓN as chairman of the CONFERENCIA EPISCOPAL, or Bishops' Conference, in 1987.

SYBILLA
Internationally recognised *couturière*, she first rose to fame during the years of the LA MOVIDA MADRILEÑA. Her clothes are now sold world-wide through an Italian company, *Gibo*.

TABACALERA

Originally a state-owned tobacco company. It is the third largest in Europe and until recently, operated as a monopoly with which all foreign companies had to deal. It controlled both wholesale and retail distribution of tobacco products. This network is now under threat and indeed TABACALERA was one of the first companies to be privatised by the AZNAR government.

TABLAS DE DAIMIEL

National park at the confluence of the GUADIANA and Cigüela rivers. Due to the recent drought in Spain, much of the 2,000 hectares of wetlands has dried up. It is nevertheless still an important breeding ground for acuatic birds. DAIMIEL was declared a national park in 1974.

TABLEROS DE FIBRAS, S.A.

This company manufactures wooden, fibre and melamine panels, drawing from 20,000 hectares of forest land throughout Spain. It also produces adhesive and various kinds of resins.

TAJO

The longest river in Spain (1007 km). It rises in the Cordillera Ibérica, flows through the central Meseta and flows out into the Atlantic near Lisbon.

TALGO

Tren Articulado Ligero Goixoechea Oriol, always known as the TALGO. It is an inter-city high-speed train, dating from 1950. It can be adapted to run on the AVE tracks which use the European, as opposed to the Spanish, gauge.

TAMAMES, RAMÓN (1933–   )

Professor of *Estructura e Instituciones Economícas* at the

University of MADRID. Communist member of parliament from 1977 to 1981 when he resigned from the party and joined IU. In 1987 he was a candidate for the post of mayor of MADRID. He joined the CDS in 1989. Among his better known works are *Estructura económica de España* and *Algunas cuestiones claves para el futuro político de España*.

TAPAS
Small portions of food (such as sardines, *chorizo* or Spanish sausage, or Russian salad) served together with a drink, either at home or – more usually – in a bar. TAPAS are also known as '*pinchos*' (in the north) or '*aperitivos*', (in the MADRID area).

TÀPIES, FUNDACIÓN
Museum of contemporary art, founded in 1990 by ANTONÍ TÀPIES and housed in BARCELONA. Besides important holdings of modern art, the foundation also has a research library and organises lectures, courses and conferences.

TÀPIES I PUIG, ANTONI (1923–   )
CATALÁN abstract painter, internationally famous for his collages and experimental work with unusual materials. He has a foundation in BARCELONA, housed in the calle Aragó. On the roof is to be found one of his works, *Núvol i cadira*. It was he who designed the monument to Picasso in BARCELONA. In 1990 he was awarded the PREMIO PRÍNCIPE DE ASTURIAS.

TARJETA DE RESIDENCIA
All foreign nationals must obtain a residence card if they intend to remain in Spain for more than 3 months, whether they intend to work or not. Any change of address must be notified to the police.

TARRADELLAS, JOSEP (1899–1988)
TARRADELLAS was *primer ministro* in the CATALÁN government during the Second Republic. In 1954 he was elected president in exile of the GENERALITAT. He returned to Spain in 1977 and was offered the presidency of the new GENERALITAT. As president, he negotiated the new statutes of autonomy for CATALUÑA.

TEATRO REAL

MADRID Opera House: it underwent a costly refitting in the early nineties and was felt to be 'cursed' after a series of mishaps, such as the crashing down of a chandelier worth £400,000 into the auditorium, the resignation of five theatre governors and that of the artistic director. The refurbishment has been hugely over budget and behind schedule but it is eventually due to reopen at the beginning of 1998.

TEIDE (PARQUE NACIONAL DEL)

National park in TENERIFE which surrounds the volcano, also called TEIDE. It is the most important park in the CANARIAS: it possesses interesting flora, peculiar to volcanic areas. The volcano itself is the highest peak in Spanish territory.

TEIDE (PICO DEL)

TEIDE is Spain's highest mountain peak (3,718 metres) in TENERIFE in the CANARIAS. It is volcanic in origin. TEIDE and the surrounding area have been declared a national park.

TEJERO, ANTONIO (1932–)

Lieutenant-Colonel (*teniente coronel*) ANTONIO TEJERO was the leader of a contingent of the GUARDIA CIVIL which stormed the CORTES on the night of the 23rd of February 1981, in an attempt to stage a coup d'état against the government. He was sentenced to 30 years imprisonment for his role in the attempted coup. He had been arrested earlier, in 1978, for plotting to take the MONCLOA while ADOLFO SUÁREZ was holding a cabinet meeting.

TELE 5

One of the three private television channels in Spain, along with ANTENA 3 and CANAL PLUS. It is very popular and has a high audience share.

TELEFONÍA MÓVIL

The licence for the commercialisation of mobile phones was awarded in 1994 to the consortium *Airtel-Sistelcom-Reditel*, in which the BANCO DE SANTANDER and the CENTRAL HISPANO each hold 13% of the shares.

TELEFÓNICA
This company is responsible for the telecommunications industry in Spain and is one of her largest companies. It has more than 75,000 employees which represent over half the sector's total employees. At present TELEFÓNICA has a crucial role to play in the modernising of the telecommunication service in Spain and in ensuring that all areas are connected to the network. This involves an investment of over 600,000 million pesetas per annum. Besides providing basic services, TELEFÓNICA is also installing optical fibres and digital transmission. Until 1995, TELE-FÓNICA had a monopoly on the telecommunications industry in Spain: by 1998, the telecommunications industry will be fully liberalized. It was one of the first companies to be privatised by the AZNAR government: currently, the state owns 20% of the company. Other major share holders are ARGENTARIA, the BBV and CAIXA. In 1997, TELEFÓNICA merged with *British Telecom* and *MCI* to form the second largest telecommunications group in the world.

TELÉFONO DORADO
A free telephone service provided for the old and lonely. It is manned by volunteers for 10 hours a day. It was set up by an organisation called *Mensajeros de la Paz* (Messengers of Peace).

TELEMADRID
State television company established in 1989, based in MADRID and funded by the autonomous region of MADRID (Comunidad Autónoma de MADRID). It is controlled by RADIO TELEVISIÓN ESPAÑOLA. In 1997 it had an audience share of 19%.

TELERUTA
State service which informs the public of the state of the road system, including traffic problems, road works and so on.

TELEVISIÓ DE CATALUNYA
Local television service which broadcasts on TV-3 and CANAL 33 throughout north-eastern Spain, in the CATALÁN language.

TELEVISIÓ VALENCIANA (TVV)

Local television station for VALENCIA, also known as CANAL 9. It commenced regular transmissions in 1989.

TELEVISIÓN DE GALICIA

Local television station in GALICIA, it broadcasts in the Galician language throughout the north-west.

TELEVISIÓN ESTATAL

There are two state television networks in Spain, TVE-1 and TVE-2 (known as *la dos*). TVE-2 is the more serious channel featuring documentaries, debates and news programmes while TVE-1 specialises in general entertainment.

TELEVISIÓN POR SATÉLITE

There are a large number of programmes which can be seen on satellite in Spain. On the *Astra* satellite are broadcast channels such as *Cineclassics*, *Cinemanía* and *Documanía*; on the *Hispasat* satellite, *Canal Clásico*, *Telesatcinco* and *Teledeporte*; and on *Eutelsat*, TVE *Internacional*.

TELEVISIONES AUTONÓMICAS

These are the television channels located in the COMUNIDADES AUTÓNOMAS. Those AUTONOMÍAS which have their own language broadcast in this language on at least one of the channels (ETB-1 for instance broadcasts only in Basque and TV-3 only in CATALÁN). TVG, on the other hand, broadcasts in a mixture of GALLEGO and Spanish. Other examples of local television are TELEMADRID, CANAL SUR (ANDALUCÍA) and CANAL 9 in the COMUNIDAD VALENCIANA.

TELLADO, CORÍN (1927–   )

Popular novelist, she has written over 4,000 novels of the type known as the novela rosa or romantic fiction. She is reputed to write at the rate of one novel per week.

TENEO

Holding company, created in 1992, for the 47 most profitable companies in INI. It was the first state company to be privatised by JOSÉ MARÍA AZNAR'S government in 1996. It later became known as SEPI. It comprises companies such as ENDESA, IBERIA, AVIACO and *Ence*.

TENERIFE
Largest of the ISLAS CANARIAS and an important tourist centre. It is dominated by the PICO DE TEIDE (3,715 m). It has 700,000 inhabitants. Important for its agricultural production (bananas, tomatoes) and its fishing industry.

TENIENTE DE ALCALDE
The deputy mayor of a town or city council. An ALCALDE may have more than one TENIENTE.

TER
The TER or *Tren Español Rápido* is one of Spain's inter-city high-speed trains.

TERCER CICLO
To enter the TERCER CICLO in higher education, the student must be a graduate or have the *título de ingeniero* or *arquitecto*. Students study a number of courses (*cursos monográficos de doctorado*) during the first two years, on which they are examined. They do research which may take a year or more after the first two years; they then defend a thesis before a *tribunal* or jury to obtain the *título de doctorado* (Ph.D).

TÉRMINO MUNICIPAL
The area administered by a municipal council.

TERRA LLIURE
Catalán political organisation which renounced the armed struggle for Catalán independence in 1991, and joined the ESQUERRA REPUBLICANA DE CATALUNYA.

TERRAZAS
Open-air cafés which spring up in all the large Spanish cities in summer, often with music and live entertainment. Activities last most of the night and can be the source of friction between customers and local residents.

TESORERÍA GENERAL DE LA SEGURIDAD SOCIAL
This autonomous body's major function is to provide the finan-

cial services for the income and expenditure of the social security system – that is, for INSALUD, INSS and INSERSO.

TEST DE ALCOHOLEMIA
Alcohol test administered at random by the police, most usually at weekends and at holiday times. Either a breath or blood sample is taken.

TIBIDABO
Hill to the north-west of BARCELONA, (1,512 metres), linked to the city by tram and funicular. It is a popular place for the people of BARCELONA to visit in the summer, partly because of the fun-fair located at the top.

TIERNO GALVÁN, ENRIQUE (1918–1986)
Born in MADRID, TIERNO GALVÁN was professor of political law at the University of SALAMANCA. He joined the socialist party in 1963 but was later expelled: he then founded his own party, the *Partido Socialista del Interior* which later became known as the *Partido Socialista Popular*. He was an enormously popular ALCALDE of MADRID from 1979 to 1986, where he was known as '*el viejo profesor, joven alcalde*'.

TIMANFAYA
National park, in LANZAROTE. Famous for its volcanic landscape and the flora peculiar to this geographical feature. It was created a national park in 1974.

TOCINO, ISABEL (1949–)
Politician, currently *diputada* for TOLEDO and *ministro del Medio Ambiente* in the 1996 government of JOSÉ MARÍA AZNAR. She graduated in law and has since specialised in questions concerning the impact of nuclear energy on the environment. She entered politics in 1983 and quickly became close to MANUEL FRAGA. She was a member of the executive (*comité ejecutivo*) of AP, responsible for women's issues.

TOCOMOCHO
Term given to a type of swindle in which a counterfeit lottery ticket with a winning number is sold to a third person for an amount which is less than the prize. The excuse for selling is that

the original owner cannot claim the prize or does not know its value.

TODOS LOS SANTOS
All Saints' Day which falls on November 1st is traditionally the day when Spanish families visit the graves of their friends and family to pay their respects. It is a national holiday.

TOMÁS Y VALIENTE, FRANCISCO (1932–1996)
Professor of the History of Law, first in SALAMANCA and then at the UNIVERSIDAD AUTÓNOMA *de* MADRID. He had been a *magistrado* for 12 years and *presidente* of the TRIBUNAL CONSTITUCIONAL for 6. He was elected a member of the *Real Academia de la Historia* in 1990. He was murdered by the Basque terrorist group ETA in his study at the University in February 1996.

TOMATITO
Stage name of José Fernández Torres, flamenco guitar player. At the age of 15, he met CAMARÓN DE LA ISLA, who was so impressed by his playing that he asked him to join his troupe. Eventually, TOMATITO replaced PACO DE LUCÍA as CAMARÓN's guitarist. The duo remained together until CAMARÓN's death in 1992. Since then, TOMATITO has pursued a solo career; in 1997 he brought out his third LP of flamenco music, entitled *Guitarra gitana*.

TORCAL
The Sierra del TORCAL is a *Parque Natural* or National Park, famous for its limestone formations which ressemble animal and plant forms. It is situated in ANDALUCÍA, near the city of Antequera.

TORRE EUROPA
These towers (also known as the *Torres* KIO) are to be found in the CHAMARTÍN area of MADRID. Built on a massive scale, they were found to contravene building regulations and have thus been the subject of a court case.

TORRENT, ANA (1966–)
Film actress. At the age of 7, ANA TORRENT was cast by VICTOR ERICE in *El espiritú de la colmena* (1973). She later appeared in similar roles in *Cría cuervos* (1975) and *Elisa vida mía* (1976). As

an adult, she has not had the same success but she did appear in the highly acclaimed *Vacas* (MEDEM, 1991). Recently, she has appeared in the prize-winning *Temas*, and in AMENÁBAR's *Tesis*.

TORRENTE BALLESTER, GONZALO (1910–   )
Writer and university professor. Member of the REAL ACADEMIA ESPAÑOLA. He has written many novels, including *Los gozos y las sombras* (later adapted very successfully for television), *La isla de los jacintos cortados* and *La saga fuga de J.B.* He was awarded the PREMIO CERVANTES in 1985.

TORRES, MARUJA (1043–   )
Journalist who first made her reputation in the FRANCO years, writing in FOTOGRAMAS and *Por Favor*. She has worked as a war correspondent in the Lebanon and in Panama. She currently writes for EL PAÍS. Her latest book was published in 1997: *Un calor tan cercano*.

TRABAJOS EN BENEFICIO DE LA COMUNIDAD
Community service orders can now be substituted for prison sentences under the regulations of the new penal code, approved in 1995.

TRANSFERENCIAS
Term used for the gradual devolution of indivual areas of responsibility from central government to the regions.

LA TRANSICIÓN
Term used to refer to the period after the death of FRANCO when Spain began the difficult process of moving from a dictatorship to a democracy.

TRATADO DE ADHESIÓN
The Treaty of Accession to the European Community was signed in 1985 and Spain became a fully fledged member of the Community on January 1st, 1986.

TREVIÑO, JOSÉ RAMÓN
Arcipreste of Irún, TREVIÑO was imprisoned for collaboration with the Basque terrorist organisation ETA. Traditionally, the Church in the PAÍS VASCO has been sympathetic to Basque nationalists.

TRIBUNAL CONSTITUCIONAL

This court is the most important interpreter of the CONSTITUCIÓN and there is no appeal against its decisions. The tribunal is consulted on organic and ordinary laws, international treaties, the statutes of the AUTONOMÍAS and so on.

TRIBUNAL DE CUENTAS

State audit tribunal, it is the supreme financial accounting body for the state and public sector. The members of this body are suitably qualified auditors, lawyers or economists with a minimum of 15 years experience. There are twelve members in all, six elected from the SENADO and six from the CONGRESO.

TRIBUNAL DE LA COMPETENCIA

Office of Fair Trading.

TRIBUNAL DE LAS AGUAS

Court dating from the Middle Ages, held in VALENCIA, which gives judgements on disputes over water rights in the surrounding countryside. It meets each Thursday outside the cathedral.

TRIBUNAL DEL JURADO

The jury system was introduced in Spain in September 1995. Local courts now use jurors (9 in all) in cases of corruption, murder, embezzlement and arson. A minimum of 7 jurors must be in agreement for a verdict of guilty.

TRIBUNAL MILITAR CENTRAL

Military court which tries members of the armed forces.

TRIBUNAL SUPERIOR DE JUSTICIA

These judicial bodies which exist in each region are divided into four courts, which deal with civil, criminal, administrative and labour matters respectively. They replace the former AUDIENCIA TERRITORIAL and are the final court of appeal within the region.

TRIBUNAL SUPREMO

The highest court in the land (also known as the *Tribunal de Casación* or Court of Last Appeal). It is authorized to rule against decisions made in lower courts and to undertake judicial reviews. It is composed of five *salas*, which cover different areas of jurisdiction (civil, criminal, litiginous-administrative, commercial and military).

TRIBUNAL TITULAR DE MENORES

Children's court.

TRICICLE

Theatre group formed in 1979 in BARCELONA which specialises in mime and pantomime and also in slapstick or farce. The three actors in the group have often perfomed on Spanish television and have toured Japan, North America and Europe.

TRUEBA, FERNANDO (1955–   )

Film director. His first film was *Opera prima* (1980), one of the so-called *comedias madrileñas*. His film *El año de las luces* received the Silver Bear award at the Berlin Film Festival in 1987. Recently, he has moved over into production: he produced the Oscar winning *Belle époque* (1992) and *Alas de mariposa* (1991).

TUBACEX-CIA ESPAÑOLA DE TUBOS POR EXTRUSIÓN, S.A.

This company manufactures seamless carbon, alloy and stainless steel tubes and pipes and is situated in the PAÍS VASCO.

TÚNEL DE SOMPORT

Tunnel through the Pyrenees from France to Spain at the SOMPORT pass. The building of the tunnel has been controversial: environmental groups opposed it, but it was eventually completed in 1997.

TÚNEL DEL SOLLER

The PARTIDO POPULAR in the BALEARES are currently under investigation for allegedly receiving kickbacks in their awarding of contracts for the building of the SÓLLER tunnel.

TUÑÓN DE LARA, MANUEL (1915–97)

Historian. He was exiled in France for many years, where he was a prominent member of the Communist party. A specialist in 19th and 20th century history, he is the author of a number of text books for students in the secondary school and university system. Among his most important books are *La España del siglo diecinueve* and *España bajo la dictadura franquista*.

TURINA, JOSÉ LUIS (1953–   )

Composer. Among his most well-known compositions are *Ocnos, Concierto para violín y orquesta* (1987) and *La raya en el agua*. He is the grandson of another famous musician, Joaquín Turina. He won the *Premio Nacional de Música* in 1997.

TURRÓN

Type of nougat, very popular at Christmas. There are two types, hard nougat, made in and around Alicante and soft, made in JIJONA. The main ingredients are almonds, honey and sugar. Since 1996, French sweet-making manufacturers have been banned from calling their nougat TURRÓN.

TUSQUETS, OSCAR (1941–   )

Catalán architect, born in BARCELONA in 1941.

TV-3

Television channel belonging to the AUTONOMÍA of CATALUÑA. It was the first regional channel to broadcast by satellite in an attempt to provide programming in CATALÁN for CATALÁN speakers outside the region.

TXALAPARTA

Percussion instrument from the Basque country.

TXOMIN See: *ITURBE ABASOLO*

UA See: *UNIDAD ALAVESA*

UBA See: *UNIDAD BÁSICA DE ACTUACIÓN*

UBRIQUE, JESULÍN DE

One of the new breed of bull-fighters, JESULÍN DE UBRIQUE is especially popular with women and has fought before exclusively feminine audiences. He has recently entered the world of show-business.

UCD See: *UNIÓN CENTRO DEMOCRÁTICO*

UCE See: *UNIÓN DE CONSUMIDORES DE ESPAÑA*

UCI

Unidad de Cuidados Intensivos or Intensive Care department in a Spanish hospital.

UGT See: *UNIÓN GENERAL DE TRABAJADORES*

EL ÚLTIMO DE LA FILA

Catalán pop group which rose to fame in the eighties: it is composed of Manolo García, lead singer and Quimi Portet on guitar.

ULTRASUR

A gang of extreme right-wing football hooligans who support REAL MADRID; their arch-enemies are the BARCELONA football team and a rival gang, the BOIXOS NOIS.

UM See: *UNIÓ MALLORQUINA*

UMBRAL, FRANCISCO (1935–   )

Writer and journalist. Among his best-known works are *Las ninfas* (which received the PREMIO NADAL), *Trilogía de Madrid* and *Ramón y las vanguardias*. In his latest novel, *Capital del dolor*, he returns to one of his favourite themes, the Spanish Civil War. It was published in 1996.

UNED See: *UNIVERSIDAD NACIONAL DE EDUCACIÓN A DISTANCIA*

UNIDAD ALAVESA
Regional party, founded in 1989 after a split with the PP in the PAÍS VASCO; the UA advocates greater rights for the province of ÁLAVA and won five seats in the 1994 regional election.

UNIDAD BÁSICA DE ACTUACIÓN
Unit in the GUARDIA CIVIL.

UNIDAD EDITORIAL, S.A.
Large media group, which publishes EL MUNDO. Despite a large deficit in 1997, it intends to bid for the new FM stations which come out for tender in 1998.

UNIDESA See: *UNIDAD EDITORIAL, S.A.*

UNIÓ DEMOCRÀTICA DE CATALUNYA
This CATALÁN nationalist party is the junior partner in the CATALÁN coalition, CONVERGENCIA I UNIÓ. The party was founded in 1931 and remained faithful to the Spanish Republic during the 1930s and to the GENERALITAT and its president, Lluís Companys. While this party is Christian Democrat in character, CONVERGENCIA DEMOCRÁTICA DE CATALUNYA, the senior partner, is socialist.

UNIÓ MALLORQUINA
Right-wing nationalist party, based in MALLORCA and affiliated to the PP. Its present chairman, Jerónimo Alberti is president of the regional assembly.

UNIÓ VALENCIANA
Valencian nationalist political party, founded in 1982 by Vicente González Lizondo. It is a centrist party with 18,000 members. It usually has one member in the CONGRESO but obtained two seats in 1989. UV is currently a partner in the regional government.

UNIÓN CENTRISTA

This centrist political party was formed in 1995 by former members of the CDS, among others.

UNIÓN DE CENTRO DEMOCRÁTICO

This centre-right party started life as a coalition of small centre and moderate right-wing parties and was headed by ALFONSO SUÁREZ. It won the first two democratic elections in Spain in 1977 and 1979, although it did not receive a majority vote. Electoral defeat in 1982 led to its disappearance.

UNIÓN DE CONSUMIDORES DE ESPAÑA

Spain's foremost consumers' association.

UNIÓN DEL PUEBLO NAVARRO

This party was founded by Jesús Aizpún Tuero towards the end of the 1970s and is a centrist regionalist organisation, preferring recently to work closely with the PP in NAVARRA. In regional elections, however, it stands as a separate party and indeed controlled the regional parliament in 1991.

UNIÓN FENOSA

Electricity company with interests in Central America, Argentina, Uruguay and Venezuela. Its principal activity is the production, transmission, distribution and marketing of electric power. The company is also concerned with research, design and development of new technologies, particularly with regard to communication and information technology. Also of interest are projects concerning water supply, urban waste treatment, and new energy technologies.

UNIÓN GENERAL DE TRABAJADORES

Founded in 1888, the UGT is one of the largest trades' unions in the country and is especially strong in ASTURIAS and the PAÍS VASCO. It was legalised in 1977 and for many years was headed by Nicolás Redondo Urbieta. It has 15 affiliated federations.

UNIÓN IBEROAMERICANA DE SEGUROS Y REASEGUROS, S.A.

Founded in 1947, this insurance company specialises in fire and other property insurance. Other interests are life insurance, transport, and vehicle and accident insurance.

UNIÓN PARA EL PROGRESO DE CANTABRIA

The UPCA is a conservative group that formed part of the PP in CANTABRIA for the 1991 regional assembly election, winning 15 seats out of 39. Its leader became president of the regional government and in June 1993 announced the end of the UPCA's pact with the PP. The party won seven regional assembly seats in 1995.

UNIÓN PROFESIONAL

This body represents the professional bodies or COLEGIOS. It has 33 constituent members out of 75 associations.

UNIÓN SINDICAL OBRERA

This trade union is fourth in size after CCOO and UGT and like them was legalised in 1977. In the past it was closely allied to UCD and was well represented in the railways and coal, iron and steel industries. It is Christian in character, many of its members having belonged to the *Juventud Obrera Católica* or the *Hermandad Obrera de Acción Católica.*

LA UNIÓN Y EL FÉNIX ESPAÑOL

This insurance company issues premiums for fire damage, multi-risk, damage to property, cars, accident and illness.

UNIPREX, S.A.

This media group owns the ONDA CERO, *Onda 10* and *Onda Melodía* radio networks.

UNITAT DEL POBLE VALENCIA

This left-wing nationalist party was founded in 1982 but is currently unrepresented in the regional assembly of the COMUNIDAD VALENCIANA.

UNIVERSIDAD AUTÓNOMA DE MADRID

Although this University was founded as recently as 1968 it is second only in size to the COMPLUTENSE and the *Politécnica.* Its campus is in Cantoblanco on the outskirts of MADRID.

UNIVERSIDAD CARLOS III

New campus university, situated in the working-class suburb of Getafe, to the south of MADRID and founded in 1989. Its founding father is the politician and professor of law, Gregorio Peces-Barba.

UNIVERSIDAD CENTRAL

Largest university in BARCELONA, with over 60,000 students on the roll.

UNIVERSIDAD NACIONAL DE EDUCACIÓN A DISTANCIA

Students at this University study through distance learning and self-study modules. There are no upper limits on numbers: to gain entry, students need only pass the SELECTIVIDAD. Classes are broadcast over the radio and contact with teachers is by phone, letter or at regional centres. Students may study for a wide variety of degrees, including Law, Economics, Business Studies, Spanish and classical languages.

UNIVERSIDAD

Tertiary education takes place in Spain in the university or in an ESCUELA UNIVERSITARIA. Currently, there are 47 public universities in Spain and 10 private ones.

UNIVERSIDADES POPULARES

'People's universities': that is, educational initiatives which arose from the needs and wishes of local people. Their work covered all aspects of education, from basic literacy and numeracy, to advanced technological training.

UPCA See: *UNIÓN PARA EL PROGRESO DE CANTABRIA*

UPN See: *UNIÓN DEL PUEBLO NAVARRO*

UPV See: *UNITAT DEL POBLE VALENCIA*

URALITA, S.A.

Large company in the building materials and services sector with several divisions: cement processing, electrochemical and agrochemical production, thermoplastic materials, tiles, plaster, ceramics, metallic seals and paint.

URDANGARÍN IÑAKI (1968–   )

URDANGARÍN was born in the Basque country, although he has

lived most of his life in BARCELONA. He is a professional handball player who has played for the Spanish national team on many occasions. He also competed in the 1992 Olympic Games in BARCELONA and in Atlanta in 1996. In 1997 he married CRISTINA DE BORBÓN in BARCELONA.

URIBE, IMANOL (1950–   )

Basque film actor, his finest performance was in *La muerte de Mikel* (1983). He directed *El rey pasmado* (1991) based on the novel by GONZALO TORRENTE BALLESTER. In 1995 his film *Días contados* won the prestigious *Concha de Oro* award in the SAN SEBASTIÁN Film Festival; in 1996 he directed *Bwana*. He is married to the actress MARÍA BARRANCO.

URRALBURU, GABRIEL

Ex-presidente of NAVARRA, he was imprisoned for receiving kickbacks from building companies, in return for contracts within the AUTONOMÍA.

USO See: *UNIÓN SINDICAL OBRERA*

UV See: *UNIÓ VALENCIANA*

VACACIONES PARA LA TERCERA EDAD
This government programme provides the elderly with holidays at reduced prices in the winter months.

VALENCIA
City with 2,000,000 inhabitants in the LEVANTE region of Spain. Important agricultural centre and port, and capital of the COMUNIDAD VALENCIANA. See also: LAS FALLAS DE VALENCIA

VALLADOLID
City of 500,000 inhabitants in the *Comunidad de* CASTILLA Y LEÓN. Headquarters of SEAT in Spain.

VALLECAS
Working-class suburb to the south of MADRID, it often appears as the locale in ZARZUELAS.

VALLEHERMOSO, S.A.
This MADRID-based company is involved in property development, and the building and rental of domestic and office accommodation for leasing or sale. Its principal developments are in MADRID and SEVILLA.

VANGUARDIA (LA)
Founded in 1881 in BARCELONA, LA VANGUARDIA is the most important regional newspaper in Spain, although it covers national and international events also. It is conservative in character. Its weekday circulation is 220,000, rising to 345,000 on Sundays.

VARGAS LLOSA, MARIO (1936–   )
Novelist born in Peru, VARGAS LLOSA has taken Spanish nationality and lives in MADRID and London. Among his most famous novels are *Conversaciones en la catedral*, *La ciudad y los perros*

and *Los cuadernos de D. Rigoberto* (1997). In 1986 he was awarded the PREMIO PRÍNCIPE DE ASTURIAS for his contribution to the arts.

VASCO
Language spoken by about half a million people in EL PAÍS VASCO and known also as EUSKERA. It has no relation to any other Indo-European language and is thought to be the language of the original inhabitants of Spain.

VÁZQUEZ MONTALBÁN, MANUEL (1939–   )
Enormously popular writer of thrillers, featuring the detective Pepe Carvalho. Very well known throughout Spain, through his writing of a weekly column in EL PAÍS. His novel *Los mares del sur* was awarded the *Premio Planeta* in 1989. His last book is *Un polaco en la corte del Rey Juan Carlos* (1996), a collection of interviews with important Spaniards. In 1996 he also published *El premio*, the twentieth novel in which Pepe Carvalho appears.

VÁZQUEZ, MANUEL (1934–   )
Cartoonist. He started his career in BARCELONA, with the *Editorial Bruguera*, designing and drawing comic strips. Among the characters he has created are the *Familia Cebolleta* and *Las hermanas Gilda* and *Anacleto*.

VEINTICUATRO DE JUNIO
St. John's Day. It has become of especial importance recently because it is the saint's day of JUAN CARLOS, King of Spain. On this day, the King invites those citizens who have distinguished themselves throughout the year to a reception at the ZARZUELA palace in MADRID.

23 DE FEBRERO 1981 (23-F)
This is the date of the attempted coup d'état by members of the GUARDIA CIVIL who invaded the CORTES and held up the DIPUTADOS at gun-point. The crisis was defused by the king, JUAN CARLOS who appeared on television and appealed to the nation and to the army to defend the rule of law.

VELASCO, CONCHA (1939–   )
Actress and TV presenter, VELASCO started her career as a dancer

in flamenco troupes and in reviews. In the 1960s she worked extensively with José Luis Sáenz de Heredia and appeared in ZARZUELAS, comedies and dramas. She made a number of interesting films in the 1970s and 1980s, including *La colmena* (CAMUS, 1982) and *Pim, pam, pum ¡fuego!* (OLEA, 1975). She is still in the public eye as a television presenter and as an actress in musical comedies.

LAS VENTAS
The bull ring in Madrid. It is the most important and prestigious in the Spanish-speaking world.

VERA, RAFAEL (1946–)
Ex-secretario de Estado para la Seguridad, VERA is heavily implicated in the GAL affaire. He was imprisoned in February 1995, accused of illegal arrest, financing the kidnapping of Segundo Marey and of embezzling public funds. He was later released on bail. See also: GAL

VERDÚ, MARIBEL (1970–)
Film actress discovered by VICENTE ARANDA who gave her important roles in a number of television series, as well as in his film *Amantes* (1991). She has also worked with other directors including FERNANDO TRUEBA, Montxo Armendáriz and Emilio Martínez Lázaro. Currently (1996) she is appearing on television in a popular series, *Canguros*.

VERINO, ROBERTO (1946–)
Fashion designer from GALICIA in the north of Spain. From humble beginnings in Orense, he now owns three companies, 19 exclusive clothes shops and 35 outlets in EL CORTE INGLÉS. He has a turnover of 3,000 million pesetas per year. He is an important employer in Verín, Orense.

VÍA DIGITAL
State-owned digital television company. It aims to provide 'pay per view' television, including new film releases and first division football matches. TELEFÓNICA, RTVE and *Televisa* (a Mexican television company) are all share-holders in the company.

VÍA LENTA
Term used to describe the so-called 'slow route' to devolution, adopted by certain Spanish regions. In effect, these were regions other than the 'historic autonomies' – GALICIA, PAÍS VASCO and CATALUÑA. The former had to wait five years before adopting any further powers other than those devolved in 1978.

VÍA RÁPIDA
The so called 'fast route' to devolution adopted by the 'historical autonomies' of GALICIA, PAÍS VASCO and CATALUÑA.

VICEPRESIDENTE DEL GOBIERNO
Deputy prime minister. His functions very much depend on the decisions taken by the current prime minister in office. In some legislatures, there have been more than one.

VIDAL-QUADRAS, ALEIX
Catalán politician, currently presidente of the PARTIDO POPULAR in CATALUÑA. He is also a member of the SENADO and a DIPUTADO for CATALUÑA.

VILLALONGA, JOSÉ LUIS DE (1920–   )
Also known as the Marqués de Castellvell, VILLALONGA is a grandee of Spain, writer, actor and journalist. He wrote the first biography of don JUAN CARLOS.

VIPS
Chain of shops, similar to the American drugstore, which has a cafeteria section and also sells books, records and stationery.

VIRGEN DE ARÁNZAZU
Patron saint of Guipúzcoa province in the PAÍS VASCO.

VIRGEN DEL PILAR
Patron saint of ZARAGOZA. Legend has it that the Virgin Mary appeared to Saint James on a pillar of jasper, as he passed through the town. The people of ZARAGOZA celebrate the Virgin's feast day on the 12th of October, by taking flowers to her statue in the cathedral: a mantle of flowers is then created for her. The VIRGEN DEL PILAR is also the patron saint of the GUARDIA CIVIL.

LAS VIRTUDES

Comedy duo comprising two women, Elena Martín and Soledad Mallol. They appear both on stage and on television and are dressed as twins, with similar clothes and black bobbed wigs.

VISCOFÁN, INDUSTRIA NAVARRA DE ENVOLTURAS CELULÓSICAS, S.A.

This group operates primarily in the field of food production and artificial wrappings, with its main activity the manufacture and sale of cellulose sausage skins. It is also involved in the manufacture and sale of tinned vegetables, marmalades and fruit and vegetable derivatives. Its factories are based in the NAVARRA region.

VIVIENDAS TUTELADAS

Sheltered housing for the elderly.

VOTACIÓN PÚBLICA POR LLAMAMIENTO

This is a parliamentary voting system in which members' names are called out in alphabetical order: they answer yes, no, or abstain. This procedure is used in motions of censure and votes of confidence. Other voting procedures are via electronic voting or ballot papers (*papeletas*).

VOTING RIGHTS

Spaniards have the right to vote at 18. Suffrage is universal.

VOTO CAUTIVO

This term is used in the south to describe the voting habits of those Spaniards who vote socialist in order to retain their state benefits, especially those related to the PER scheme. See also: PLAN DE EMPLEO RURAL.

VOTO DE INVESTIDURA

The CORTES votes on the programme presented by a candidate for the premiership in what is known as the vote of investiture. If the programme is accepted, the candidate is duly appointed prime minister by the reigning monarch.

XUNTA DE GALICIA
The Parliament of the autonomous region of GALICIA. XUNTA is the Galician word for *junta* or council. At the time of writing, MANUEL FRAGA IRIBARNE is President.

YA

Formerly an important Catholic newspaper. Due to falling sales, it went bankrupt in 1996 and was forced to close.

YANES, ELÍAS (1928–)

Archbishop of ZARAGOZA since 1977, YANES is also presidente of the CONFERENCIA ESPAÑOLA EPISCOPAL, the representative body of the Spanish bishops which pronounces on ethical issues and questions of interest to the church. He is known to have liberal views and played an important part in the discussions with the government on the changing role of education in Spain.

YAÑEZ, LUIS (1943–)

Socialist member of parliament in the CONGRESO from 1977 to 1986, *presidente* of the *Instituto de Cooperación Iberoamericano* from 1982 to 1985 and *secretario* of the *Instituto de Cooperación Internacional y para Imberoamérica* from 1985. He was president of the commission set up to organise events for the 500th anniversary of the discovery of America in 1992.

YESERÍAS

Name of the women's prison in MADRID.

YOYES (1954–1986)

YOYES was the nom-de-guerre of María Dolores González Cataráin. She had been a leading member of the Basque terrorist group ETA but left the organisation in the early 1980s and attempted to live normally in the Basque country as part of the policy of REINSERCIÓN. She was gunned down in the street by José Antonio López Ruiz, as a warning to others who might also wish to abandon their membership of the party.

ZABALA ARÓSTEGUI, JOSÉ IGNACIO
Along with JOSÉ ANTONIO LASA, ZABALA was kidnapped by the GAL in Bayonne (France) in 1983 and killed. Their bodies were exhumed in Busot (Alicante) and identified in 1995. Later evidence suggests that they were shot by the GUARDIA CIVIL.

ZABALETA, PATXI (1947–   )
Leader of HERRI BATASUNA in NAVARRA, ZABALETA is a lawyer, poet and novelist. He belongs to the more moderate wing of the movement for Basque independence.

ZAMBRANO, MARÍA (1907–1991)
Essayist and philosopher, disciple of Ortega y Gasset, she worked on the differences between ideas and beliefs. She lived in exile for many years in America, France and Switzerland and only returned to Spain in 1984. She was awarded the PREMIO PRÍNCIPE DE ASTURIAS in 1981 and the PREMIO CERVANTES in 1988.

ZAMORA VICENTE, ALONSO (1916–   )
Philologist and literary critic, member of the REAL ACADEMIA ESPAÑOLA, he was awarded the *Premio Nacional de Literatura de Novela y Narrativa* in 1980. Among his most important works are *Dialectología española* and *Mesa sobre mesa*.

ZAPLANA, EDUARDO (1956–   )
Presidente of the COMUNIDAD VALENCIANA since 1995, ZAPLANA was previously ALCALDE of BENIDORM. He is a member of the PARTIDO POPULAR.

ZARAGOZA
800,000 inhabitants. Situated on the EBRO river. Headquarters of the *Academia General Militar* which trains soldiers and officers for the Spanish army.

ZARZUELA
Home of the Royal Family. The palace takes its name from the ZARZUELAS or light operas which were performed there in the 17th century.

ZARZUELA
The Spanish form of light opera or musical comedy, it was especially popular around the turn of the century.

ZETA
A media group which controls popular magazines such as INTERVIÚ. It also has an important stake in ANTENA 3 television.

ZONA AZUL
Areas in which one must pay to park one's vehicle during shopping hours. The name comes from the colour of the kerb, which is painted blue.

ZONA FRANCA
Free industrial zones have been established in BILBAO, BARCELONA, Cádiz and Vigo. Merchandise can be kept in these zones for up to six years. During this time, small samples can be withdrawn either to enter Spain or other countries and normal packing and sorting operations can be effected within the zone. Industrial operations changing the nature of the merchandise may be authorised in accordance with the governing laws and regulations.

ZONAS DE URGENTE REINDUSTRIALIZACIÓN
These zones were designated as a result of the LEY DE RECONVERSIÓN Y REINDUSTRIALIZACIÓN. They were areas felt to have been particularly affected by the restructuring of industry and they qualify for government grants to attract investment.

ZONAS HÚMEDAS
Spain has a number of wetlands, of special importance because of Spain's location on the routes of migratory birds. Unfortunately, many of these areas are threatened by modern agricultural practices and lack of rainfall in recent years.